# Experiencing Rome: A Visual Exploration of Antiquity's Greatest Empire

Steven L. Tuck, Ph.D.

THE GREAT COURSES®

**PUBLISHED BY:**

**THE GREAT COURSES**
**Corporate Headquarters**
**4840 Westfields Boulevard, Suite 500**
**Chantilly, Virginia 20151-2299**
**Phone: 1-800-832-2412**
**Fax: 703-378-3819**
**www.thegreatcourses.com**



Printed in the United States of America

## Steven L. Tuck, Ph.D.

Associate Professor of Classics
and the History of Art
Miami University

Steven L. Tuck is currently Associate Professor of Classics and the History of Art at Miami University, where he was named a University Distinguished Scholar in 2005 and an Outstanding Professor in 2007 and 2008. He was educated at Indiana University, where he received his B.A. in History and Classics; the University of Missouri-Columbia; and the University of Michigan, where he received his Ph.D. in Classical Art and Archaeology. He held the postdoctoral Arthur and Joyce Gordon Fellowship in Latin epigraphy at The Ohio State University. He has taught at the University of Missouri-Columbia (where he won a Graduate Teaching Award), the University of Michigan, the University of Evansville, and Miami University.

Professor Tuck frequently gives public lectures on the classical world and has for more than four years served as a national lecturer for the Archaeological Institute of America, traveling around the country giving academic and popular lectures on archaeology and ancient art. He was also a regular lecturer for the Continuing Education program at the University of Evansville, presenting lectures on a vast range of topics including ancient social and political history, archaeology, and public spectacle. He has conducted fieldwork in England, Italy, and Greece and has led more than 10 study tours to Italy and England. He has served a term as president of the Vergilian Society, an international academic organization, and is the author of many articles in international journals, including ones on the spectacle schedule at Pompeii, the decorative program of the amphitheater at Capua, and triumphal imagery across the ancient Roman world. He is the author of *Latin Inscriptions in the Kelsey Museum: The Dennison and De Criscio Collections*, published by the University of Michigan Press in 2006. ■

# Table of Contents

## INTRODUCTION

Professor Biography .......... i
Course Scope .......... 1

## LECTURE GUIDES

**LECTURE 19**
Small Town Spectacle—Games at Pompeii .......... 4

**LECTURE 20**
Aquatic Displays .......... 18

**LECTURE 21**
Roman Circuses—Arenas for Chariot Racing .......... 33

**LECTURE 22**
A Day at the Races .......... 46

**LECTURE 23**
Theaters and Plays .......... 60

**LECTURE 24**
Emperors as Performers .......... 75

**LECTURE 25**
Imperial Forums—Power and Policy in Rome .......... 90

**LECTURE 26**
Imperial Arches, Columns, and Monuments .......... 105

**LECTURE 27**
Imperial Baths in Rome—Spas for the Masses .......... 119

**LECTURE 28**
Roman Engineering—Linking the World .......... 134

## Table of Contents

**LECTURE 29**
Roman Military Forts and Fortifications ........ 148

**LECTURE 30**
Images of Warfare—Roman Military Monuments ........ 163

**LECTURE 31**
Roman Colonies—Small Romes ........ 177

**LECTURE 32**
Local Baths and Roman Bathing Culture ........ 192

**LECTURE 33**
Roman Harbors—Liminal Monuments ........ 205

**LECTURE 34**
Putting It All Together I—A Day in Pompeii ........ 219

**LECTURE 35**
Putting It All Together II—A Day in Rome ........ 234

**LECTURE 36**
Conclusions and the Images of Empire ........ 249

**SUPPLEMENTAL MATERIAL**

Timeline ........ 264
Glossary ........ 269
Biographical Notes ........ 275
Bibliography ........ 278

# Experiencing Rome: A Visual Exploration of Antiquity's Greatest Empire

## Scope:

The ancient Roman world, which lasted more than 1,000 years, was one that at its height spanned three continents (Europe, Asia, and Africa), contained millions of people, and included a range of local customs, laws, coinage, languages, and religions that would overwhelm a modern government. Despite these numbers, most of its inhabitants were illiterate and spoke a variety of languages, with only a minority knowing Latin. It makes sense then that, even more so than ancient Greece or other ancient societies, ancient Rome was organized around what one could see, especially extravagant and carefully controlled spectacle. This course therefore combines cutting-edge scholarship with breathtaking images to offer an understanding of the Roman Empire through the medium it relied on—sight.

The lectures are organized thematically and explore every topic of Roman life and culture, from the sports played to the houses and the details of family life to the weapons and armor used to conquer the empire. The lectures are richly illustrated with images of monuments, relics, artworks, and maps. This visually intensive approach brings the Roman world to life in a way that complements more traditional courses on ancient Rome. The course begins with an overview of the Roman Empire—its cultural foundations, expectations, and mores—and explores the daily lives of ancient Romans, from the clothes they wore to the rituals they observed. From there the course broadens, considering Roman towns, cities, and the countryside as shaped by Roman armies. The course concludes with an examination of the empire as a whole—exploring visual and other representations of the empire at that time, later, and down to the present day.

After two introductory lectures on the nature and extent of Roman spectacle and the geographical and chronological ranges of the material, we focus on spectacle throughout the various key components of Roman culture. Lectures 3 and 4 provide a case study in a key component of the Roman world—

military conquest—and how it was configured into spectacular displays to reinforce the power and status of the military commanders and to transmit the values and outcomes of victory to the people in Rome, who were far from the front lines. Lectures 5 through 8 turn our attention to spectacular display in the domestic world of Roman residential space. Starting with imperial palaces, we see how emperors established their identities and virtues through the design and decoration of their palaces. From there we move to private domestic space and see many of the same patterns, as lower-ranking Romans also configure their homes and gardens into elaborate stages to project emulations of imperial identity. The final lectures of Part I move out from the house and explore the interactions of individuals in the Roman city through religious observances and funerals. Part I culminates in the central civic space of Rome, the Forum Romanum.

Part II, comprising Lectures 13 through 24, concentrates on the largest buildings in Roman cities—the entertainment venues of amphitheater, circus, and theater—and the events that utilized them. These spaces hosted the largest and most extravagant of public spectacles in the ancient world, serving to reinforce Rome's laws, political system, social ranks, military power, and religious beliefs. As a building type created by the Romans and housing their own unique entertainment, the amphitheater gets primary attention, with the major events of gladiatorial combat, animal hunts, and prisoner executions each analyzed for their roles in projecting and sustaining Roman culture. With this as the basis, a lecture on Christian martyrdom analyzes the world-altering cultural conflict that took place as the Romans' exemplary punishment—intended to create a deterrent to Christian belief—instead provided a venue for Christian martyrs to demonstrate their virtues to the audience. The second half of Part II examines spectacle entertainment outside of the Colosseum, with an exploration of games at Pompeii, chariot racing in the circus, aquatic spectacles, and plays. Part II concludes with a lecture on emperors as performers, providing a synopsis of the public spectacle entertainments and a cautionary tale of conflicting priorities as emperors, invariably later assassinated, violate social norms and perform in public.

Moving beyond the arenas for spectacular entertainment, Part III explores visual display and Roman spectacle through the grand public building and engineering achievements of the ancient Roman world. Lectures 25 through 28 illustrate the intersection between the practical and the spectacular, with an examination of the use of large-scale building to display and advance images of imperial power, control, and beneficence. Lectures 29 and 30 examine the specifically military application of the visual vocabulary, from the elaborate forts and boundary markers on the borders of the empire to the illustration of these same monuments and their contexts within the framework of Roman cities and along key road systems. Lectures 31 and 32 examine how Rome used the methods of colonization to create reflections of Rome and the benefits, stability, and integration of its rule throughout a new urban world. In these small towns, we find direct emulation of Rome in bathing culture. We examine the form and use of a series of bathing establishments and their roles in creating communal identity, reinforcing political power, and defining one as a Roman. After pausing to travel virtually through the massive and extensively decorated harbors that link the towns and cities of the empire, the course culminates in Lectures 34 and 35, each of which allows us to gather our themes and subjects in a day in Pompeii and Rome, respectively. These demonstrate the rich intersections between the myriad subjects and venues for visual display throughout the cities and towns of ancient Rome. We see the Roman city as the Romans did from the street, passing through both public and private spaces and noting how each projects Roman values and identity.

We end the course with a consideration of the inheritance of ancient Rome's visual culture. A brief survey of the transmission and reception of these forms and messages finds its most recent and arguably greatest statement in the public buildings and monuments of Washington DC. ■

# Small Town Spectacle—Games at Pompeii

## Lecture 19

**Pompeii provides us with a model of a small city with extensive evidence about games—how and when they were held and by whom. Through the written advertisements found on the walls of the city, as well as the evidence from the amphitheater and the gladiatorial school, we can explore the critical role that games played in a small community.**

Pompeii hosts the oldest extant Roman amphitheater, dated to 80 B.C. It reveals the importance and role of spectacle in the community. As in the Colosseum at Rome, the seating at Pompeii was divided by class, with the elites close to the action and on display themselves. Despite the class restrictions in seating, the entrances and passageways were limited by the design of the amphitheater. Spectator comfort was clearly an issue, with evidence of awnings as at Rome. The painted decoration is notable; animal hunts and posed gladiators were painted in panels along the arena wall.

The population of Pompeii clearly identified with the gladiators, although they were distant from them socially. An amphitheater riot in A.D. 59 pitted the Pompeian supporters against those of a neighboring town, Nuceria, leading to a 10-year ban on gladiatorial contests at Pompeii. Graffiti throughout the city celebrated the local gladiatorial school and specific gladiators, whose statistics were recorded by fans.

The painted announcements of gladiatorial spectacles, *edicta munera*, provide unique evidence of the details of *munera*, their sponsors, and the community's expectations. On walls throughout the city, and even outside the walls, we find the *edicta munera* of upcoming gladiatorial games. These announcements were painted by professional sign painters on the exterior walls of both public and private buildings. Many of them were not painted over for decades, enabling us to compile a gladiatorial schedule at Pompeii for decades prior to its destruction in A.D. 79. The announcements are formulaic, giving the sponsor of games and the elements offered, including the number of pairs of gladiators, the length of games, prisoner executions, and added features.

Analysis of the *edicta* demonstrates the link at even the local level between gladiatorial games and politics. None of the announced games are funerary in context. All of the sponsors are local elites who are known from records as office holders at Pompeii. The importance of offering games is clear from the response to the 10-year ban; Greek athletics and animal hunts were substituted for the gladiators who were formerly the headliners of the games.

**The gladiatorial school at Pompeii was evidentially a source of great pride and civic identity, with the gladiators remarkably integrated into the community.**

The *edicta* support the crucial role of the games for Pompeii as a whole and not just the local politicians. They advertise games at Pompeii and neighboring communities, suggesting that hosting games was an important role for the city. The scheduling of games was careful to avoid major local events, such as elections and agricultural activities, when the majority of the workforce could not spend two or three days in the amphitheater. The event schedule also avoided conflict with religious festivals and markets at Rome, suggesting that these drew the same audience and that therefore people from as far as Rome came to Pompeii for local gladiatorial games.

The gladiatorial school at Pompeii was evidentially a source of great pride and civic identity, with the gladiators remarkably integrated into the community. The earliest gladiatorial barracks identified is in a converted house at Pompeii. The house was converted into gladiators' barracks around the time of Augustus. The graffiti found on the interior walls make it clear that perhaps 20 gladiators, including free men, slaves, and former slaves, lived in the house. Their residence in the house probably ended with the earthquake of A.D. 62, but there is evidence that they outgrew it and moved to a larger facility created from a public square.

The placement of the school showed the city's willingness to give up valuable public space for gladiatorial training of a troupe that was probably needed for the expanded games held under Nero. The central place of the school on public land made it a visual marker of the city's identity in an entertainment complex. The gladiators lived and trained in this central facility where their arms were also kept, demonstrating that any fear of a gladiator insurrection was probably remote. Any such fear was mitigated by a desire for their display: Their training was probably witnessed by the public, which was the case in Rome. ■

## Suggested Reading

Bomgardner, *The Story of the Roman Amphitheatre.*

Jacobelli, *Gladiators at Pompeii.*

## Questions to Consider

1. Analyze how gladiators were integrated into the life of Pompeii both physically and politically.

2. What do the schedule, advertising, and audience for their spectacles reveal about their importance for various components of the Pompeian community?

# Small Town Spectacle—Games at Pompeii

## Lecture 19—Transcript

Welcome back. In this lecture, we're going to explore the topic of games at Pompeii, more specifically, spectacle entertainment at the city of Pompeii. Pompeii provides us with a superb example of a model of a small city with extensive evidence of a very, very rich variety for their games, for the spectacle entertainments that occur at the amphitheater at Pompeii. We know, thanks to the evidence preserved by the eruption of Mt. Vesuvius, when the games were held, what types of games we have, how many, and who the patrons are. This sort of material evidence we don't have from anywhere else. It's all within a relatively narrow period of time, from the founding of the colony in 80 B.C. to the eruption of Mt. Vesuvius in A.D. 79.

First, we're going to take a look at the venues for spectacle in Pompeii, the amphitheater, which is a superb example. We're going to take a look at the wealth of additional evidence for the games throughout the city, and it does go throughout the city. And then we're going to take a look at the gladiatorial school and think about the role of these spectacular entertainments in a small town; how they serve a number of functions to reinforce the personal prestige of Roman patrons, to bolster the political system, and as an outlet for community identity.

Pompeii has the oldest extant amphitheater we have from the Roman world and I suspect the oldest one that will ever be found. It dates to 80 B.C., when the Roman colony was founded and, therefore, is a signature monument for the colony. When the Romans put a military unit here and establish their colony, one of the first buildings they build is an amphitheater, so it's really a projection of Roman cultural identity that they build this immediately.

As with the Colosseum at Rome, the amphitheater at Pompeii illustrates a microcosm of the Roman world, the hierarchical separation of the classes. If we look at the interior of the amphitheater at Pompeii, we'll see that. There's a lower seating area, the lower cavea, which is restricted for the upper classes, a middle seating area, and then an upper one.

I should point out that when we look at a view of the interior of the amphitheater at Pompeii we don't see a lot of the seating area. This is because it was largely robbed away after the excavations. The amphitheater was one of the first things excavated almost exactly 250 years ago when Pompeii was first discovered and excavations begun. At that time, if there was material that was not particularly useful or necessary, it was reused somewhere else in the Kingdom of Naples, and so much of the seating area here is gone. I think that if you went around the neighborhood you would probably find some of these blocks. I've done this myself at various archeological sites in the area; gone around and found reused material in the fronts of people's houses as their front doorsteps and things. So when we look at the amphitheater today we're not really seeing it as it was in the ancient world. It would have been complete. In addition, we're not seeing it as the way the Romans would have because there are parts of it that are missing because they were ephemeral.

If we take a look at the inside, we'll see that there's a wall that separates the arena floor from the seating area, but there should be a fence that surmounts that wall to keep the spectators away from the spectacle, particularly large animals, and that's missing. There's also missing some of the aspects of the arena that went to spectator comfort, most notably, all of the material that made up the awning is gone, and we'll see an image of that a bit later.

If we look at the inside or the outside of the amphitheater at Pompeii, what we see is a building that's much simpler than the Colosseum at Rome. If you have in your mind a vision of the Colosseum, remember that gleaming white exterior facade. It's four stories tall. It had 160 life-sized statues outside, 80 entrances. It really made a visual impact about spectacular display and let's you know going in that this was going to be something special. The amphitheater at Pompeii is much earlier and much simpler. It takes almost exactly 160 years before the games are inaugurated in the Colosseum, and technically, it's a lot simpler. The arena floor is solid. There's no substructure, so you don't have any of those great trap doors or any of those things that you have for special effects. The exterior is also solid. The building is built on a core of concrete, but what we do have on the outside gives us a sense about what's going on here besides just the games inside, and that is, on the outside we have not a full arcade, but a line of barrel vaults that supports the building. Thanks to the evidence that's preserved inside them, we know these were used at shops. This gives us a sense of the extent of this spectacle outside the walls of the amphitheater itself because a day of games is effectively a holiday in a small town. So if people came for a day of games, they would see the amphitheater here, but each one of those little arcades with those little barrel vaults on the outside would have somebody in it selling something: food, or wine, or perhaps souvenirs. We don't know everything that's in there, but there is a variety of commercial activity supporting the structure.

To get into the amphitheater was a much simpler affair than the Colosseum. There were only sets of four large staircases on the outside. I want you to take a look at this just briefly so you can recognize the staircase. It projects out because there are no good interior passages in the amphitheater, and you ascend the stairs on the exterior of the building, and then enter the cavea, the seating area, at the very top, and then you descend through the cavea into your seats. Everyone would do this except for the highest classes. Those people who were seated in that low seating area surrounding the arena, members of the local city council, local priests, and so on have interior passageways so they can get directly into their box seats. So spectator comfort is important. We've got the awning over there. We know it's supposed to be a day of games, but it's not as grand as what we've seen at the Colosseum in Rome.

There is, however, additional decoration. The arena wall that you see all the way around, separating the performers from the spectators, was painted all on the inside with great scenes of animal hunts and gladiators. Interestingly, [there were no scenes,] as far as we can tell, of gladiatorial combat, but just gladiators striking poses like musclemen, trying to look good, and that kind of thing. It's an interesting idea. The Romans never seem to illustrate their amphitheaters with gladiatorial combat, just gladiators in these dramatic poses. It's a curious notion.

We do know, however, from a literary account of the historian, Tacitus, that for the Pompeians, the gladiatorial school is an important and critical component of their entire social system. Tacitus gives us a very vivid account of a riot that occurred here at Pompeii in A.D. 59. Pompeii has its own gladiatorial school. Campania, the area where we are, is the origin of gladiatorial combat as far as we can tell. It's the origin of the form of the amphitheater, and so it's a very rich area for gladiatorial combat. Spartacus, the gladiator who revolted against Rome, came from Capua, which is here in Campania, the major city of Campania.

In A.D. 59, there was a set of games at Pompeii in the amphitheater where two gladiatorial schools were present: the gladiatorial school from Pompeii and the gladiatorial school from Nuceria, a neighboring town. Tacitus tells us in his very matter-of-fact way exactly what happened, and that is, in the amphitheater the crowds are cheering on their teams and they begin to taunt one another. Eventually, words are exchanged, then blows, and finally, weapons are pulled and a full riot breaks out. For this riot in 59, the Roman Senate intervened into the games at Pompeii and gave Pompeii a harsh penalty: a 10-year ban against gladiatorial combat. Here is a community that has its own gladiatorial school that much of the social and economic life is centered around, and they get this incredibly harsh punishment; 10 years no gladiatorial contests at Pompeii. This is a truly devastating punishment for the people of Pompeii.

We have, by chance, a wall painting preserved on the walls of a house at Pompeii that shows us the amphitheater, and I want you to take a look at this if you can. It shows us a sort of split perspective, almost a bird's eye view, of the amphitheater. I pointed out to you before the exterior stairways leading into the amphitheater, and we can see that very clearly. We look at this and we see instantly this is the amphitheater at Pompeii. This gives us a great sense of what was here originally. You can see the seats are all still there. We see that arena wall. It's all painted. In this case it's painted like faux marble all the way around to give that sense of luxury. We see the awning over the amphitheater itself, instantly recognizable as Pompeii's amphitheater. There's a quadraporticus, or a portico, next to the amphitheater with a swimming pool in the middle. That's still there so we can know where we are.

The really amazing thing about this painting is that it doesn't just show us a generic view of the amphitheater. What it seems to be showing is that riot of 59. If you look at the painting initially, you see guys on the floor of the arena fighting. There are pairs of individuals down there, some people on the ground, other people beating them up, but then when you pan around and start looking around in the plaza outside and all the way around, you see those same figures. Fighting figures are all over the place. This is not a set of gladiatorial games. This is the riot of 59 taking place. We can see individuals fighting with one another throughout this area of the city. So this is an exciting source for us because it gives us evidence about what the amphitheater looked like and what the economic activity is for a set of games. We see little temporary stalls set up. We can see how the arena fit into its urban context. We can see the lines of trees that were planted around and have now been replanted. And, of course, we have the only visual source for this tremendous riot that took place. So material from and about the amphitheater gives us a lot of information about Pompeii and the games that occur here.

This is all good, but with the exception of this wonderful wall painting, it's not especially unique. A lot of places have amphitheaters. What sets Pompeii apart is the depth of the evidence that we have. This is what allows us to explore the role of games in the local community as we can nowhere else in the Roman world. We have evidence, not just at the amphitheater and not just about the amphitheater, but thanks to the careful excavation of particularly recent work at Pompeii, we can recover graffiti about gladiators, for example, where people stop and scratch on the sides of buildings, probably just using sharp instruments like a stylus, the Roman equivalent of a pen. They scratch little pictures of their favorite gladiators with captions having the individuals' names, and very often their career statistics, so you get a nice little graffito with an image of a gladiator and somebody's career stats down below. In some cases, where people have scratched on the walls on the inside of what seem to be inns or bars, we get a whole sequence of bouts where somebody has recorded a day's gladiatorial combat; scratched and kept a tally there on the inside of a bar.

We also have decoration throughout the city that is of gladiators that's more formal. Gladiators make an appearance in more formal wall paintings, and most notably, in tomb reliefs. There are many tombs around the outside of Pompeii that are decorated with the images of gladiators. Some of these we can believe are the tombs of patrons, individuals who sponsored games and want to be commemorated with this throughout their afterlife, to be associated with that great set of games. But with others, there's no evidence that's the case. They just seem to have really liked gladiators. This should be familiar to us and we should think about this. I saw an ad recently where you can buy a casket with your favorite college sports team's logo on it, so that when you go into the afterlife, presumably you go with the logo of your favorite sports team. That level of identification is what the Romans have toward their gladiatorial teams.

We also have from Pompeii something else that's unique to the ancient world, and that is on the walls throughout the city, and even outside the walls of the city, we have painted announcements, socalled "*edicta munera*," the announcements of games. These are painted announcements done by professional sign painters, for lack of a better term, who are paid to go around and announce sets of games. They're always written in red paint because the background color of Roman walls is generally white plaster. They paint these everywhere. We see them on the outside walls of houses and public buildings and, most surprising for us, tombs outside the walls of the city. Many of them preserved a number of these *edicta munera*, and so as we look outside the walls and walk along that line of tombs heading into the gates, we can see lines of these throughout the entire city.

These are a great source that we don't have anywhere else. Fortunately for us, the Pompeians seem to be very cavalier about replastering or repainting their walls because we can collect these *edicta*. I have done so myself; collected them and created a database of them. Archeology, by the way, is not all bullwhips and such. I have to tell you it's a lot of time in the library. What I found is that many of these *edicta* go back for decades. Remember, Vesuvius erupts in 79. Some of these announcements of games actually date back to the time of Augustus, so people are being rather cavalier about repainting their houses.

The announcements are fairly formulaic, and that's great for us because what they tell us is a number of key pieces of evidence about local spectacle entertainment. Again, this is material we get nowhere else. Even at Rome we don't know this level of detail. We always get the name of the sponsor of the games, and that makes sense. If you're paying some guy to go out and paint a big sign announcing a set of games that you're sponsoring, your name is going to be prominent, and so we see that. The name of the sponsor of the games is always the most prominent element, and the first one, and often about twice the size of the rest of the announcement of the games. So we get the name of the sponsor, and then an enumeration of the elements in the games, usually the number of pairs of gladiators. Very often it comes down to 10 pairs of gladiators a day, so if there's an announcement of a set of games that goes over three days, we have 30 pairs of gladiators.

The length of the games, how many days long they are, is announced. One, two, or three days is fairly common. Here at Pompeii, a small community, we can have games that go up to five days long, so that's quite an investment on the part of the patrons.

We also have announcements of additional elements besides gladiatorial combat, whether there are going to be prisoner executions as part of the spectacle. This is obviously not a regular occurrence, but something that occurs periodically when presumably you've saved up enough condemned prisoners. There are also added features that we find besides prisoner executions: the use of awnings. Sometimes there will be features that say at the end, "the awnings will be up" to entice you to come and sit in the shade and emphasize that spectator comfort.

We also see things that announce whether gifts will be thrown to the crowd. We talked about this at the Colosseum in Rome, whether or not they will have those wooden balls with the names of prizes on them that they sling into the crowd and someone will grab one and be the recipient of a month's worth of bread, or a slave, or an apartment house, whatever. I suspect the gifts here at Pompeii were somewhat more modest than the ones we know of at Rome. Nonetheless, this is obviously a feature that entices people to show up.

So we get these sorts of announcements. What we can do with these announcements is analyze them for a number of factors. We find out some key things. First, none of the games at Pompeii are funerary. Under the republic, of course, gladiatorial combat in particular, is exclusively funerary. By the time of Augustus, even in a small town like Pompeii, there is no funerary context whatsoever. It's purely political. All of the sponsors are local elite, and they're all people, thanks to the work on the *edicta* by other individuals, that we know of as office holders at Pompeii. They're individuals who are sponsoring games because they're running for office or because they're currently holding office. So that tells us that the games are part of the political system as an obligation of office or as a promise by somebody running.

The importance of offering games is obvious from the response of the 10-year ban. When gladiatorial combat is banned for 10 years starting in 59, that doesn't stop magistrates from offering games. Instead, we see substitutions for things like Greek athletic games—they announce certain Greek athletes are coming—or animal hunts. One of these *edicta* says bear hunts. So they shipped in some bears instead of gladiators.

The *edicta* also support the crucial role of the games for Pompeii as a community, not just for local politicians. The reason they do that is because many of these announcements advertise games not at Pompeii, but at other surrounding communities: Herculaneum, Cumae, Capua, Nola, Nuceria, and so on. So what we're seeing here is really a community exchange network. People are traveling back and forth between these communities. That makes sense when we think about the size of the amphitheater at Pompeii. We don't know precisely how many people it held, but it could have been twice the population of the city. Pompeii itself may have had a population of about 10,000 people, whereas the amphitheater could have held about 20,000. So we know that people are coming from the whole region.

If we make a calendar of the *edicta* and all the dates that they fall on, what we see, something even more surprising, is that we can create a schedule of the games over this almost 80 year period. We see that they fall in particular places. It's not based on weather. It's not like the games are always held in April or September when you think it would be nice out. They go all year round, from January to December, but there are key dates that they miss. Games are never held on election day. They're never held on the date that local officials take public office. They're never held opposite important agricultural dates. We know this from agricultural calendars. Games are never held opposite the harvest and things like that, and that all makes sense.

What I think is more surprising is the fact that games are never held opposite key festivals and markets at Rome itself. Never, in this long line of games at Pompeii do we see any conflicts with the major religious or economic festivals that we find in the city of Rome. This is really interesting material because what it tells us is the range people are traveling. Rome is over 120 miles from Pompeii. But if they're concerned about audience overlap, clearly people are moving that far or going that distance to attend games. I don't think it's just the Pompeians going to Rome. There's evidence of people from Rome coming down to the Bay of Naples; people from Rome going out. You would think they themselves would have enough games, but it seemed not to be the case. So this material in and around the amphitheater itself and the material throughout the city allows us to establish just how important gladiatorial combat is to the people of Pompeii.

The third piece of evidence I want to touch on is the archeological evidence of the gladiatorial school at Pompeii. It's a remarkable source of tremendous pride and civic identity for the Pompeians. The evidence for the gladiatorial housing and training facilities at Pompeii has forced us to re-evaluate what we thought we knew about the status and treatment of gladiators in the Roman world. Gladiators, of course, are technically slaves outside the normal social system. It was thought, well, forever as far as I can tell, that because they're slaves, gladiators were chained up, or kept locked way, or excluded from society. At Pompeii, at least, that seemed not to be the case. They're integrated into the community.

We have two locations that we can readily identify as gladiatorial barracks at Pompeii. The earliest one is just simply a house that looks like any other Pompeian house, but it seems to have been renovated inside about the time of Augustus. Thanks to the graffiti on the inside, it makes it clear that this was a house where approximately 20 gladiators lived, both free men and freedmen, that is, slaves and former slaves, as well as just men who were free. They live in this house in a regular neighborhood, coming and going. There's no evidence that they're chained up or anything.

The residence in that house probably ended in 62 with the massive earthquake that hits this area, and the house is probably no longer habitable. At that point is probably when the gladiatorial school moves into its largest facility, and stays there from 62, at the end of the earthquake, until the eruption in 79. This facility also tells us about the centrality of the gladiatorial school for the people of Pompeii because they took the quadraporticus, the four-sided portico, which was attached to the theater, and they separated it off from the theater. This was a standard component of theater design going back to the 4th century in Athens, to have a covered portico so people could leave the theater and find some place to stand in the shade. The Pompeians have taken that element off and turned that large quadraporticus, that four-sided portico with a courtyard in the center, into the gladiatorial school and barracks, at least from 62 to79.

This decision shows the city's willingness to give up valuable public space for gladiatorial training. It suggests the centrality of this community identity that's invested in the gladiatorial school. It also probably suggests the ramping up of gladiatorial games that occur under Nero, and that seems to be the case. Nero's wife, Poppaea Sabina, is actually from Pompeii and there are a lot of connections between Nero, Poppaea Sabina, and Pompeii that we can see. Nero seems to invest a gladiatorial school down here.

So the fact that they've moved the gladiatorial barracks into public land, into this large, prominent location that, as far as we can tell, is open to the public, is notable. It creates a new entertainment complex for the city of Pompeii. It also tells us something very important, and that is that our previous constructs of the fear of gladiatorial insurrection, informed by the revolt of Spartacus, seems not to be a problem at Pompeii. There are elements that some of the cells, or little rooms, around this do have some chains in them, but only a few of them. They seem to be for punishment, not for regular use. It's not as though every gladiator here is chained up at night. So there doesn't seem to be any great fear of insurrection.

Instead, what the Pompeians seem to be doing is advertising their gladiatorial school. Their training seems to be on display. If you look at the gladiatorial barracks at Pompeii, the gladiatorial school as we have it, or better yet, if you go and take a look at it yourself, you will see that it's readily visible from all around; from the theater, from the triangular forum next to it, and we know that people would come out and watch gladiatorial training. We don't know exactly what they're doing in there to train, but we do know that the public is witnessing this very carefully. It's a lot like people today going out to spring training for baseball, going out and seeing the training take place, and that's what's going on here at Pompeii as well.

So the evidence for the city is tremendously rich. It's unique from anywhere in the Roman world, and it provides us with tremendous sources to demonstrate the role of spectacle entertainment outside the city of Rome. Spectacle entertainment is the glue that unifies the community. Unlike at Rome where their grand entertainments are provided almost exclusively by the emperors themselves, at Pompeii we see this system in a small town where the duties of providing spectacle entertainment are those of the local political officials, but they're shared among local officials for the local and regional populous, for the surrounding communities, and for travelers who apparently come from at least as far away as Rome itself.

This suggests that the games here are more than just a reinforcement of the political system. They're very much a central part of creating a regional identity for a Roman community.

# Aquatic Displays

## Lecture 20

**Although gladiators and animal hunts were the most popular and famous of Roman spectacle entertainments, the grandest might have been the aquatic displays.**

Aquatic displays of all kinds called for special venues: theaters and amphitheaters plumbed for water or large artificial basins. Some ancient writers refer to the Colosseum and theaters in Rome hosting aquatic displays, but these venues seem illsuited to have done so. The substructures of the Colosseum that were integral to its functioning would have made submersion unlikely. The remains of the theaters show no evidence of the retrofitting necessary for aquatic displays, and their small size makes them poor facilities for hosting any largescale spectacles.

The only amphitheater in the vicinity of Rome that was plumbed for water in the arena seems to be that at Capua. As a slightly smaller copy of the Colosseum, it might represent the type of engineering that could have been used at the Colosseum. Its extensive aqueduct and drain systems reveal a facility, perhaps unique in the Roman world, designed for both land and water spectacle.

Literary, artistic, and archaeological evidence supports that certain emperors constructed and used for their spectacles large artificial water basins (*naumachiae*). Each was large enough to be one of the largest manmade structures in Rome. This tradition was initiated by Julius Caesar, whose *naumachia* was large enough to host a naval battle of thousands of men.

Augustus followed this model and left us more details about his basin. As he reported in his *Res Gestae*, he had an area 1,800 by 1,200 feet excavated and filled with water. This space was large enough for a battle of 30 ships and over 3,000 combatants in addition to the rowers. Later *naumachiae* were used by Claudius, Nero, Titus, and Phillip the Arab, although it is unclear whether Phillip was using previously constructed basins.

Many of the aquatic spectacles were animal-based, generally nonlethal displays, emphasizing extensive animal training that exemplified the control over nature by Rome and ultimately by the emperor, sponsor of the spectacle whose rule made this possible. Wild animals were trained to act against their normal behavior as an example of Roman conquest of nature. Some of the displays required animals to act like other animals—generally land animals to act as sea animals. For some spectacles, bulls and horses were trained to swim as though they were on land, violating their nature and providing novelty.

Other spectacles made use of animals trained to act like people or mythological figures, demonstrating control of nature by placing animals in human tableaus. The water ballets performed by land animals created a spectacle of human-like behavior. Titus's games at the inauguration of the Colosseum included a mythological spectacle of animals trained to be sea monsters and sea horses pulling the chariot of the sea king.

**Since 1810 scholars have debated whether the Colosseum was used for aquatic displays. Today there are still two schools of thought on the issue.**

The largest aquatic spectacles were the naval battles, also called *naumachiae* after the basins in which they were held. These included reenactments of historic battles, fantastic matches, and simple spectacles with no historical connection. The motivation for these shows was to demonstrate Roman control over the resources necessary to pull off these spectacles, enhancing the honor and position of the sponsoring emperor. Literary accounts emphasize the technical achievement of providing these displays. The size, including exact dimensions and placement, of the basins are prominently mentioned by authors celebrating novelty and accomplishment. The discussions of the *naumachiae* feature particular mentions of the wonder evoked by turning land into sea, a major factor of the imperial beneficence.

The battles demonstrate Roman ability to control history and to provide firsthand opportunities to witness distant events. Famous historic naval battles, such as the Athenian and Persian battle at Salamis in 480 B.C., were reenacted for Roman audiences, allowing the Romans control over history that preceded theirs and the ability to witness distant events as safe spectators. Fantastic battles between opponents who never fought could also be staged as *naumachiae*, extending Roman control over history. Many of these naval battles were presented in the context of triumphal celebrations, allowing Romans to witness and admire the ability of their armed forces from Rome itself. ■

## Suggested Reading

Coleman, "Launching into History."

Futrell, *The Roman Games.*

Jennison, *Animals for Show and Pleasure in Ancient Rome.*

## Questions to Consider

1. How does the creation and display of aquatic spectacle serve the purposes of Roman emperors and solidify their rule?

**2.** What lessons would a Roman crowd draw from these displays? Are the animal ballets celebrations of nature or of Roman control of it? What values and qualities do reenacted naval engagements celebrate?

# Aquatic Displays

## Lecture 20—Transcript

Welcome back. In this lecture, Aquatic Displays—Naval Battles and Swimming Bears, we're going to look at a different type of spectacular entertainment, one that is, in fact, apparently not a competition the way gladiatorial combat, or chariot racing, or so on was, but, in fact, is merely a show. It's not really a sport, but just pure spectacle. What we'll see here is defined not by the activities, but by the venues, and that is, the aquatic. We're going to look at a series of events that the Roman emperors sponsored that are some of the most fantastic of all the spectacle entertainment in the Roman world, and that is these aquatic displays. We'll look first at the venues in which they were held, both the theaters and amphitheaters that might or might not have been flooded, as well as the ready-made basins that are used for these tremendous naval spectacles. Then we're going to look at the spectacles themselves, both the non-sport aspect of animals in the water, as well as tremendous mock naval battles that were held under the empire. Then we're going to take a look at the meaning of all this; what the significance is and what these spectacles tell us about the Roman imperial world.

There is a tremendous number of aquatic spectacles of all kinds that we have mainly literary evidence for in the Roman world. Some authors refer to these as particularly Roman events, and I think that's apt, this Roman idea of theatricality that informs the notion of the aquatic spectacle.

We need to think about the venues where these were held. Some authors—and these are highly debated accounts—make it sound as though these spectacles were held in theaters and amphitheaters, most notably the Colosseum. If you look at the Colosseum today, what you see is—under the floor of the arena, and the floor itself is long gone, but restored in section—a whole gallery of rooms that are designed for animal storage, cages, cells for gladiators, armories, areas for the doctors to work on wounded gladiators, and so on. For this to be actually used for aquatic display, that is, for the entire arena to be filled with water for a mock sea battle or some performance by trained animals, all of that would have to be submerged. That presents a difficult problem.

I have to tell you that there are two schools of thought about whether the Colosseum and theaters were flooded in the Roman world, and that the argument about this goes back to 1810. So we're probably not going to solve it today. Frankly, it's enough to make me tear out my already thinning hair to think about these issues, but there really are two schools.

The first school is the purely literary, where you read the accounts of Martial where he writes in his five-book set of poems on the inauguration of games at the Colosseum. He tells us very precisely that the arena is flooded for a mock naval battle. That seems very circumstantial. There are individuals, authorities, for example, Kathleen Coleman, the world authority on spectacle entertainments, and who really believes Martial and thinks we should take his eyewitness account seriously and believe that he is accurate. Others look at the archeology and see that there's no apparent way that these could be flooded. There's no water source that seems large enough to flood these. Technically, there's nothing that supports the arena in order to support the tremendous volume of water. Water of that amount would be a tremendous weight. There's nothing there that tells us there was a drain system that would allow the Colosseum to be drained as well. I'm, I guess, of that second school. I'm agnostic in this. I don't find the evidence, either literary or archeological, compelling or persuasive enough that I can say that they did flood the Colosseum for games.

That being said, there are remains of buildings that do show us evidence; case in point, the amphitheater at Capua. Capua is a superb example, and it's very useful for us because it is certainly plumbed for water. There is an aqueduct that leads right up to the amphitheater at Capua to deliver large quantities of water very rapidly. There's also an extensive drain system that's still preserved. We can go down—and I've done this—into the basement of the amphitheater at Capua and trace the drain system. I realize it's not the most dramatic or exciting thing in the world, but it was fun and it led to some tremendous insights into how this works. Capua is important for this. It's also important because it's actually, with the exception of its well-preserved drain system, almost a carbon copy of the Colosseum. It was built perhaps 10 years later into the same plan. So if Capua was flooded, perhaps the Colosseum was as well. But I just don't know.

In any event, what we do see is a facility where we do know that aquatic displays were held in an amphitheater, so Capua is exciting evidence for that. We have literary evidence that theaters and amphitheaters are flooded, and then, of course, we have the evidence from Capua itself. Even I, skeptical as I am, am convinced that Capua was the site for some great nautical displays.

There are, in addition to what we might term "retrofitted buildings," specially made buildings designed for aquatic displays. These are referred to in the singular as a *naumachia*, and in the plural as *naumachiae*. Unfortunately for us, the name for the building forum, the "*Naumachia*," is the same name for the mock naval battles that were held in the basin, so it's completely ambiguous in the use of the term. I always tell my Latin students that if you have a low tolerance for ambiguity, Latin is probably not your language because they like to use the same word for a variety of meanings. It's as though they just don't care if we learn the language or not.

*Naumachia* is the name for the particular basins that we know of that are ready-made for these grand aquatic displays. The first of these was constructed by Julius Caesar, whose *naumachia* was used for a *naumachia*, a mock naval battle. The best understood of these, however, was built by Augustus. Augustus, in his *Res Gestae*, an interesting document that Augustus left, is a list that tells us his *res gestae*, that is, the things he accomplished. It's a wonderful list of all of the accomplishments he takes credit for during his lifetime. He wrote it himself, apparently, and left it with the Vestal Virgins, and then upon his death it was published. We have a couple of copies in fragments where it was carved out and placed on large slabs of marble so people could come by and read what Augustus had done.

In his *Res Gestae*, Augustus tells us that he constructed a *naumachia* right on the edge of Rome. If you look at Rome you will that most of the city as you're facing it is on the right hand side of the Tiber River. This, of course, is valuable urban space. Augustus built his *naumachia* over in the area that is now Trastevere, which is a word meaning "across the Tiber." That's what he did. He built it over on the west bank of the Tiber. He built an aqueduct system leading directly up to this basin. How big this basin was he also goes to pains to tell us. It was 1,800 Roman feet long and 1,200 Roman feet wide, so it was a tremendous, large area here on the edge of the Tiber, not filled by the Tiber, but filled by a separate aqueduct that kept the basin full.

If you want to see the remains today you can do so. If you go down the Viale di Trastevere, the main road down there, you'll see a Standa, which is a grocery store chain in Italy. Go into the Standa and go down into the basement to the house wares section, and there are all those plates and everything down there, and you will see in the wall are actually the foundations for the *Naumachia* of Augustus. I've done this myself a couple of times. It's fun to go down there and to see that they've built effectively an entire block along this main road based on the remains of Augustus's naval display basin, his *naumachia.* So that's something you can look for next time you're in Rome.

As I say, this space, which is about 1,800 x 1,200 Roman feet, seems to have been large enough for a battle for 30 warships. We also have evidence of later *naumachia* built or perhaps just used by Claudius, Nero, Titus, Domitian, and most intriguingly, perhaps even Philip the Arab. Philip the Arab was an emperor in the 3rd century during a period of great turmoil and crisis for Rome. It's unclear whether Philip used or renovated Augustus's *naumachia.* I think he actually renovated it rather than build his own. Philip is important in this history of aquatic display because if we leave him out, what we see is a very restricted range. The history of *naumachia*, aquatic performances, starts with Julius Caesar in 46 B.C. and goes up to Domitian in A.D. 89. So it's a very limited time period, except for this intriguing evidence of Philip the Arab, who seems to renovate the *naumachia* for Rome's great secular games during his rule.

These are the venues as far as we know about them, the number of basins, and we have just some fragmentary evidence and some marvelous reconstructions that might give us a sense of what these originally looked like.

What we do have is quite a bit of literary evidence that tells us about the events themselves, the activities that are taking place in these basins or perhaps in the amphitheaters. Many of these aquatic spectacles are animal-based, that is, they're not competitions or animal hunts, but they're generally what we might term non-lethal displays, emphasizing animal training. The notion here is the Roman idea of control of nature. I've mentioned this with the notion of Roman animal hunts, how they bring in exotic animals from specific far lands to display Roman power and control over those areas. This is a different sort of perspective on that idea of Roman control of nature. What we see is the Roman control of nature through training animals to do things that are completely unnatural to them. These aquatic animal displays are really only a component of the trained animal shows that we see on land. There is a tremendous tradition in Rome of land-based animal shows, and we have some very good literary, as well as visual, evidence of these.

The trained animal shows in Rome were regularly held at the Circus Maximus, and they provide the source for our use of the word "circus." The space, Circus Maximus, referred first to the building and then was transferred to the events that were held there. The animal shows were then called "circuses." From there, the word passes into our usage and that is the circus for the entertainment as opposed to the venue.

Examples of these land-based animal shows give us a sense about what the Romans are trying to accomplish. They're trying to accomplish a presentation, a spectacular display of animals trained to act in unnatural ways. These unnatural ways fall into one or two categories: either animals trained to act against their nature, but still as animals, that is, trained to act as though they are other types of animals. For example, carnivores are trained not to eat other animals. One of the standard forms of entertainment, apparently, is to train a lion to hold its mouth open while rabbits leap in and out of its mouth. Of course, you have to train the rabbit, as well as training the lion. There are also examples that suggest that they're training animals to be like humans, that is, elephants trained to walk along tightropes, bears playing with balls, and a variety of animals trained to do human activities.

Turning back to our aquatic displays, what we see in the literary descriptions of these animal-based aquatic events is the two types again: animals trained to act like other animals and animals trained to act as humans.

The first type is animals trained to act like other animals. In the aquatic events, what we see are land-based animals trained to act like animals of the sea. In particular, we have literary accounts of bulls and horses, which are trained to swim in spectacles, violating their nature and providing novelty.

The descriptions make them sound as though they're just swimming. But there are other descriptions that make them sound as though the animals are trained to act like people or mythological figures; not living people, but mythological individuals, where their training was one of control of nature to create animals in part of a human tableau, the aquatic version of those elephants walking along tightropes.

My favorite accounts of these are bears. Apparently, there is this tradition of training bears to synchronize swim, that is, a form of a bear water ballet that we have evidence of under Titus and, if the accounts are correct, under Domitian.

Every once in a while I fantasize about time travel with a video camera and when I do I have to tell you that this is at the top of the list of things that I would go back and film. I have sort of a three-step plan for this. Go back and film animals trained to synchronize swim, return here and put it on pay-per-view, and then retire rich. That's my three-step plan, so if any of you have mastered time travel, let me pitch this to you as a potential place to visit.

In addition to animals trained to act like humans, we also see animals trained to act like mythological figures. At Titus's games at the inauguration of the Colosseum, the poet, Martial, gives us a description about mythological spectacle. Animals—and I'm unclear on which ones; I think it's horses—are trained to be sea monsters. Then other horses—and we're certain about this—are trained to be seahorses, to pull a chariot of the sea king. We don't know who is acting as the sea king in this case, but what they're doing is creating a mythological tableau of these animals moving through the water.

The notion here, of course, is an extension of that Roman idea of control. It's informed by the theatrical spectacle that was received from the time of Nero on, where the Romans are emphasizing not just the novel or presentation of animals in zoos or anything like that, but really making these things do what the Romans want. That is the key aspect here.

This is certainly a form of aquatic spectacle and aquatic display that we have evidence of in the *naumachia* basins, as well as in the amphitheaters or perhaps even in the theaters, animals trained to act as sea animals. The largest of all these spectacles, of the aquatic display or, in fact, of any variety of spectacle, are the naval battles called *naumachia* themselves that are held in those artificial basins. These are extraordinary in what they represent about the Roman world. They're extremely sophisticated performances requiring huge resources and massive Roman infrastructure. Also, it's of special equipment, these special suitable venues, these large artificial basins created just for this purpose, and casts of thousands of specially trained performers, all so that a very large Roman audience can come out and witness this display.

We see in these mock naval battles reenactments of actual historical battles, about which I'll tell you more later, fantastic matchups between naval foes that never met one another, as well as nautical spectacles that seem to have no historical connection whatsoever. So the Romans were playing with what's going on in history with these notions.

The motivations for these seem slightly different than what we see with the animal displays. For these shows, the purpose seems to be to demonstrate Roman control over the resources necessary to create the spectacle itself. Remember that Augustus emphasizes in his *Res Gestae* the size of his basin, how great an undertaking it was just to create this wonderful venue for his aquatic display. So the notion seems to be that just by pulling this off successfully, the emperors have enhanced their public reputations.

I want to emphasize that idea about the emperors because this is a key point about *naumachiae*. They are all sponsored only by emperors. Nobody but the emperors controls the resources necessary to pull off one of these tremendous mock naval battles. In addition to that, they are all presented only in the context of special occasions, most notably, triumphal games. Unlike chariot racing where someone apparently walked by the emperor, Caligula, one day and said, "How about we have chariot racing today?" and Caligula said, "Sounds good to me," and they had a day's races. You can't do that with *naumachia*. We're talking about something that's an undertaking that might be years in preparation. So by just pulling this off, what we see is an emphasis on the technical achievement and emphasis on the command that the emperor has over the resources of the vast and far flung Roman Empire.

What we also see is a sense of something that we don't really think about much today, and it's the sense of wonder that's evoked by these. We don't use that word much, I think, any more, this notion of wonder. It's really been out of fashion, but this notion of awe or just being struck with some tremendous construction or achievement. We have the Seven Wonders of the ancient world, but we don't really celebrate things that way. We analyze them and criticize them and debate them. But for the Greeks and the Romans, something that just created a sense of wonder in its beauty, and its size, and its complexity could be contemplated openly with a sense of open wonder. That's the description we get about the *naumachiae* in the literary sources.

The other thing about these battles that I think is more sophisticated—and I'm going to ruin the sense of wonder here by analyzing them—is that they demonstrate the Roman desire and ability to control history. They provide the Romans the opportunity to really reenact historical events, sometimes as they were and sometimes, as I say, in the fantastic realm. They also provide the Romans something that we saw with triumphal processions: the ability here in Rome to witness, firsthand, distant events, something that is occurring somewhere else, in this case, not just geographically, but chronologically. Let me just briefly describe a few of these to you to give you a sense of what we're talking about, with these mock naval battles.

The first recorded public *naumachia* was offered by Julius Caesar, as I mentioned, in 46 B.C., as part of his great triumphal celebration, so, again, only part of a special occasion. It featured a battle between two fleets representing Tyre and Egypt, prominent Hellenistic Greek city-states. Tyre is along the Phoenician coast and, of course, the Ptolemaic kingdom of Egypt. The fleets were manned by 4,000 oarsmen and 2,000 marines. All of these individuals were prisoners of war, captured by Julius Caesar in his battles, most notably the Battle of Zela, and were convicted and condemned to death. So all these prisoners of war were expected to die. That, I think, points out the triumphal aspect that we have here, as well as the fact that this is not a competition; this is just pure spectacle. So Julius Caesar gives us the first one of these in a *naumachia*, the first *naumachia* in a *Naumachia* at Rome.

The second *naumachia* occurred under the emperor, Augustus. In 2 B.C., to celebrate the inauguration of his Temple of Mars Ultor, his votive temple which he had vowed in his attempt to overthrow and kill Julius Caesar's assassins, which, of course, he did, Augustus staged a reenactment of the Battle of Salamis, the battle in 480 B.C. between the Athenians and the Persians. In this case, in his new basin in *Naumachia*, Augusti, that is, Augustus's *Naumachia*, he has a battle with 30 ships and 3,000 marines. This is that basin that's 1,800 by 1,200 feet, so in there he has a lineup of 30 ships, so there must be 15 on a side. If they're set up the way a normal Roman battle line is, what we have is them divided into three large groups, so the units are spread out. So there has to be enough room in here for actual naval vessels to maneuver in this basin. This is, again, a tremendous idea. In addition to the basin, of course, there has to be room for seating around that as well.

We've got Julius Caesar and Augustus. The grandest of all *naumachia*, however, is sponsored by the emperor, Claudius, in A.D. 52. In this case, what we have is the largest of all of these. Claudius had two fleets, each one of which had 50 ships, so altogether 100 naval vessels, with a total of 19,000 marines. Now, given the number of vessels and the number of marines, this probably meant that he had upwards of 40,000 oarsmen as well. So approximately 60,000 men are involved in this naval battle, again, a mock naval battle: 60,000 men, 100 ships, all brought into this basin along the edge of the Tiber for a tremendous spectacle.

In this case, what we see is that movement from the historic to the fantastic because in Claudius's *naumachia* what we see is that his mock battle is between the forces representing the island of Rhodes and the island of Sicily. It's a completely non-historical event. We don't know what informed Claudius's idea here, whether or not he just wanted to do something wondrous. It's a curious account, but nonetheless, it's a very interesting one because it does show us this extension beyond just the historic.

I think this idea is not one that's ahistorical, however. I don't think the Romans here are creating something that is purely fantastic because they're actually picking real places. Rhodes and Sicily are famous for having tremendous navies. The island of Rhodes really controlled the eastern Mediterranean for over 100 years until the Romans destabilized it. Sicily, similarly, led by the city-state of Syracuse, had a tremendous navy.

So what I think we're seeing here is not just an attempt to create this fantastic idea of a foreign peoples, but to control history. Claudius, who was, himself, a historian and a published one, is apparently rewriting history to create this sense that he can control what's going on in these battles.

I want to point out one critical thing about these. In none of these battles do we see Roman fleets. They're all foreign peoples. The reason for this is that this is not like the displays that we see in a triumphal procession where they are directly celebrating triumph over foreign peoples. In this case, people on both sides are going to die. Most, if not all of them, are eventually going to die. So it would be inappropriate to have the Roman navy out there against, say, the Carthaginians. We don't see a reenactment of the First Punic War or anything like that. What we see is the Romans have their place as the spectators and the foreigners are the spectacle. In this way, it's much more parallel to what we see in gladiatorial combat under the republic where the categories of gladiators are named for Rome's enemies and the Roman citizens themselves are watching this spectacle.

It's clear, I think, that both types of spectacle, the animal-based, as well as the mock naval battles, are similar to their land-based counterparts of animal hunts and gladiatorial combat. They give emperors an opportunity to celebrate control over a variety of natural and historical acts and events. The animal performances demonstrate control over exotic, foreign, wild nature.

The battles that were reenacted for Roman audiences allow the Romans control over the history that preceded theirs and the ability to witness distant events as safe spectators. The fantastic battles, therefore, show the extent of the Roman desire to project their control across their world, both geographically as well as chronologically. The past and the present are under Roman control here.

As I said, many of the naval battles are presented in the context of triumphal celebrations, allowing large audiences of Romans to witness and admire the ability of their armed forces, that is, it's a celebration of Roman military victory, although their military isn't involved here, from the safety and security of Rome itself. Ultimately, the spectators in these, the largest of all forms of spectacle entertainment of the Roman world, are playing the role of beneficiaries of the entire Roman imperial system.

# Roman Circuses—Arenas for Chariot Racing

## Lecture 21

**Chariot racing at Rome was only the final stage in a very large and intricate system designed to support these massive entertainment spectacles.**

Chariot racing at Rome was controlled by four factions, which ran their own stables, recruited drivers, imported horses, and provided teams for public spectacles. The four teams—red, white, green, and blue—competed for centuries as the exclusive proprietors of chariot racing. Each imported horses from Spain, Africa, and the Near East; kept separate stables and training facilities; and hired and trained charioteers. Like modern professional athletes, charioteers could change teams during their career, racing for those who paid the best.

The fan base was large, intensely supportive, and probably based on class. With only four teams, Romans tended to support one color as a personal favorite. Some fans were so fervent they paid for spells cast against the opposing teams. The four teams divided into pairs of bitter rivals: red versus white and blue versus green. It seems clear that the green team had deep support among the poorer classes in Rome, and emperors who supported them were viewed as pandering to the urban mob. Because of these intense feelings, violence did break out over chariot racing, so imperial authorities kept tight security in the circus.

The circus itself, exemplified by the Circus Maximus, was designed to host the enormous spectacles of chariot racing while supporting a carefully devised system ensuring equal chance through the races. The Circus Maximus, located in the valley between the Aventine and Palatine hills, was integral to Roman spectacle. According to Roman tradition, Romulus held the first games on this spot. The Circus Maximus was a key location along the triumphal procession route. Processions passed through the circus, and some triumphal games were held in it.

In its finished form in the imperial period, the Circus Maximus seated as many as 250,000 spectators, making it the largest gathering place in Rome, yet it was less openly ideological than events in the arena. Unlike at the Colosseum, seating at the circus was open, so men and women of all classes and nationalities sat together. Without the emphasis on patrician class, senatorial membership, or citizenship, this seating created an open social atmosphere. Admission was free and open, except in the reserved boxes for the imperial party and the statues of the gods.

**In its finished form in the imperial period, the Circus Maximus seated as many as 250,000 spectators, making it the largest gathering place in Rome.**

The Circus Maximus was designed for chariot racing, with attention paid to drivers' needs and to ensuring a fair race. The track was almost 600 yards long and almost 100 yards wide to minimize accidents. It was divided down the center by the *euripus*, a low barrier over 350 yards long and 10 yards wide that kept chariots from head-on collisions. The *carceres* (starting gates) lined one end of the track almost 200 yards from the near end of the barrier, allowing the chariots time and space to pick up speed and an opportunity to race for an optimal position at the starting line. The *carceres* were curved in a long arc, ensuring that each was an equal distance from the starting barrier.

The Circus Maximus was also designed with care for the needs of the spectators. It was lavishly decorated for a luxurious experience, with columns, obelisks, fountains, and statues lining the *euripus*. All of the decorations were carefully selected to avoid impeding the view of the track. Spectators could follow the course of the race by the lap markers on each end of the barrier. Markers counted down from seven laps, the standard length of a race. Some of the many images of chariot races show flagmen on the track, who seem to be indicating the leaders.

Although arguably less central to the state than *munera* in the arena, the chariot races had critical religious and political aspects, as seen in the Circus Maximus. The major races at Rome were one component of key religious festivals such as the Roman and Plebeian games. These games were among the oldest and most vital of religious festivals, ensuring Rome's continued existence and prosperity from year to year. In addition, the circus hosted games associated with triumphs and many major religious events of all kinds before the construction of the Colosseum. All of these took place under the watchful eyes of the gods, whose major cult statues were seated in their own reserved box.

The chariot races in the Circus Maximus had a key political component through sponsorship, connections to the election cycle, and political dialogue. The major races were sponsored by the emperor and his family, who used these as an example of their beneficence and success at providing the benefits of empire to the Roman people, essentially offering the greatest good to the greatest number. The emperor was on display in a reserved box and engaged the crowd by starting the races and presenting the prizes to the winning charioteers. Because so many of the citizens and their leaders were present, the Circus Maximus became an important location for political dialogue between emperor and audience, sometimes with significant results for the Roman state as emperors were forced to respond to public appeals during the races. ■

## Suggested Reading

Auguet, "Chariot Races, Stables and Factions."

Cameron, *Circus Factions*.

Humphrey, *Roman Circuses*.

## Questions to Consider

1. In what ways does the Circus Maximus act as a political venue? How does this differ from the situation in the Colosseum?

2. What role did chariot racing play in the Roman world? Do the teams or factions have modern counterparts that we can use for comparison?

# Roman Circuses—Arenas for Chariot Racing

## Lecture 21—Transcript

Welcome to this lecture on Roman Circuses—Arenas for Chariot Racing. For sheer scale and audience appeal, no regularly scheduled spectacle in the Roman world competes with chariot racing. The *naumachiae*, the mock battles that we see in the great naval basins, are larger, but we can count on both hands the number of those that were held throughout Roman history. Chariot racing is a regularly established part of Roman spectacle entertainment and, as such, it's essential that we take a look at it because it is enormous in its scale and in its appeal. What we're going to do in this lecture is explore the idea of chariot racing in the Roman world, how this Greek entertainment becomes an organized Roman institution, and then we are going to look at the venues for spectacle, in particular the Circus Maximus and see how the religious, political, and social aspects work together in that venue. We're going to try and touch on notions of the circus as a stage for political theater and the key role of the races as they serve to create a common experience for much of the population of the city of Rome.

I've lost track of the number of times in my career that I've said something along the lines of, "If you could just see this yourself it would all make sense," or, "I really wish you could be there and experience this space, or this building, or this wall painting, or whatever." In the case of the Circus Maximus, forget about that because time and time again in my life, I've taken people from my father to groups of students to the Circus Maximus in Rome, and their universal reaction is one of immense disappointment because we have the space where the Circus was, in a little valley between the Aventine and Palatine hills, but the there is nothing left of the building itself. The grand Circus Maximus itself exists really as a big dirt spot. This is tremendously upsetting to everybody who goes there, and it's really a shame because what should be one of the highlights of the study of the public Roman world just doesn't come across at all. So what we're going to do is to rely largely on reconstructions to give you a real sense of what the Circus was like, the venue itself, as well as the events that took place there.

We need to be aware that chariot racing in the Roman world is only the final stage of a very large and intricate system designed to support a very massive entertainment spectacle. Chariot racing in Rome is also different than it is in the Greek world in that it is tightly controlled. For the Greeks, chariot racing is a form of elite competition associated with religious festivals like the Olympics, or Pithian games, and whatnot; only the very wealthiest people could sponsor a chariot. If their team won they would, of course, become famous, and get a prize, and make a dedication to the sanctuary.

In the Roman world, chariot racing is tightly controlled by four teams. This is the case for centuries; there are only four chariot racing teams that import their own horses, recruit their drivers, run their own stables, and provide the teams for the public spectacles. These teams never had names. They are only known by the colors of the tunics that the drivers wear. We have the Reds, the Whites, the Blues, and the Greens; and that's it. These are the exclusive proprietors of chariot racing. We have a marvelous mosaic that shows a Roman consul, in a chariot himself, flanked by riders from these four teams on horseback, all displaying themselves and their colors, the red, blue, green, and white tunics that they wear and, of course, their association with this political figure to make that case.

Each of these great chariot racing teams are factions, as they are called in the Roman world. It is an important term to know because it's the same one used for political parties. Factions refers to chariot teams and it also refers to one's political organization. Each one of these imported horses from around the Mediterranean world, from Spain to Saudi Arabia, they went and sought horses for their chariot teams; North Africa, all the way around the Mediterranean. Each one keeps its own stables and training facilities, recruits and hires its own charioteers, and when we learn about these charioteers and understand who they are, we get a sense of how this spectacle conforms to Roman institutional ideas. The charioteers, like the gladiators and animal hunters that we know of in the arena, are noncitizens, or at least they start as non-citizens. Some eventually make their way to citizenship, but they start out as non-citizens. Like modern professional athletes, charioteers could be free agents, that is, they would be hired by one team and then hired away by another one.

We have wonderful records of the career of one charioteer in particular, a charioteer whose name is Diocles, Diocles the charioteer. We have his epitaph. I won't read you the entire thing because it records his entire 24-year career in disturbing detail and it's just amazing. Somebody is counting every one of his races; where he placed, what happened, who won, the entire thing, and it's an extraordinary document. If you get a chance to see the epitaph of Diocles, you should do so. It makes for some amazing reading. What it tells us is quite a bit about chariot racing in the Roman world, starting with his name. Diocles is a Greek name and his full name, Gaius Apuleius Diocles tells us, because he has this Greek third component to his name, that he was born a non-citizen with his Greek name Diocles, and was later adopted into Roman citizenship. That is, he becomes a Roman citizen with a full Roman name, Gaius Apuleius Diocles. And so it tells us about the status of charioteers in a very clear way, understood by people who study Roman naming practices.

His career also tells us some very interesting details. He raced chariots for 24 years, and died at the age of 42. During the 24 years of his career, racing four-horse chariots, he started in 4,257 races. He won 1,463 of them. I've done the math and this is just over one-third of his starts. So one-third of the races he starts in, he wins. If you do the math, 4,257 races divided by 24 years, you come up with one race every other day on average during that 24-year career. I would think Diocles would be in any world athletic Hall of Fame just for that record alone. In fact, the length of his career and the number of wins, I think, makes him really a candidate for athlete of the millennium; of his millennium, at least.

So we know a bit about the charioteers, we know about their status, we know about their careers, and we know about some of the details of chariot racing. We should also think about the fans because the fan base for chariot racing is large. These are the largest audiences we see in the Roman world for any spectacle, with the possible exception of the *naumachiae*. The fan base is large and they are intensely supportive. By intensely supportive, I mean to the point of killing rival fans, if we can term that intensely supportive. The fandom also seems to be class-based. With only four teams available, Romans selected and supported one team as a personal favorite, and this seems to be pretty consistent. That somebody doesn't have a preference is extraordinary and almost unique. The emperor, Marcus Aurelius, who displays his stoicism and his Greek philosophical calm, points out that he doesn't have a favorite team and this is an example of how exceptional his is. Everybody else picks one of the four. We have remarkable evidence of how rabid the followers are. They do things like purchase spells to curse rival teams; things like that.

The four teams are largely divided into bitter rivalry. The Reds seem to be in rivalry with the Whites, and the Blues versus the Greens. It seems clear, from the literary evidence and some of the epigraphical evidence, and I've studied the inscriptions of Roman chariot racing, that the Green team has deep support among the very poorest classes in Rome. The plebeian classes seemed to be rabid supporters of the Green team. The emperors who supported the Green teams as well, notably Caligula, were viewed as pandering support from the urban mob by the senators who wrote about them. So there seems to be a real class conflict going on there. We have comparable things today, of course, in teams and in cities that have dual major league baseball teams. In New York and in Chicago there seems to be a real class consciousness about whether you support the Cubs or the Socks or the Yankees or the Mets. Because of the intense feelings and the immense amounts of money that are at stake here, violence breaks out around chariot racing, so there is a real social aspect. Chariot racing seems to not unify people into an entire Roman community the way the Roman government seems to hope. And so the imperial authorities keep tight security around chariot racing, or at least they attempt to do so.

One of the most famous examples of urban violence in the Roman world occurs under the Emperor Justinian, in 532, the so-called "*Nika* riots." "*Nika*" is the Greek word for victory. It's the chant that teams made, or their fan base made, to their charioteers. In the Hippodrome at Constantinople there was a massive riot, a mob action by the supporters of the Greens and Blues. Justinian tried for days to subdue the mob and finally just sent in the troops and killed about 35,000 people. He sealed off the entrances to the Hippodrome and killed everybody inside to take care of the problem. So there's really an intense fan base; strong feeling for these four teams. That gives you a sense about the role of this in the Roman world, the social and political aspects of being involved in supporting one team or another.

We need to think about and take a look as well at the venue for chariot racing, the circus itself really exemplified by the Circus Maximus in Rome.

The Circus Maximus is designed explicitly and precisely for the enormous spectacles of chariot racing while supporting a very carefully devised system of ensuring equality in the races, so let's take a look at how all that works. As I mentioned, the Circus Maximus—and we looked at an image of it today in its current state—really looks better on a model, if we can take a look at it there. It's in the valley between the Aventine and Palatine hills in Rome, and it's integral to Roman spectacle and Roman history. According to Roman tradition, Romulus held the first games here in the Circus. It was here, in the Circus, that the rape of the Sabine women occurred, this famous event when the Sabines were invited for a religious festival and games. At a prearranged signal, the Romans, having no women of their own, snatched all the Sabine women, and rushed them back behind the walls of the Palatine hill to become the mothers and wives of Rome under Rome's first king. So the Circus itself has a very old history for the Romans.

It's a key spot in the triumphal procession route. All triumphs, which gathered down on the southern part of the Campus Martius outside the walls of the city, make their way as they're passing into the city, through the Circus Maximus. Some triumphal games are held here as well, reinforcing that triumphal aspect. There's a triumphal arch built into one end of the Circus itself. The Circus develops gradually when Romulus was here, of course, if Romulus was there. It's just an open field down in the floor of the valley. Throughout the republic, it seems to have just been an open, low field. Gradually, however, it's architecturally articulated. The valley floor is leveled, the little stream that runs through is covered over, and stands began to be built.

The Circus itself seems to reach its greatest size under the Emperor Trajan. At that point, it probably held about 250,000 spectators. Some people have difficulty believing this number; I do not. Some sources say it could not have been over 150,000, but I think it must have been about 250,000. The reason I think this is because I've been down there in that space with over 300,000 people on a couple of different occasions. They hold free concerts down in the Circus Maximus in Rome in the summer, and on one occasion the official count down there was almost a half a million people. It was really quite extraordinary to see that number of people all on the slopes of what had originally been the seating area down there for a free concert. It was really tremendous to be surrounded by that number of people for a shared experience in a public spectacle, in my case of course, a rock concert. But nonetheless, 250,000 people is a lot. It's effectively one-quarter of the population of Rome during the early imperial period.

And so the Circus is quite extraordinary because it brings in a much larger proportion of the city of Rome than any other area in the city in terms of spectacle. It also brings them together in a different way than other spectacular venues do. In the Colosseum, of course, seating is hierarchical. It is strictly status-based, with the lower classes in the upper level of seating, all the way down to the patricians and public officials down on the edge of the area. At the Circus, what we have is open seating. Men and women, all classes, citizens, noncitizens, slaves, foreigners, all together in open seating. There is no emphasis on patrician class, on senatorial membership, or citizenship. So it really creates an open, social atmosphere, which is missing at the other spectacular venues, so I think the Circus is unique in this way. Admission is free, and it's open, and so people just come and pour into the stands, apparently, until they're full. The only exceptions are two boxes which are reserved seating: one box for the imperial family and one box for the gods. This is the only reserved seating. The gods are here in the form of cult statues, which make an appearance in the Circus in the seating area and, of course, the family of the emperor, his extended family, are all seated in a special box called the *pulvinar*, which means cushioned seat. The *pulvinar* is articulated by its own little roof system so that you can tell where the emperor is. It's generally, we think, lined up on the starting line, which is also the finish line, so the emperor can start the races and give prizes.

Such a vast number of people, 250,000, naturally supports a range of subsidiary activities. Around the exterior, if you look at the model, you'll see that there is a line of barrel vaults on the ground floor around the Circus supporting the seating area above. In those barrel vaults we have commercial activity, people selling food and drink and a variety of things. We know that prostitutes used those barrel vaults for business as well because there is an inscription that survives from Rome proclaiming a senatorial decree to tax the prostitutes for the upkeep and the repairs on the building. They are using it, they are getting the benefits, therefore, they should pay some taxes.

The Circus Maximus itself is used for a variety of entertainments, including animal hunts, gladiatorial combat, and a range of things, but it was designed for chariot racing, mindful of the needs of drivers and teams for a fair race. So we need to take a look at how the track is set up on the inside to make this happen. The track itself is just about 600 yards long and it's almost 100 yards wide, so we have a huge open space. The idea seems to be to allow as many as 12 chariot teams to go around in a race simultaneously to reduce the possibility of accidents. Also to reduce the possibility of accidents, and to keep the chariots going in one direction separate from one another, there is a long *spina* or *euripus*, a long low barrier which separates or runs down the center of the track. This is about 350 yards long and about ten yards wide, and it keeps the chariots from running into one another as they go around.

At one end of the track, we have what is called the *carceres*. "*Carceres*" is Latin for jail cells, actually, but these are the starting gates for the race. The starting gates line one end of the track and they are actually about 200 yards from the near end of the turning post at the end of that *euripus*. This is to allow the chariots time to get up to speed because the starting line is actually right there at the end of that barrier, and so all that 200 yard area is for them to jockey for position when they get up to that starting line. The starting gates are curved in a precise arc to ensure that each one of the starting gates is exactly the same distance from that barrier, from the starting line at the end of the barrier. So there's a real refinement going on here to make sure that everybody gets an equal opportunity no matter where they are along that line.

There's a lot going on in terms of subtle refinements to make sure that this is a fair race and that the race is completed. There's also quite a bit here that is mindful of the needs of the spectators to insure that what they see is a spectacular entertainment. There's quite a bit of lavish decoration. If we look at the decoration that we see illustrated in our reconstruction, or mosaics, or carved gems, or whatever medium we have of illustrations from the ancient world, we see that along the *euripus*, we have a lot of decoration. At each end there are three tall, thin turning posts, the *meta* at each end, and then along the line of the *euripus* we have obelisks, little freestanding columns, and things like that, all decorations that are long and thin. They're carefully designed not to obstruct the view across that barrier to anybody on either side. And I think that makes sense to you.

We also have elements of the circus that allow the spectators to keep track of what is going on in the race. If you look in the center of most every illustration of the *euripus*, what you see are lap markers: dolphins and eggs. Why they're dolphins and eggs we simply don't know, I have to tell you, but eggs usually on one end of the track and dolphins on another. There are seven of them in line. The dolphins seem to rotate so that you can turn them down to count down the number of laps remaining, and the eggs can be removed so people can, at a glance, see how many laps are left in a particular race.

Some of the images of chariot racing also show us men standing in the corners holding basins of water. They seem to be throwing it on the track to keep the dust down. We believe this is actually for the spectators so that the dust doesn't obscure the view.

There are also individuals that we see in some of the images who seem to have flags, one flag of each of the four colors, and these guys seem to be indicating the leader of a race. This makes sense because once you've started a race and you've gone a few of the seven laps, the chariots would spread out. It wouldn't be immediately apparent who was in first place and so you have a flag guy down there holding up the color of the leading team. This sort of refinement makes sense and shows that there is a lot of thought going into making this a great venue for the spectators. The notion of the flag guy is very similar in what you see in stock car racing, the leader board, or Indy car racing, where you see a list of who is currently in what position in the race. We see details of this in a marvelous terra-cotta plaque which showing a lion hunt taking place in the Circus Maximus, but it also shows us that line of eggs, a slender column, and you get a sense of the decorations as well.

Although it is arguably less central to the State than the games in the area, the *munera* of gladiatorial combat, chariot races have a critical religious and political role as well in the Roman world. The major races at Rome are one component of religious festivals. The two great religious festivals in ancient Rome, particularly in the republican period, are at the Roman games and the Plebian games, and they are each celebrated with chariot racing. These games are among the oldest and most important of all Roman religious festivals, and they insure Rome's continued prosperity and existence from year to year, so these chariot races play an integral part in religious festivals.

In addition, we see the political aspects. There are triumphal processions and games that are hosted by emperors, about which more in just a minute.

In addition to the fact that they host religious festivals, the games, particularly in the space of the Circus Maximus, as opposed to other circuses, we see a variety of religious shrines. The Circus Maximus itself hosted a number of religious shrines, notably a very old shrine to the god, Consus. Consus is a god of grain storage, a god so old the Romans themselves did not know what his name meant or why he was worshiped there, but his shrine was there.

I mentioned the key political aspects of the races, as well as the religious. Through the sponsorship, their connections with the election cycle, and the political dialogue that goes on here, is a lot of political maneuvering. Major races, particularly under the principate, under the emperors, are sponsored by the emperor and his family, who used these as an example of beneficence and to reinforce their success at providing the benefits of their rule to the Roman people. So we see them in the races, and we know from the literary accounts that they are active, and we also see them in the visual record. We have statues and mosaics and paintings that show us magistrates, sometimes senators and consuls, often emperors, throwing down the *mappa*, the starting flag, effectively. It looks like a big white towel that they throw down from their box to mark the start of the race, the opening of the starting gates and everybody coming out.

The emperor starts the races from his box and also provides the prizes. He presents the prizes to the winning charioteers; he doesn't just pay them money for them. We have a marvelous relief from the Hippodrome at Constantinople which shows the emperor in the *pulvinar*, in this exclusive reserved box, and he's standing there in the center and he's holding in his hand a wreath that he's going to use to crown the winning charioteer.

A lot of emperors strove to be associates with chariot racing. Caligula, Nero, and Domitian, most notably, are fanatics about racing. Domitian gives us the first example in the ancient world of expansion league sports. He expands the number of teams from the canonical four to six. He creates the Purples and the Golds. And then, of course, shortly afterwards he is assassinated so those teams drop out. So expansion league sports teams are not always a good idea.

Domitian also institutes something that does stick. He builds his great palace up on the Palatine Hill overlooking the Circus Maximus. He still has his reserve box in the Circus, but he has what is the world's first sky box up in his palace on the edge of the Palatine. And so Domitian, who was really a nut about chariot racing, could come and watch the races just sitting in the palace in his own private space looking out over the valley down below. It's really a extraordinary space and that actually is worth going to see if you want to see something related to the Circus Maximus in Rome. Go up on the Palatine Hill and experience Domitian's skybox. You can do that today. But the Circus itself is a disappointment.

Because so much of the city and so many of its leaders are present here in the Circus, as I say, about one-quarter of the entire population, the Circus Maximus becomes a very important location for political dialogues as well. We find constant references to political exchanges taking place in the Circus. The best example of this occurs under Septimius Severus. Rome was in the midst of a great civil war from A.D. 193 to 196. Septimius Severus hosts a series of games in 195, and the account of the historian, Cassius Dio, tells us that the entire audience spoke with one voice, begging the emperor for peace. That form of political dialogue is really extraordinary, and it shows us the power that's involved here in the Circus and, in fact, the civil war was over shortly afterwards. That seems to have occurred in the fall of 195, and the civil war was over by January of 196. Whether or not Septimius Severus took this to heart or the people just happened to get what they wanted afterwards, nonetheless, Cassius Dio really does preserve for us a the best anecdote we have about this massive political use of the Circus, not just on the part of the emperors to project their notions of authority, but on the part of the populous as a whole to create a dialogue with their rulers. That's the great thing about the Circus Maximus, it's that it becomes a great open space for everybody in Rome to come to and to use in a variety of ways all in the context of this greatest of regularly held spectacles chariot racing.

# A Day at the Races

## Lecture 22

**From gambling, to cursing opposing chariot teams, to picking up girls, to promotions, to actually watching the races, we follow our Roman guide through a day of racing under the emperors.**

For the spectators, a day at the races began long before the starting gates opened, and some of the most important aspects occurred outside the Circus Maximus. The evening before the races, the sponsor and the owners of the factions would host a celebratory dinner in the factions' stables. This provided a proximity to the horses and charioteers that would be rare in the life of an ordinary Roman. It was an opportunity for additional beneficence through inviting peers and associates to dine in this elite company. Prior to a day of racing, the names of the charioteers and their horses for each race were posted outside the circus. The list served as a form of advertisement if a prominent driver was scheduled to appear. This listing gave the writers of curse tablets the information needed to prepare these before the race, either for personal use or for sale to those entering the circus. The tablets were then nailed into the ground of the track before a race.

The open seating and social aspects of racing also began outside the circus. The poet Ovid describes hanging around outside the circus waiting to meet an attractive woman he can follow in and sit next to. Spectators could rent cushions and footstools before they entered the circus. Vendors selling refreshments set up shop outside in the ground-floor arcade of the circus, as did prostitutes.

Once inside the circus, spectacle started before the races themselves, with a *pompa* (procession) that had political, religious, and racing components. The *pompa* was led by political figures, reinforcing their roles and the power of the state. The sponsor of the games was accompanied by the other magistrates for the year, each bearing the symbols of office and creating a display of Roman political power. For major festivals, the young men who were about to come of age followed as visible reminders of the military strength of Rome.

Following the political and military imagery was the religious component, an integral part of every festival. The *pompa* started on the Capitoline Hill next to the Temple of Jupiter Optimus Maximus and proceeded into the circus from there. Cult statues of the major deities came next, borne on floats, each carried by a team of four men. The statues included Mars and Venus, the ancestors of the Romans, along with other key images, especially Victory.

The racing factions made up the final element of the *pompa*. The team owners, outriders, and auxiliary personnel all walked or rode in the procession. Finally, the charioteers in their chariots pulled by their teams concluded the procession. After passing into the circus and making a lap on the track, the charioteers went to the starting gates while the magistrates and gods took their places in reserved boxes.

**The emperor was expected ... to answer petitions and requests handed or shouted to him. Shouted petitions could escalate to the level of large-scale political demonstrations requiring immediate response.**

The course of the race involved both the sponsoring magistrate and the crowd but had the possibility of interruption for political theater or dialogue. The magistrate sponsoring the races took an active part throughout. He signaled the crews, who opened the starting gates by dropping the *mappa*, the cloth that signaled the start of the race. Once each race was concluded, the sponsor presented the prize money and a victory palm to the winning charioteer in his box, thus associating himself with victorious athletes.

The crowd responded to the action but also could affect the course of a race. Ovid records the cheers of the crowd as he counsels cheering for the team of the woman you wish to impress. He also makes it clear that in the case of a bad start, the crowd could signal for a restart by waving their togas, giving them control over the course of the race. As at games in the Colosseum, the crowd in the circus expected giveaways thrown to them at regular intervals.

Interaction between the emperor and the crowd, much of it political, would occur on a regular basis as these otherwise distant rulers would be in close proximity to the ruled for an extended period of time. The emperor was expected to attend to the action and to answer petitions and requests handed or shouted to him. Shouted petitions could escalate to the level of large-scale political demonstrations requiring immediate response. ■

## Suggested Reading

Futrell, *The Roman Games*.

Wistrand, *Entertainment and Violence in Ancient Rome*.

## Questions to Consider

1. In what ways did chariot racing encourage spectator interaction with the course or outcome of the race or with their political leaders?

2. How was the spectacle of chariot racing used to reinforce the core values of the Roman religion, military, and government?

# A Day at the Races

## Lecture 22—Transcript

Welcome to this lecture on A Day at the Races. Having established the basics of Roman chariot racing and the venue in which it occurs, what we want to do now is turn to the experience of a day at the races and try and follow through what might be a day of full racing for an average spectator, from gambling on the races, to cursing your opponents, to picking up girls, to even watching the races themselves. We follow a Roman guide through a day of racing under the emperors. The experience allows us to see what the races really meant to a Roman, to an urban inhabitant of the city of Rome, under the early imperial period. The races serve as an opportunity for spectacular diversion, as well as a chance to address otherwise distant political leaders.

Before I start on that, I need to say something about how we know what we know. I talk about spectacular entertainment to a lot of people, mainly students, and I find that most of what people know falls into two groups. If people are of a certain age, they've seen *Ben Hur* and have an idea of what chariot racing looks like from that. If they are, perhaps, of the demographic of my students, they've seen a particularly regrettable episode of *Xena Warrior Princess*, where she races Caligula. I want to point out that neither of these is a documentary. We get an excellent view of chariot racing to a certain extent from *Ben Hur*, but if we really want to understand chariot racing in the Roman world, we need to go back past *Ben Hur* and *Xena Warrior Princess*, back to the primary sources, the literary and visual sources and what they tell us. So what we're going to do here is try and do that as best we can.

One of the emperors who was the most fanatical fan of chariot racing was Caligula, so what I've decided to do is to pick a putative day of racing under the Emperor Caligula. Caligula ruled from A.D. 37 to 41, was enamored of chariot racing, and identified with the charioteers himself. He hosted games in the Circus Maximus, as well as his own circus outside of Rome, and he was a real follower of the Green faction. We can picture ourselves here, I think, under a series of chariot races, under a set of games under Caligula. Just for effect, we'll select the Roman games, the great *ludi Romani*, which Caligula himself would have sponsored in the fall and early September of A.D. 38. So picture yourself on a crisp fall day.

To flesh out what we know about Caligula and chariot racing, we're going to also use the source of Ovid. Ovid, the great Roman poet of love, wrote before the time of Caligula. He passed away almost exactly 20 years before Caligula came to power, so he is almost contemporary. He gives us a first hand account of what happens in a day of racing and what the average Roman thought about it, so he's really an invaluable source. Between the literary, visual sources of racing under Caligula and what Ovid tells us about a day at the races, I think we can get a good sense of the sequence of major activities here.

For spectators at a day of racing, the actual spectacle begins long before the starting gates open for the first race, or even before they open up the Circus for people to rush in and claim those open seats. Some of the most important aspects of the race at the Circus actually start the day before. The evening before the races, the sponsor and the owners of the factions would host a dinner in the factions' stables. The idea of having dinner in a stable is perhaps not the most appealing thing, but this was, for a lot of people, a wonderful opportunity to get close to professional athletes, the charioteers, close to the horses, and close to the patron of the games, the emperor.

It's an opportunity on the part of the emperor for additional beneficence to host this dinner for his clients and for his—the emperor doesn't have peers, but for his associates in the stables. That idea of proximity to the horses and the charioteers appeals to Caligula particularly. So Caligula himself, we know, hosted dinners in the stables the night before races. In his case, he's a fanatical supporter of the Green faction, and he hosts dinners for the charioteers and the faction owners and everything. Then he'd call out the Praetorian guard and have them patrol the streets all around; not to protect him, but to protect the horses. So the Praetorian guard, the bodyguard of the emperor, would be out all night in the streets around the stables of the Green faction, making sure nobody disturbed the animals' sleep. So there would be this great dinner where everybody would recline on their elaborate, formal dining couches right there in the stables, and talk about horse racing the night before in this great, I suspect, boozy dinner event. Well, that's sort of the night before ceremony and what's going on there.

We also see, before anyone enters the Circus Maximus in the morning—we have ample evidence—that the list of the charioteers and the horses themselves, all by name, are posted outside the Circus Maximus. Famous charioteers like Diocles, who I've mentioned to you, have worldwide reputations, but horses are also famous. We have a number of images, and mosaics, and wall paintings, and such that show us not just the names of the charioteers, but the names of their horses as well. These would all be posted outside of the Circus, giving people a sort of a teaser of the day's races to come. It serves as a form of advertisement of a particularly prominent driver, or particularly prominent team of horses that is to appear, and it also serves as an opportunity because outside the Circus, among that commercial activity that's taking place—the people selling snacks and wine and the prostitutes, and so on—are witches, that is professionals who will, for a fee, cast a spell. They will write out a curse tablet cursing a particular team.

Picture a putative young man who is coming to the races and he is a follower of the Blue faction, which seems to be particularly popular among the nobles. He might stop and see the announcement outside the Circus of who is going to be there that day and note the names of the drivers for the Green faction, the hated rivals of the Blues. He notes the names of the drivers and the names of the horses, and he might go to one of these witches and pay for a curse tablet. This is just simply a flat sheet of lead in which a spell is scratched with a little iron stylus. The witch would cast a spell and then what they do is take that flat piece of lead and fold it in half a couple of times and drive a nail through it into the surface of the track. That spell details the name of the driver and the names of the horses.

Roman magic, much like Roman religion, in terms of prayers, has to be specific; you have to really invoke particular actions for specific individuals, so you must list what you want. "I want all the drivers of the Green faction [and list their names], "and all their horses [and list their names], "to all be struck deaf, dumb, and blind," and list it all very circumstantially or the spell won't be effective. Then somebody, perhaps the witch we suspect, would go onto the track and drive that nail into the surface of the track itself so that the curse is actually there and ready to be engaged once the horses run over it. I think this is a remarkable event. We know about this because we've discovered a number of these curse tablets, some of them *in situ*, actually in position in the surface of tracks.

I think this is quite extraordinary, not for the notions of Roman spell casting and magic and ritual cursing in the Roman world, but simply for the fact that there is that much access to the track. I know that in thoroughbred racing today you can't get near the track. You can't get near the horses. I've been down to the Kentucky horse farms on a number of occasions, taken my daughter down to see the thoroughbreds, and they are always guarded by these guys with automatic weapons. I mean, they have machine guns keeping you away from the horses down there. They're very careful about access. And so for the Romans, that doesn't seem to be a problem. They let people onto the track. It's a very different idea.

So, we are with our putative young man, he's a follower of the Blues, he's just cursed the Green team, and now he's hanging around outside. The open seating and the social aspects of the races really start outside. If our young man is similar to Ovid, he is waiting outside to meet a young woman. Because of that open seating possibility, Ovid tells us you come to the Circus to pick up girls. Going to the amphitheater or to the Colosseum to pick up girls would be a complete waste of time. You can see one, but you couldn't sit next to her. At the Circus, you can sit next to her. And Ovid tell us that you can meet an attractive young woman outside, and you can treat her nicely. You can buy a cushion or a foot stool, which are, apparently, available for rent, or a program. There's a Latin word "*libellus*," meaning little book, that Ovid used to suggest that somebody is out there printing programs for sale. So you find a young woman and you buy her a cushion, and a foot stool, and a program, and you follow her in, and sit next to her. And Ovid tells us that you can buy refreshments as well; food and drinks and snacks and sweets. And because of the seating at the Circus, and it sounds a lot like the seating at, for example, University of Michigan football games, where I think you get 16 inches to your seat, you are all pressed together. Ovid thinks this is ideal because you are sitting right next to this young woman.

So far, we're now finally inside the Circus Maximus itself and the spectacle hasn't really started. There's nothing that's gone on beyond the social and the magical so far.

The first component of the games is a *pompa*, that is, the procession, that occurs. This is the great parade that starts any day's racing. The great *pompa*, or procession, is an opportunity for political, military, religious, and of course, the racing components to all come together. The *pompa* is led by political figures reinforcing their roles as patrons of the games. In the case of Caligula, we know that he did this. Caligula would be right out there in front, allowing everybody to see him as the patron of the games. He loved that role, not just at formal festivals, but at the drop of a hat. We know on one occasion somebody walked by Caligula and made a random comment saying, "How about a day's racing?" Caligula said, "Good idea. Let's do that." So they had an impromptu day of racing at the Circus Maximus, quite an extraordinary event for the Romans.

This *pompa*, or large procession, is going to start with the sponsor of the games, accompanied by the other magistrates for the year: the consuls, and *praetors*, and *aediles*, and so on, making a real display of the political power. In Caligula's case, of course, it's going to be himself and members of his immediate family, as well as the local magistrates, all carrying the symbols of their office. So you can see the political power there.

If we are in fact at the *ludi Romani*, the Roman games, then we would have the young men who are about to come of age, that is, about to be old enough to join the military. They would be the next group because they would represent the future of Rome. So we have the public officials , then we have all the young men about to come into their adulthood. Caligula, in fact, made a point of speaking to these young men. There is an account in Suetonius's *Life of Caligula* where he stops and greets a group of these young men. So we know that Caligula is particularly attentive to them as well.

Following the political and military imagery is the religious component, an integral part of every festival. This religious component is of two types: first, the spectacular, that is, the kinetic, the participatory aspect, and second, from the location because the *pompa* gets its start at the Temple of Jupiter Optimus Maximus up on the Capitoline Hill. Everybody gathers up there at the Temple of Jupiter and from there makes their way down to the valley of the Circus Maximus.

In addition to that association with the Temple of Jupiter, we also have the cult statues of the major deities, all carried in the procession because they are going to make their way into the Circus to their own reserved seating. Ovid describes this to us and he tell us about the deities that are here: Mars and Venus, the ancestors of the Romans, along with other key figures. In particular, a statue of Victory, the personification of victory is here. Ovid describes how the *pompa* comes though the Circus and everyone sees the statues of the gods and stands and cheers for their particular deity, their patron deity. And Ovid, of course, being who he is, stands and cheers for Venus, as our young man might, sitting next to his young woman, would stand and cheer for Venus.

The final component of the *pompa* is the racing component. The team owners, the outriders, the support staff, the flags, the auxiliary personnel are all there and then finally, the big finish, the charioteers themselves. In their chariots, pulled by their teams, they conclude the procession. As it passes through the Circus, everybody makes a lap along the Circus and that's quite a lap actually; I've done this myself. It's just over a mile making that lap, so we are talking about quite a distance. At this point the magistrates and the gods peel off for their reserved seating; the charioteers go into the starting gates and prepare for a day's racing. At some point the starting gate assignments are made. This seems to be a random draw, but it's not part of the spectacle, so our guide wouldn't witness this and nobody really talks about it, but we do know that there is some sort of random assignment of starting gates.

The course of the race involves both the sponsoring magistrate and the crowd, but it had the possibility for quite a bit of interruption for political theater or dialogue. The magistrate is starting the races and in this case, of course, Caligula is going to be very prominent. Caligula loved the Green faction and cheered for them wildly, and would make a real spectacle about supporting them, standing up and heckling the supporters of other factions and cheering for the Greens and throwing those gifts to the crowd, particularly to the fans of the Greens, and doing those things that really made it really clear that he was a partisan.

He, of course, would also start the races. Caligula would be up there in his box and at the start of the first race, he would take the *mappa*, that big white flag, and throw it down from the box so that it landed down on the floor of the arena. The starting gates burst open and then all of the teams burst out. There are as many as 12 teams at once, so there could be as many as three chariot teams of four horses from each of the factions. So you could have three charioteers and three chariot teams for the Reds, three for the Whites, three for the Blues, and three for the Greens in a full line of races.

We have a marvelous image for you about what a race might have looked like. This is not actually an episodic image; it's not a snapshot, it's synoptic. It's a synopsis of what is going on at the races because in the background we've got Victoria's charioteers holding her hand up, but what we have in the foreground is chaos. I think this really gives us a good sense of probably what it was like once those starting gates opened and all the chariots rushed up to that near end of the barrier so that they could make the shortest possible lap. They are all rushing for that one point at the end of the barrier, which is really the starting line, so that they can cut the corner and get the quickest race out as possible.

Normally, an emperor or magistrate who is supervising the games would stay up in his box and when a charioteer won a race, the charioteer would come up and get his prize. In Caligula's case, this is not what he does. We have a marvelous mosaic image which actually shows a magistrate down on the floor of the arena, and this is exactly the type of thing that Caligula did. It's a complete violation of his social and political role. The performers that are down there on the floor of the arena are not Roman citizens; they are, in fact, outside the Roman system. But Caligula was so desperate to associate himself with these individuals that he descends down to the floor of the arena. And in this image we have an unknown individual giving the prize, but it could well be Caligula because we know that he goes down there and associates with the charioteers and even, horror of horror, races a chariot himself. So this is a marvelous image of the end of a race and it really shows us that association of the emperor with the winning charioteer.

We see the winning charioteer standing in his chariot. He still has the reins tied around his waist, which is how they hung on to the four charging horses. They were actually strapped onto the horses. Each of the horses has a branch of some flower, probably laurel or palm, in his headdress, and then the magistrate is giving the prize to the charioteer. The symbolic prize is a palm branch, but in his other hand he has something that actually looks kind of like a dinner roll, but it's actually a purse of money. That's the real prize for a charioteer. We know that some of these chariot races actually paid huge sums of money, and in the case of Diocles, we know that his lifetime earnings amounted to 35 million sesterces, which is one of the biggest fortunes we know of for a non-elite in the Roman world. It's really a tremendous amount of money.

In a day's racing, the crowd responds to the action, but it could also affect the course of the racing and not just through the curse tablets, although there is always that hope as well. Ovid tells us that the crowd cheers for their teams, of course, and there seem to be particular team-specific cheers, as well as general cheers. But he also tells us, and gives advice to our young man, to cheer for the team of the woman you are trying to pick up. In this course of giving this advice about how to cheer for the team of the young woman, he tells us something very clear, and that is, in the case of a bad start, the crowd could signal for a restart by waving their togas. Remember all the men are wearing these long white, woolen togas which are made up of 15 yards of wool, and they could stand up and somehow signal for a restart. We don't know how this was decided, but at some level there must have been some technical problem; one of the starting gates didn't open, a scratch start we might call it in sports today. What's quite remarkable is that the crowd can call the charioteers back. This gives them an immense amount of control over the spectacle. Ovid makes it clear that if your girl's team gets a bad start, you stand up and wave your toga, hoping for a restart so that that she'll be happy later on. He's a genius.

What we don't know about a day's racing is actually quite a bit, but I did want to cover some of what might happen during the course of a day's racing in terms of the actual race itself. How long might a race be, how many would there be in a day, and that sort of thing.

As I said before, there are 12 starting gates, so you can have up to 12 chariots at a time in a race, three from each of the four factions. A standard day's racing is, throughout the early imperial period in the 1st and 2nd centuries, 12 races. Later on, this doubles to 24. The question is, how long would a race go on? If we use a comparison from the Kentucky Derby today this might give us a rough estimate, if we could do the math correctly. The Kentucky Derby is about a mile and a quarter long and it's run in about two minutes. The mile and a quarter is almost exactly the same distance as one lap at the Circus Maximus. A race is seven laps instead of one and the horses are carrying a chariot as well as the driver, although the chariot, as far as we can tell, is fairly light, probably weighing no more than 100 pounds complete. So we have the driver and the chariot divided between four horses. If they can do a lap all together in a coordinated team in about four minutes, or double the time of the Kentucky Derby, then what we might have is a race being completed in roughly 30 minutes. So we have 30 minutes for the race, then we have the prize ceremony. We have people out collecting the broken chariots and the broken charioteers who have wrecked or crashed during the course of the previous race, and then we have to get people back to the starting gates.

I cannot a imagine that a good seven-lap race, plus the beginning and ending ceremonies and so on, and the cleaning up, could be conducted in less than an hour, which suggests to me that these 12 races in a day must have taken about 12 hours. I think you could push it if you wanted to, but it's really going to take an extraordinary amount of time. Those times later on where they are doubling to 24 races in a day; I think what we are seeing is shorter races and also a shift from four-horse chariots to two-horse chariots, which seem to move faster.

So what we have is a rough idea of how long a race lasts and how long a day's racing is. This is a full day of festivities. There is also, Ovid tells us, as well as the accounts of the epitaph of Diocles, an emphasis on the first race after the *pompa*. The first race of the day seems to have been particularly important, and so that gives us evidence that it's likely that subsequent races after the first one would feature less famous charioteers to kind of fill out the card. This, of course, is opposite to the way we do, for example, horse races. The first race of the day is not always the most prestigious. It could be the last race of the day. Same thing with boxing cards; you have warm-up bouts and things like that. But for the Romans it's the opposite.

This seems to indicate to me that people are not just sitting there on that bench for 12 hours watching the races. They're watching the first one, they're watching some in between, but there are also a lot of social things going on here, some of them social, some of them political. In the case of Ovid, he is there trying to pick up girls. But there is also a tremendous amount of political dialogue taking place. Interaction between the emperor and the crowd would occur on a regular basis where otherwise distant rulers, and even people who were as common as Caligula, are still distant to the vast majority of Romans. You don't see Caligula everywhere.

You are here in close proximity between the ruler and the ruled for an extended period of time, so there's lots of opportunity for dialogue and exchange. Part of this exchange is what we might term ritualized or expected kind. Caligula is famous, of course, for throwing out prizes to the crowd. He loved to do that and to give these lavish prizes of slaves and villas and apartment houses and things like that all written on these wooden balls. He would really get the crowd stirred up. On some accounts, he would like to throw these wooden balls into empty seats and watch the people rush down into the seating area after them. I could see Caligula doing that.

The emperors were also supposed to attend to what the crowd has to say. And we know that there is repeated dialogue going on between the emperor and the crowd. For example, in Caligula's case, he's a die-hard supporter of the Greens, and if the Greens lose, he gets really petulant and the crowd mocks and laughs at the supporters of the Greens. If, for example, the Blues were to win, Caligula gets really angry and shouts at people and threatens them and acts, in our estimation and that of elite Romans, inappropriately. This gives us a marvelous sense that this is not just a one-way street. There's real dialogue going on here, and even emperors who aren't considered to be the best follow the rules of answering. They have to be in attendance, they have to be paying attention, and they have to answer what the people say. Whether or not they answer appropriately is, of course, based on their character. But shouted petitions could also escalate to the level of large political demonstrations in the Circus, and we see this, as well under a number of emperors, requiring immediate response.

A day's racing in the Circus Maximus, particularly under Caligula, where we have a lot of evidence of what's going on, provides a huge swath of the Roman population a pleasant day of competition and entertainment, and a shared experience with 250,000 of their closest neighbors. It's really an extraordinary idea. It's in a venue designed to create the best possible racing experience, combined especially with religious associations and interaction with the imperial officials, creating an inclusive Roman identity for a large part of the entire population of the city of Rome, a unique experience in any spectacle entertainment in Rome.

# Theaters and Plays

## Lecture 23

**The Romans adapted Greek comedy and tragedy to better fit audience expectations for spectacular entertainment.**

The forms of Roman theater, like the building form, were derived from Greek examples but were altered for Roman needs. The Greek theater building was a seating area and orchestra set into a hillside with no freestanding superstructure. The performance space was the orchestra floor of the theater with no sets, props, or effects, only doors for entrances or exits.

Greek plays focused on mythology-based tragic theater with limited theatricality. They were set within a 24-hour period and used just one set. They featured no action, only dialogue; all scenes of violence, for example, occurred offstage. Greek tragedy used mythology metaphorically to refer to contemporary problems but did not directly address them.

Roman theater, based on Greek antecedents, emphasized spectacular display and diversion. Roman theaters were freestanding buildings with elaborate facades and awnings shading the audience, similar to the Colosseum, creating luxurious settings for the performances. Roman plays were performed on stages with elaborate, multistory stage buildings as backdrops. Expensive props, sets, and special effects would heighten the drama of the performance, creating a spectacle entertainment out of a philosophical tragedy.

The Roman interest in and desire for theatricality and spectacle probably contributed to the eventual popularity of comedy over tragedy. Tragedy was probably more popular in the republican period, but none of the plays and few sources survive. The evidence makes it clear that the tragedies were versions of Greek plays performed at Athens in the $5^{th}$ century B.C. Tragedies were Romanized with local references and Roman stories. Plays became a component of the major religious festivals during the republic as early as 364 B.C., probably starting with tragedies, in imitation of Greek festivals.

Comedies were also originally based on Greek models but developed into particularly Roman products. The stories, of clever slaves outwitting their masters while aiding love-addled young men, became stock plots. The comedies used a number of comic techniques, such as *stichomythia* (dialogue with short lines like a tennis match), slapstick, and songs substituted for the Greek chorus. All 27 of the extant comedies are by two playwrights: Titus Maccius Plautus and Publius Terenius Afer (Terence).

**Audience comprehension was aided by the selection of stories from Greek mythology, which was known to all the spectators.**

Starting in the 1st century B.C., forms of Roman theater called pantomime and mime became increasingly popular, eventually supplanting tragedies and sharing the stage with comedies. Pantomime was a performance form similar in many ways to modern ballet. It portrayed themes of love, adultery, and mythology through dance and gesture. Pantomime grew in popularity in the late republic and early empire as a dance form. It originally consisted of a solo dancer accompanied by music (flutes, pipes, cymbals) and a chorus. The performance was without dialogue, but the story was conveyed through music, dance, costume, movement, and attitude. The stories could be either comic or tragic, and audience comprehension was aided by the selection of stories from Greek mythology, which was known to all the spectators. Spectators would recognize characters by conventional costume and masks.

Mime was, despite the name, a spoken form of theater that rose in popularity throughout the imperial period. It consisted of spoken, usually short vignettes that could be either serious or comic but were often satiric. Unlike pantomime, dance and masks were not used by the large casts, which included women. The satiric nature of the performance and the depiction of sex and violence probably contributed to mime's popularity. The performances became increasingly spectacular, with special effects and witty references to current emperors and, later, the Christian church. ■

## Suggested Reading

Scodel, *Theater and Society in the Classical World.*

Slater, *Roman Theater and Society.*

## Questions to Consider

1. What qualities and components did Roman theater owe to its Greek antecedents? Where did it strongly diverge from them?

2. How did the performance space and selection of theater types reinforce our notions of Roman spectacle?

# Theaters and Plays

## Lecture 23—Transcript

Welcome back. In this lecture, we're going to explore theaters and plays in the Roman world, or more precisely, theatrical spaces and the theatrical performances that take place in them. We're going to look at what these spaces are like. We're going to look at the types of performances there are, and we're going to try and place them a bit in the context of the Roman world.

Before we do that, I think it's important for us to think about what, perhaps, we know and where the Romans got their ideas for theaters and for performances. I would wager that much of what you know, as with me, comes from Greek theater. We know a lot about Greek theater spaces and about Greek theatrical performances. Much of this, of course, is due to the generations of high school English teachers who have insisted that we read *Oedipus Rex*, or at least in my case, in $10^{th}$ grade, or at least the Cliffs Notes versions of *Oedipus Rex* and look at pictures of Greek theaters. So this is a good place for us to start.

It's also a good place for us to start because it's where the Romans started. They directly developed their theatrical spaces and traditions largely from the Greek, and so we'll establish the Greek model first and then build from that. So we'll start from that brief survey of what Greek theater buildings are like and Greek theatrical performances, and then see what the Romans did with all of that.

For the Greeks, what we see in terms of their theaters is something that's recognizable, but actually distinct, from the Roman tradition. If we look at an image of a Greek theater, for example, what we see is these are invariably built within hillsides. They're not freestanding structures. They're always built within a large hillside with the slope of the hill making up the seating area. Down below, at the base of hill, is the orchestra. This is the performance area. It's invariably a round area. "Orchestra" means dancing floor, and it gives you some idea of the origins of Greek theater. Greek tragedy in particular comes from Greek dance, and so we have this great circular area where the action takes place and that, I have to tell you, is a misnomer. There is no action in a Greek play, about which more in a moment. Everything takes place in that big round area with the audience seated almost all the way around.

There is generally a building behind that serves as a screen to screen off the orchestra and the theater itself from the surrounding buildings. But there are no sets, there is no stage, there is no real staging of any form, and so it's very different than what we're used to for a theater. If we look at another image of a Greek theater from the perspective of the audience, we get a good sense of that. Picture yourself seated up here on the top row of a theater looking down on that orchestra and the performances all taking place down there below.

We've got a good reconstruction that I like to share with people of a theater in Athens. It gives you a sense of what it was like to attend a theatrical performance in Athens in the 5$^{th}$ century B.C., the period and place where we know the most about Greek drama. What we see here is an open air theater built into the side of a hill, with the orchestra down below. The seating area is filled with perhaps 5,000 individuals. Everybody inside that theater is male. This is an important distinction from Greek to Roman. All the performers are male. The entire audience is male. It's a male form of performance designed by men for a male audience, and so I think that's significant and something worth thinking about.

In terms of the performance that we see in Greek theaters, the Greeks wrote comedies as well as tragedies, but tragedies are, in fact, the primary form. In a performance that you might find at a Greek festival you have three tragedies for one comedy, and that gives you a sense of the primacy of tragedy over comedy. In that play—let's just pick a generic tragedy—all of the action, as it is, takes place within a 24-hour period. Again, there are no sets; there are no props. That building that frames the back of the orchestra serves to give space for entrances and exits, but there's no way to change the scenery or anything like that. Everything is taking place right out there in the open.

This is effectively theater without theatricality because what we have is all dialogue. This should be familiar to us if you attend theater. This is what we might call the *Glass Menagerie* school of theater. It's discussion as opposed to the *Phantom of the Opera* musical theater. I think more people, however, are familiar with film than with live theater, and I think that's probably a better way to think about it because film is our genre of communication and entertainment. What I refer to Greek theater is the *My Dinner With Andre* school of theater. I don't know if you've seen the film, *My Dinner With Andre*. It's a great movie if you get a chance to see it. It consists of two men seated at a dinner table talking for two hours. And that's all they do is they sit there and they talk. No action takes place, but it is fascinating.

The alternative to what I refer to as the *My Dinner With Andre* school is the Hollywood blockbuster, the *Raiders of the Lost Ark* school of film making with special effects, and a large cast, and all these sorts of things, a real spectacular performance. This is not a qualitative distinction. I'm not saying *My Dinner With Andre* is superior to, say, *The Lord of the Rings*. *The Lord of the Rings* is an amazing achievement in film making, but they are, in fact, quantitatively very different, and Greek theater is like *My Dinner with Andre*. The reason for that is because Greek theater is a mythologically-based story. Greeks never present contemporary individuals in their tragedies, and so the theater is, for example, the Greek plays that we're familiar with: *Oedipus*, and *Antigone*, and *Medea* are all based on Greek mythology. And so what we see are stories in Greek mythology that the audience is supposed to already know.

What's the point, then, of telling you about them or showing them? The point is because these act as mythological metaphors. You, as a Greek audience, are supposed to leap in and fill in this mythological story as a contemporary metaphor. *Oedipus* is a story about fate versus free will, *Antigone* as duty to the State versus duty to the family, *Medea* about the limits of human experience and what it means to be a human, and that sort of thing. This, again, is the Greek tradition, and the Romans take this and build off of it, so it's important that we understand that.

We know that the Romans were interested in Greek theater, and in fact, carried on these traditions because we have marvelous images. There's a great wall painting from Pompeii that shows a scene from the tragedy of *Medea*. Medea, of course, is jilted by her husband, Jason, who leaves her for what we would call a trophy wife, a young princess, and Medea, to get back her husband, decides to kill their children. Not that she doesn't love her children, but she hates her husband that much.

We have this marvelous wall painting from Pompeii that shows us a pensive scene of Medea here, reflecting, holding a dagger in her hand and looking at her children. As a Greek play, you would never see any of that horrific action of Medea killing her children, or of Oedipus blinding himself, or anything. All that occurs offstage, and messengers just report back. So the Romans are familiar with these stories, they know the tradition, and this is the tradition they develop their theater from. For the Romans, the tradition is developed. As I say, they make major alterations, so we need to talk about those.

Roman theater emphasizes spectacular display and diversion over the political and personal reflection that these Greek mythological-based tragedies emphasize. Naturally, of course, Roman emperors are going to frown on the type of political engagement that you find in Greek theater. Roman emperors are not keen on the audience going home and reflecting on tyranny and its limits, or whether or not you should overthrow the State, and at what point. Greek tragedy does this all the time. Roman drama, not so much. Roman emperors are very keen on ignoring the man behind the curtain. So what we find instead is an emphasis, again, on the spectacular.

That starts with the building itself, the actual theater that we find in the Roman world. We have an excellent example, still extant today, in the theater of Marcellus, and we have an image of that you can see. The theater of Marcellus is just down from the Capitoline Hill in Rome. In fact, the theater is just down the hill between the Capitoline and the Tiber River. It's a free-standing theater. It's not built into a hillside, and this is important because being free-standing, Roman theaters can be built anywhere, not just into that hill. That means that theaters can be used to change the topography of a city. You can create monumental performance spaces where you want so that they, themselves, act as markers within that urban fabric to establish identity and values. You can see Roman emperors building theaters throughout not just the city of Rome, but other cities as well.

Being themselves spectacular, and we get a good sense of that from a reconstruction cutaway of the theater of Marcellus, we can see that there is an elaborate stage building behind the stage. The orchestra is cut in half, and the actual performance takes place on a raised stage, with a stage building usually two or three stories tall behind it. So the building itself is much more spectacular and grand than a Greek theater. The cavea, or seating area, is all freestanding, so you have marvelous arcades that wrap around. On top of that—and in this reconstruction you can see these projecting poles—you have an awning that covers the seating area. So it's spectacular and it's luxurious. Being so, they are a natural outlet for imperial beneficence, as well as a venue for political theater.

Let me touch on those two things. First, being spectacular. Because the Romans have a stage with a stage building behind, they can have special effects. There is a great anecdote from the life of Nero where we read in Suetonius's work about a theatrical performance taking place where Nero, being no slouch on spectacle himself, is there, and there's a fire in the stage building as part of the performance. Rather than in Greek theater having somebody run in and say the building is on fire, the Romans actually lit part of the stage building on fire, and that became part of the performance. It was a really spectacular effect. You could also have all sorts of entrances, and exits, and sets, and props, and all sorts of things that the stage and stage building make possible. You have people up on those second and third floors. There's a great example from the theater at Sabratha, a three-story stage building with arcades, and people would be up there as well as part of the performance, and you would see them in illustrations up there in those arcades.

Another anecdote from Suetonius's *Life of Nero* tells us about the theater as a venue for political theater. Nero is hosting the king of Armenia in this particular event, and they go to the theater of Pompey, the first stone theater in Rome. This was built only in 52 B.C., very late as these things go because the Romans were opposed to theaters and didn't want to have a permanent one. Nero takes the king of Armenia to the theater of Pompey, which apparently, according to Pliny the Elder, is one of the three buildings in Rome you take people to when they visit the city. He had the awning replaced with one that was dyed purple, with gold embroidery throughout, and they had this elaborate theatrical performance where the king of Armenia knelt to Nero and Nero put his crown on him, accepting his authority. Then he stood up and they both stood there flanked by members of the military and all the legionary standards. It was a spectacular display of imperial power, and the theater was the appropriate venue for that. So these buildings are important in the distinctions between the Greek and the Roman.

One last distinction I want to make about the Roman theater is in the seating area itself, and this image from Sabratha makes this very clear. You see a wall separating parts of the cavea, or the seating area, and that is, as at the Colosseum, in a theater the seating is by class. Only members of the Patrician or highest class are seated down below on their curial chairs, or their chairs of office that would bc carried in for them. And then the middle classes are seated above them, and then finally, the lower classes are seated at the worst seats up above.

We've talked about the theater building, how Romans are interacting with it, how they're seated, and things like that. We need to cover the performances, as well as the space. There are four basic forms of theatrical performance that we have in a Roman theater. We're going to start and carry these through by their period of popularity, from the earliest to the latest.

The earliest popular form of theatrical performance is tragedy. In Rome, tragedy is more popular in the early and middle republic as far as we can tell. We don't have any of these early tragedies extant, which is unfortunate, but we have references to them. We know that the Romans are, in fact, adopting tragedies directly from the Greek models. They're taking Greek tragedies and rewriting them with Roman locations and, of course, in Latin, Roman names, and things like that, and then performing them. So they're Romanizing Greek plays of the type that we would see in Athens in the 5$^{th}$ century B.C. They are also performing them in a manner, in a context, which is also Greek, and that is, as part of a religious festival. For the Greeks, tragedies are performed as part of major religious festivals. The Romans do this starting, as far as we can tell, in 364 B.C. That's the earliest event that we know of where the Romans adapt a Greek tragedy and perform it as part of a festival. And so the Romans, with tragedies, are adapting both the Greek forms and the Greek context in their tragedies.

Tragedies, as I say, are popular in the middle republic. From them what we begin to see is the rise of comedy. These comedies that we know of are actually more popular, eventually, than tragedies. This is, again, the opposite of the situation that we see in Greece. Comedies are also based on Greek models, and the Romans take these and adapt them as far as we can tell.

We're actually very fortunate because we have the opportunity to see, in a film version, something that is probably close to what a Roman comedy was like. If you have the opportunity and can find it, go out and see if you can get a copy of *A Funny Thing Happened on the Way to the Forum*. *A Funny Thing Happened on the Way to the Forum* is, in fact, based on a Roman comedy, and they have just taken this Roman comedy, put it into English, changed a few subplots, and that's it, and filmed it. It's wonderful. It's still hilarious today. Well, opinions vary on that. I think it's hilarious today. Anyway, it still plays. It played on Broadway and it plays on film, and it has all of the elements of a Roman comedy. It has the standard plot. It has mistaken identities. It has wacky entrances and exits, lots of slamming doors, sort of French farce-like. It's really tremendous. It's also got, as I say, the standard plot of pretty much every Roman comedy, and I'll give you that right now.

The standard plot is this. There's a clever slave. There's a member of a family. The two most important other members of that family are the father, the paterfamilias, who is a stern upholder of traditional Roman values, not too bright, though, and a young man, probably 18–20 years old, desperately in love with an inappropriate young woman. He's also not terribly bright. The slave is smarter than both of them.

We have the beginnings of a conflict here: A love-addled young man, the stern father who doesn't approve of his choice of girl, and the clever slave. So you know, of course, what's going to happen because we're still using this plot. By the end of the comedy, the young man will have reconciled with his father, who will have approved of the girl, they will be married, and the slave will get his freedom. I'll save you two hours.

This is the standard plot, not only of Roman comedy. Actually, P.G. Wodehouse wrote almost 90 books, many of which are based on this exact same plot. Instead of a slave, he substituted a British butler, Jeeves. Instead of the not-too-bright young man, he has a not-too-bright young master, Bertie Wooster, but it's the same plot.

These comedies use a number of techniques that I think would be familiar to us today. We actually have quite a few images of these comedies. There is one I wanted to show you here of a comedy taking place. There are a lot of these in the Roman world. There is a particular technique called *stichomythia*. *Stichomythia* is short bursts of dialogue given back and forth like a tennis match. *Stichomythia* is used in tragedy, but also in comedy, and it gives you that wonderful cross-talk routine.

If you think about that famous comic routine, *Who's on First*, think about it in Latin, if that's possible. That's *stichomythia*, a wonderful word play and confusion, and back and forth dialogue, often boiling down to slapstick. Somebody is going to get hit by the end of this, and we see this in Roman comedy as well, a lot of slapstick and that sort of thing.

Roman comedy also takes the Greek forms like the chorus, for example, and substitutes for the chorus, songs. So Romans really developed the first musical comedy. If you've appreciated musical comedy sometime in your life, thank Roman authors.

I should mention those authors here because we have two playwrights from the Roman world whose works are still extant. All of the existing 27 comedies that we have from the Roman world were written by two authors. The earliest, not by much, is the author known as Titus Maccius Plautus, who died about 184 B.C., so in the second quarter of the 2nd century B.C., and his slightly younger colleague, Terence—Publius Terenius Afer—who died in about 159 B.C., so again, the second quarter of the 2nd century. Both of them, as I say, wrote all of the extant comedies that we have, and they are really responsible for developing that Roman form of musical comedy, which is popular from their lifetimes in the 2nd century B.C. really through to the end of the Roman Empire.

Those two forms of theatrical performance, tragedy and comedy, are both derived from the Greek. What we see are two other forms that I wanted to mention called, confusingly, and I would like to personally apologize for this, pantomime and mime. I know, it couldn't be any more confusing, could it?

Starting in the 1st century B.C., what we see is these two forms, pantomime and mime, supplanting tragedy. They take over as a native form of entertainment. Let me describe these to you. You can, hopefully, distinguish between the two of them.

Pantomime is a dance performance. That's the best way to think about it. It is equivalent to modern ballet. What we have are pantomimes that are dance performances that are on a variety of themes—love, tragic love, comic love, lots of mythological scenes—that could be expressed through dance, music, and gesture. Pantomime starts, as I say, in the late republic and grows throughout the early empire. It originally consisted—and we have a wonderful image of this—of a solo dancer accompanied by music—flute, or pipes, or cymbals, or perhaps all three—along with backup singers, of chorus. The performance, as I said, is called pantomime; it is completely without dialogue. I think the equivalence to ballet helps. I don't know if you've ever attended a ballet, *Cinderella*, or *Swan Lake*, or *the Nutcracker*. For the Romans, it would be a mythologically based story as it was for the Greeks and they wouldn't need to have the story told to them. They would know it already. If you attend the ballet *Cinderella* you're going to know the story. So the performers, in this case an entire company, can convey the story to you through gesture, through costume, through movement, through their interactions, and through the music. You don't need to know the story. *The Nutcracker*, some of the finest times I've had at the ballet have been at *The Nutcracker* in a warm auditorium on a December afternoon. I had some fine naps at *The Nutcracker*. That's probably not what they wanted to hear, but in any case, you don't need to know the story of *The Nutcracker* beforehand because it's all there in the masks, and costumes, and everything, and so there's really no need for a synopsis of it.

The Romans were the same way. They knew the stories from Greek mythology and they could be conveyed, originally by a solo dancer, and then gradually throughout the Roman Empire, as there's an interest in novelty and spectacle, by entire companies of dancers. And so we know that these performances increased in popularity, in size, and in spectacular scale throughout the empire. By the time of the 2nd century A.D. what we have are public companies of pantomime dancers, which include men and women together. Of course, we have men and women in the audience in the Roman world as well, and so again, there's a key distinction between the Greek and the Roman.

The final form of performance I wanted to talk about is mime. Despite the name, mime is a spoken form of theater. I mentioned in my lecture on Roman funerals mimes as actors. Mimes would perform as professional mourners in the funeral context.

Mime is an incredibly popular form of Roman theater, again, like pantomime. It really takes off in the 1st century B.C. and develops throughout the imperial period. It consists of spoken, usually very short, vignettes. These could be serious or comic, but they're always satiric, and as far as we can tell, the comic ones were the most popular. I think it's effective here to think in modern terms. If you think about modern sketch comedy groups—*Saturday Night Live*, or standup comedy, or Carrot Top. I try not to think about Carrot Top too much, but that's the idea that we're thinking about here with mime—people that tell jokes, make satirical comments, a lot of commentary on authority. If you're familiar with the work of George Carlin, he was always talking about government or religion in his stand-up routines. When he appeared in a movie, I think one of his film roles, *Dogma*, he spent the whole movie skewering the Catholic church, for two hours. This is the type of thing that mime does, troupes giving short vignettes of action, again, always satirical, skewering authority figures.

You might appreciate that this would be more popular under the empire than the republic. Under the republic, when all government is representative and everybody can go down to the forum and argue about things and talk everything out, there's really no need for this form of humorous attack on government because government is everywhere, it's everyone, and you can go down and attack it directly. But under the empire things are less direct, so there's a real boom in this notion of satiric attacks on authority, not just Roman government, but eventually the Christian church as well. There are particularly a lot of satiric attacks in the 3rd and 4th centuries on local priests and bishops and things, local Christian authorities.

The satiric nature of the performance, along with the comedy, fueled the attractiveness of this form of theatrical performance. There is also a lot going on in mime that is attractive in a spectacular way. Mime is not bounded by the traditional boundaries of tragedy and comedy. There is a lot of sex in mime, not necessarily full nudity, although there is evidence of that, but actually of display of the human form. There are a lot of revealing costumes, a lot of bawdy humor, a lot of fart jokes and that sort of thing. There is also a lot of violence that takes place in these mimes, and it takes place directly on stage where everybody can see it.

Again, if we take a page from Suetonius's *Life of Nero*, Nero attends one of the mime performances one time and the subject is the fall of Icarus. Icarus, with his father, made wings out of wax and feathers, and flew to escape their captivity. Icarus, the son, flew too close to our sun. The wax melted, and he fell and died. In this performance, according to Suetonius, *The Fall of Icarus*, the performer actually did that. He leapt off the stage building and he fell, apparently by accident, and splattered right there on the stage and died, and Nero himself was splattered with the man's blood. It was considered to be an extraordinary spectacle, unexpected, but not unappreciated.

This is a tragic form of mime, but again, the most popular form, as far as we can tell, is the comic form. It's satiric; it allows people to, in a safe way, attack their authority figures, whether they are the Roman government or the Church, eventually. So this mocking of authority and the love of mocking authority is common for the Romans, as it is for us. Again, if you think about sketch comedy like *Saturday Night Live*, I think you get a good sense of what mime would have been like. This was enormously popular. Mimes could themselves become some of the wealthiest men in Rome, and certainly, celebrities in their own right.

If we think, therefore, about Roman theater, and we'll finish up here with a nice image of the Roman theater at Orange. We see a lot about it that is characteristically Roman—spectacular spaces, large buildings that are lavish and grand in scale, luxurious in their awnings, seating by class, decorations, including images of the emperors themselves worked into the images of the buildings, and then at the Roman performances. The earliest forms of tragedy and comedy are based on the Greek models, but then the later forms, the more native Italic forms that we see that become the most popular, are the characteristically Roman. Pantomime, has marvelous dance and music performances. It tells stories. And, of course, I think the most characteristic and eventually the most popular of all the Roman forms, mime, which gives us our best sense of the role of the theatrical performance in the Roman world.

# Emperors as Performers

## Lecture 24

**On occasion, emperors such as Caligula, Nero, Domitian, and Commodus left the box and descended into the performance area. This lecture focuses on those emperors who left their seats to perform in the arena, theater, and circus as gladiators, animal hunters, singers, and charioteers. It covers their motivations, their performances, and the result of violating social norms, including—inevitably—losing their lives.**

Rarely did emperors descend from their reserved boxes to act as performers in Roman spectacle. From the four who did, we get remarkable insight into Roman rulers and the expectations for their behavior, along with their responses to cultural values. The usual pattern of imperial behavior at spectacles in the Colosseum and Circus Maximus was strictly prescribed. The emperors followed the rigid class structure of Roman culture, reflected in the Colosseum and Circus Maximus, where they sat on display in box seats surrounded by family and civil and military officers. The expected behavior of the emperor as patron of the games was to administer games, give prizes, distribute largess to the crowd, and answer petitions. Each of the four emperor-entertainers (Caligula, Nero, Domitian, and Commodus) illustrates and accelerates an important shift in Roman culture: the changing definition of what it meant to be a Roman man.

The republican definition of manliness, *virtus*, was virtually unchanged for several hundred years, with its demonstration only in battle. Under these four emperors, we see the deliberate shift to a broader definition as each associates the imagery of triumph and *virtus* with other activities: chariot racing, gladiatorial combat, musical performance, and hunting. An analysis of the circumstances of each of the four reveals parallels in their situations and insight into the motivations for their extraordinary behavior.

Caligula, Nero, and Commodus were very young, the latter two in their teens when they came to power, and none had military experience although all succeeded successful generals or conquerors. Caligula, Nero, Domitian, and

Commodus each succeeded emperors who were family members; unlike Trajan or Hadrian, they were selected not for competence but for dynastic reasons. The result of these factors was a set of emperors with unstable successions, no natural constituencies, and little experience in government.

Caligula (r. 3 A.D. 7–41) was the first emperor without military experience. Through a series of public actions, he denigrated the military in favor of chariot racing and gladiatorial combat. His denigration of the military seems to have been one component in the plan to redefine *virtus* away from the battlefield and toward his own values. He personally mocked the commander of the army units in Rome. He called the army out on maneuvers to collect seashells and then held a faux triumph for their achievement. His great triumphal procession was to parade across the Bay of Naples wearing the breastplate of Alexander the Great.

Instead of training as a soldier or commander, Caligula was a great supporter of the chariot races in Rome and a charioteer. Caligula's support of the green faction was notorious, as they were associated with the lower classes. He built a second circus outside Rome and trained himself as a charioteer. He hosted lavish feasts at the stables and used the army to secure the stables before races. Most scandalously, he trained and performed as a gladiator, specifically a *thracian*.

Nero (r. A.D. 54–68) accelerated Caligula's pattern of behavior, appearing as a charioteer, animal fighter, and singer and emphasizing the triumphal imagery. Nero assumed the roles of charioteer and animal fighter in the circus and arena. Nero left his reserved seat in the Circus Maximus to dress and act as a charioteer, to the delight of the crowds. He also appeared as an animal fighter, imitating Hercules and his labor killing the Nemean lion; this occurred in the context of mythological reenactments seen in the arena.

Nero's major spectacular entertainment occurred when he performed as a singer in theaters in Rome, Naples, and Greece. Starting in Rome and privately, Nero eventually moved his performances into the public sphere. From Rome he moved to Naples, which was originally a Greek colony and still hosted Greek-style competitions, including musical ones, which Nero entered and won. Finally he traveled to Greece, where he participated in all of the major musical contests that were rescheduled on his behalf, winning all of the prizes. Nero's motivation was clearly redefining *virtus*, as seen in his use of the military and reaction to his victories: They were celebrated as triumphal processions.

Domitian (r. A.D. 81–96) was by all accounts obsessed with games in the arena, presenting huge numbers of *munera* and chariot races. His obsession led to emphasis on the Circus Maximus and Greek games. He built his palace with the first skybox, which overlooked the Circus Maximus in the valley below, allowing him to watch the races from the palace. He created the first expansion teams in Roman chariot racing, the gold and purple teams. He also built the first public stadium in Rome for Greek athletic games.

**In his largest games in November 192, [Commodus] killed 100 bears with exactly 100 spears.**

Domitian also performed for the public as an animal hunter. He was famous for his ability with the bow, one of the weapons of Hercules, with whom he identified himself in public sculpture. A bronze statue of Domitian as a lion hunter was placed in the courtyard of a temple to his deified brother and father. He also kept a game park outside Rome, where he staged at least one public lion hunt.

Commodus (r. A.D. 180–193) is the best documented of the public performers, appearing as a gladiator, charioteer, and animal hunter. Commodus appeared repeatedly as a gladiator. He was dressed and performed as a left-handed *secutor*. He went on to win more than 1,000 bouts. This was largely attributed to his position as emperor rather than his ability as a *secutor*. His appearances were conflated with the identity of Hercules, whose lion skin and club were carried before Commodus or placed on display in the imperial box when he appeared in the arena.

Commodus raced four-horse chariots in the circus while dressed as a charioteer. His appearances as an animal hunter also used the Hercules imagery and emphasized the emperor as protector of the empire. Dressed as Hercules, he killed dangerous wild animals. In his largest games in November

192, he killed 100 bears with exactly 100 spears. He also killed bulls, a tiger, a rhinoceros, a giraffe, two elephants, and five hippopotami.

These emperors clearly needed to distinguish themselves from previous emperors, with Domitian and Commodus creating a mythology of themselves as sons of Jupiter and Hercules. The result of their behavior for *virtus* and its definition was the successful redefinition toward hunting and the expansion of the worship of Hercules and Greek culture in general. ■

## Suggested Reading

Köhne and Ewigleben, *Gladiators and Caesars*.

Wiedemann, *Emperors and Gladiators*.

## Questions to Consider

1. How do the accounts of emperors as entertainers represent variances from their traditional roles and subvert Roman personal values?

2. What parallels to we find between the biographical details of these emperors and their adoption of the identity of Hercules?

# Emperors as Performers

## Lecture 24—Transcript

Welcome back. In this lecture on emperor performers we're going to be looking at what is some of the most transgressive behavior that Roman emperors undertake, behavior that transgresses tradition, and almost all Roman social and cultural boundaries. So it's going to be quite a ride here.

We're going to take a look at what's expected of Roman emperors when they attend performances. We're going to look at four case studies of particular emperors: Caligula, Nero, Domitian, and Commodus, who transgress those boundaries of acceptable behavior. We're going to try and assign motivation for what they do and see how their actions, how these very transgressive behaviors actually serve to change Roman culture in the long run. So it's quite a bit to cover here.

The first thing we need to do is cover what is expected. What are the traditional roles for a Roman emperor at public spectacular events, spectacular performances? That pattern of accepted behavior for emperors is very prescriptive. There's a set limitation of what they're supposed to do. They, themselves, are also on display, as are the performers in the Colosseum, the circus, or the theater, but the emperor is on display in a particular location and context is key. He is on display in his box. The good emperor, so to speak, sits up in his box and does everything that he is supposed to in association with the performance. He, along with his officers, his court appointees—his flunkies we would call them—his immediate or extended family, sit there and enjoy the performance. But they also engage in the performance. We have this marvelous reconstruction that shows an emperor seated in a box in the Colosseum. The emperor's job is, in many cases, to start performances like chariot racing and drops the *mappa*, or to end things by giving prizes to successful performers, gladiators, charioteers, animal hunters, to give recognition at the end of a play and things like that. The emperor's role is important, but it's ceremonial and it's distant. He is not supposed to descend to the level, quite literally, of the performance area itself, of the arena floor, of the chariot track, of the stage itself.

We do, however, have four emperors who do just that, who violate those notions. Rather than distributing largesse and being on display, they become part of the performance. What we need to do, I think, and it's very important, is to analyze the circumstances for these emperors. Why is it that these four emperors transgress accepted behavior and become part of the performance?

I think the standard thing that people say—and by "people" I mean scholars—is that these people were mad. Caligula was mad, or Nero was mad, or Commodus was mad and they just dismiss this behavior. I think this is unacceptable because if they are truly mad, they're not going to be basing their behavior on what other people are doing. What we see—and we'll develop this chronologically from Caligula to Nero to Domitian to Commodus—is really that, a development of behavior as emperors look back on previous attempts to transgress and to become performers and develop their own public personas based on those. So I don't think what we're seeing here is an element of madness. What we're seeing here, I think, is method. That method is really an attempt to redefine one component of Roman culture. That component is *virtus*. *Virtus*, which is literally manliness, is for hundreds of years, from the founding of the republic down to the 1st century A.D., only defined by its application in battle. *Virtus* could be demonstrated only as a successful military official. But starting with Caligula and moving on, we see attempts to redefine *virtus* away from purely the battlefield. I believe that what we're seeing with these four transgressive emperors is just that: an attempt to redefine *virtus*. I say that because in addition to acting as performers, they simultaneously denigrate the military, they adapt the ultimate reward for military achievement, that is, the triumphal procession, to their own forms of unique achievement, and the result is a change in the definition of *virtus*.

We need to think about these four emperors as a group. What do they have in common? What is it that joins all of them together? There are a number of factors that when we analyze the circumstances of these individuals it puts them all together and makes them, first, insecure emperors, and good candidates for attempting to come up with another venue for male achievement besides the military.

First, three of them come to power when they're very young. Caligula, Nero, and Commodus are very young, in their late teens or early 20s, when they come to power. Domitian is somewhat older, but Domitian, like Nero and Commodus, also succeed emperors before them who are members of their dynasty, that is, members of their extended families, who were deified. The emperors who served before Nero, Domitian, and Commodus were considered so successful that they made that elite group of emperors who, upon their deaths, were voted by the senate into deification. They were declared to be gods and given public cults. So the young men who followed them had an enormous burden following an individual who wasn't just a successful emperor or successful military commander, but was literally declared to be a god.

In three of these cases—Caligula, Nero, and Commodus—we have young men who have no military training following successful generals. They have no training in the military, they don't seem to value it, and so it seems very clear to me that what they're doing is trying to look for another venue to establish elite male achievement.

Let's take a look at the patterns that they come up with and what these venues are, how they seem to come up with a new model for what an emperor and, arguably, any elite Roman should achieve. We're going to see a survey under these four emperors, starting with Caligula and then moving through to Commodus in these forms of transgressive behavior.

We'll start with Caligula. Caligula rules for a short period of time, from A.D. 37–41. He is the first emperor without military experience. He followed two successful generals, Augustus and Tiberius, the first and second Roman emperors. Caligula comes to power because of dynasty. There's nobody left alive in the family other than Caligula and his uncle, Claudius, is believed to be an idiot. So things fall to Caligula.

What we see with Caligula's public actions is a consistent pattern that combines, as I mentioned, the denigration of the military with new forms of male achievement. Let's talk about that denigration of the military. Having never served in the military and seeming to have no value for it, under Caligula we see a number of events that I think are inspired by humor on his part, but really show us an attempt to downplay the power of the military. He personally mocks military commanders, both in Rome and commanders in the field. This strikes me as perhaps like rule number one of bad things to do, and that is to mock men who are armed and who command large numbers of armed men. But Caligula, as I said, was a man with a keen sense of humor. So he personally mocks a number of military officials. He calls the army out in one brilliant event for maneuvers and lines them all up as if for battle and sends them out to collect seashells on the seashore. They bring all the seashells back to Rome and he holds a faux triumph for their great achievement. Again, really systematically mocking the whole institution of the Roman military.

Caligula has another great triumphal procession where he builds a great bridge over the Bay of Baie and rides back and forth on a horse or on a chariot. In one case, he wore the breastplate of Alexander the Great instead of Roman triumphal dress. He was very clearly searching for another model for elite male identity. Rather than modeling himself on Augustus or Tiberius, he seems to select Alexander the Great and the notion of driving chariots.

Instead of training as a soldier or as a military commander, Caligula is a great supporter of chariot races in Rome. He's a supporter of the Green faction. There are four great chariot-racing factions in Rome, the Reds, the Whites, the Blues, and the Greens, and of all of these the Greens seem to be the most common. They seem to have support largely from the lower classes. By doing this, Caligula is just dismissed by our Patrician sources who say he's just slumming. But what Caligula could be doing here is attempting to appeal, to create a constituency, which he doesn't otherwise have, with the lower classes. And so he is cheering for the same team that he sees the lower classes cheering for, the Greens. We see the same thing with governors. When their football team makes the NFL playoffs, they show up and wear a jersey or whatever. I don't see that in my state because our team never makes the playoffs, but I heard about this and I think it does occur. I have good sources that tell me this.

In addition to supporting the chariot races, Caligula actually raced himself, again very transgressive behavior. He appears as a charioteer, first in private, and then in public, racing chariots in the Circus Maximus, and he also builds a second circus outside Rome. What today is the Vatican, if you go to St. Peter's and stand in the piazza, you will see that St. Peter's is actually built on a rise. Standing down there in that enormous piazza underneath St. Peter's, you're standing on Caligula's chariot racing track. That's his circus down there at the base of the Vatican Hill. And so you can go down there and take a look at that.

In addition to racing chariots, Caligula also hosts great banquets in the stables of the Green team, and he calls out the army, another mocking thing for the army to do, and they're supposed to guard the stables all night so the horses of the Green faction can rest. So the army is lowered to guarding stables. There's a tremendous denigration.

Along with his pattern as being a charioteer and denigrating the military, Caligula also appears as a gladiator, particularly a *thracian* gladiator, a type that's instantly recognizable by the curved sword that they carry. He apparently fought a number of bouts as a *thracian*, and replaced his military bodyguard with a bodyguard of *thracian* gladiators. There I think we can see that pattern where Caligula is acting here in another way, creating a parallel for military achievement and military bonding with gladiators and with charioteers.

Caligula doesn't last terribly long. He mocked one too many military officials and was assassinated. Shortly afterwards, in A.D. 54, Nero becomes emperor. Nero also succeeded a very popular and, apparently, a very good emperor, Claudius. Nero accelerates Caligula's pattern of transgressive behavior, appearing as a charioteer, as an animal fighter, and also as a performer, as a singer on stage in the theater. Nero's performances are very rich. Again, he leaves that box, descends to the floor of the Circus Maximus, and drives chariots just as Caligula had done, a very Greek form of behavior, not at all appropriate for the Romans.

Nero also appears as an animal fighter. There is one instance where he appears to be imitating Hercules as an animal fighter, and Hercules's first labor was killing the Nemean lion, and so Nero seems to be holding a form of a mythological reenactment where he descends down into the arena and kills a lion as Hercules did with the Nemean lion. This is a sort of spectacular event, the type of thing that would appeal to Nero, who lived his entire life as this sort of theatrical performance, part of it acceptable and part of it not, even on to his death when Nero's last words were apparently, "What a great actor dies with me."

Nero's greatest transgressive behavior and, apparently, most common, is performing as a singer. This was his major public activity, and he performs as a singer in theaters in Rome, in Naples, and then eventually, on a tour. He goes on tour; Nero on tour. That would be a T-shirt to have, wouldn't it? He starts in private in Rome as Caligula had done with chariot racing, but gradually he wants to perform in public, so eventually he does, originally leaving the city of Rome and going down to Naples. Naples was originally a Greek colony on the Bay of Naples in southern Italy, and still hosted Greek-style competitions, including singing competitions, and Nero goes down there with his lyre and sings and, of course, wins all of the prizes down there, which really fuels his ambition.

Finally, he has a tremendous performance tour where he goes to Greece and performs in all of the great spectacular games in Greece. You're familiar with the Olympics, which we hold every four years. We do that because the Greeks held the Olympics every four years, and in the intervening years there were other major games: The Isthmian Games, the Nemean Games, and the Pythian Games, so four major sets of games and you'd go once a year to one of these major games. For Nero, they rescheduled them all into one year so Nero could attend all of them on his grand tour and, of course, he won, apparently hundreds of prizes, and came back to Rome.

This looks just like indulgence, but when he returns to Rome, what he does there is what tells us what he's trying to accomplish. That is, on his return he has a triumphal procession into Rome in which he combines the traditions of Roman military triumph, including using the chariot that Augustus used in his great triumphal processions, at this point 100 years previously. Nero combines those Roman triumphal traditions with Greek traditions given to victorious athletes or performers in the Olympic games. A section of the city wall is taken down because he's a conqueror, and so he comes through the city wall. He combines these Greek and Roman elements together in a transgressive performance as a triumph. Clearly, what Nero is trying to do here is what Caligula had done, but again being Nero, on a grander scale as to perform in a new form of male elite achievement outside the battlefield to create a new form of achievement based on Greek elite achievement, and Nero was a great supporter of things Greek, a great Hellenophile. You may see a pattern here. Nero also dies in office. In A.D. 68, he commits suicide before he can be assassinated.

The next emperor who performs as well is Domitian. Domitian succeeds his brother, Titus, who was deified, whom Domitian was rumored to have killed in order to get the throne of emperor. Domitian rules from 81–96. What we see with Domitian is an individual who again extends this form of transgressive behavior in some of the same areas, but one new one from what we have seen previously.

With Domitian we have an individual who shares the love of chariot racing that Caligula and Nero had. Domitian loves the chariot races. I mentioned this in the lecture on chariot racing and the Circus Maximus, he built his palace on the edge of the Palatine Hill with a great skybox so he could look out and watch the races from up in the palace. He created the first expansion teams in Roman chariot racing, adding two new colors, Purple and Gold, to the four factions. He built the first stadium in Rome, the first dedicated venue to Greek athletic contests that we see in the city of Rome. He imported Greek athletes to perform for people. So, again, he's very clearly attempting to create a new form of Greek-inspired cultural achievement. It was different than the Roman tradition.

Also in his palace, and this is something that continues after his death, he is such a nut for chariot racing that he built a sunken garden shaped like a circus. That's a pattern that actually continues after his death. We find those later on in 2nd-century palaces as well.

These are things that Domitian did to support these forms of behavior, but he also performs. He performs most importantly as an animal hunter. I mentioned that Nero had done this as well. Domitian was famous for his ability with the bow. The bow, of course, is one of the weapons of Hercules, and he identifies himself very strongly with Hercules. Hercules, of course, is the son of Zeus, or Jupiter in the Roman world, and Domitian has a little statue of an infant Hercules, with Domitian's facial features, placed on the lap of the statue of Jupiter in the Capitolium in the Temple of Jupiter Capitolinus. Because Domitian's father, Vespasian, is himself a god and was deified upon his death, Domitian, like Hercules, is also now the son of a god. So he adopts this Herculean identity and performs in public as a great animal hunter, shooting his bow.

We also have evidence of him not just shooting his bow and killing deer and harmless animals like that, but as a lion hunter as Nero had done. There is a marvelous bronze statue from the Secellum of the Augustales from a shrine to the cult of the emperors down on the Bay of Naples. We see Domitian there in this bronze statue on a rearing horse with a spear in his right hand. We don't have it any more, but there should be a lion crouched underneath the rearing horse and Domitian is about to dispatch it with a spear. This notion of a lion hunt is a particularly masculine notion. It's a very powerful image.

Domitian also had public lion hunts and had staged lion hunts that he had at his game park outside the walls of Rome. We have quite a few images that show the popularity of lion hunting in the arena, and it was a very popular form of animal hunt and spectacle. Domitian is building on this and combining it with his imagery as the new Hercules.

The altogether champion of all of these, of behaviors, and because I think he is developing what we saw earlier with Caligula, Nero, and Domitian, is Commodus. Commodus was emperor from 180–192, almost exactly 100 years after Domitian. Commodus also succeeded his father, Marcus Aurelius, a successful general and commander who was deified upon his death. Commodus is the best documented of these performers, who appears as a charioteer, an animal hunter, and a gladiator all together. We have some great reconstruction images showing us Commodus in the arena.

One of Commodus's behaviors is as a gladiator. He dressed and performed as a left-handed *secutor*. I think I mentioned this in my lecture on gladiatorial combat, a *secutor* is a heavily armed and armored gladiator who fights with a short sword, or a long dagger. The distinction is a little vague. He pursues the *retiarius*, the lightly armed and armored gladiator who fights with a trident and a net. A *secutor* is that pursuer gladiator, so he's very heavily armed. Commodus, in addition to being emperor, which probably gave him a distinct advantage, was also left handed, and this also is a real problem for an entire world where everybody is right handed. To actually have to face somebody in combat who is left-handed throws everything off. Commodus apparently made the most of this as a left-handed *secutor*. I speak from experience when I say that this is actually an enormous advantage when you're fighting. I've won a number of fencing contests against much better opponents because they didn't realize I was left handed initially, and had about five seconds of confusion on their part where nothing was where it was supposed to be. You can actually do pretty well like that. I recommend it to you. Commodus apparently fought over 1,000 bouts as a gladiator, and again, as this left-handed *secutor*.

We're fortunate to have a couple of images of left-handed gladiators. There are not many, but we're really fortunate to have something that I think is particularly interesting, and it may actually reference Commodus directly, and that is a carved ring. This is a ring that shows a *secutor* against a *retiarius*. It's a carved gem that you would use to impress in wax as a seal to seal letters and things like that. On the image that we have of the gem, it looks like we have a right-handed *secutor* against a *retiarius*. But if you press down into the wax and look at the reverse, what we actually have here is a left-handed *secutor*. I don't know for sure, but this is exactly the type of ring that emperors' supporters would wear. We know of this type of image of loyalty on the part of imperial supporters where they would wear rings with the emperor's birth sign, or a monogram, or a patron deity, and things like that. This image is particularly exciting because it could—it might, in fact—be a reference to Commodus himself, something worn by a member of his court.

In addition to performing as a gladiator, Commodus, as with Domitian, conflates his identity with Hercules, and this is perhaps the most famous of the transgressive behaviors that Commodus displays. He dresses as Hercules, presents himself as the new Hercules. As with Domitian, Commodus's father is a god, and he himself is the son of a god here on earth bringing the benefits of his rule and power to all people. It's a marvelous bust of Hercules/Commodus in the Capitoline Museum in Rome, where Commodus is dressed with the lion skin and club of Hercules, and holds out in his hand the golden apples of the Hesperides, the golden apples that brought life after death. Hercules's greatest achievement was to bring that life after death to his followers and, eventually, believers. Commodus picks up on this enormously powerful imagery and begins to dress as Hercules, not just casually—I'm not sure how you could actually dress casually as Hercules—but in staged performances. We have the bust, we have coins that show Commodus with the lion's skin, the club, and the bow, the classic weapons of Hercules. He also performs as Hercules in the arena.

This is a much later image that we have of a reconstruction from, I believe, the early 16th century of Commodus firing a bow and killing, in this case a tiger. Clearly, the artist isn't familiar with a tiger, either. We know that Commodus appears as a great animal hunter in the arena where he used Hercules's imagery. He emphasized the notion of the emperor as a protector figure, that is, the killer of these wild animals that threaten human life and agriculture, lots of tremendous wild animals, and he kills a number of dangerous wild animals.

The most famous event was in November of A.D. 192, and we have an eyewitness account of this in the historian, Cassius Dio, who was there at the games. Commodus comes out and kills 100 bears with 100 spears. You can be appalled by this, and we probably should be, but it's also a remarkable achievement. It's pretty extraordinary to be able to do that. He also killed wild bulls, as I've mentioned, a tiger, a rhinoceros, a giraffe, a couple of elephants, and five hippopotami, all of these single-handedly. I'm not sure how you would single-handedly kill an elephant. The hippopotami might perhaps be the ones that cause people to smirk the most, but you shouldn't. Hippopotami are incredibly dangerous animals. They're territorial, and hippopotami kill more people in Africa than crocodiles do. They float in the river and look really peaceful until they think you're a threat, and then they just run over you, and they keep coming until they're dead or you're squashed. They're really powerful, very dangerous animals, and Commodus descends into the arena and kills these dangerous, wild animals as a symbolic gesture of his role as protector of the Roman world.

Commodus has two major public roles here that we see: that of Hercules and that of the gladiator, the *secutor*. We're fortunate to have, and I must credit the producer of this course, James Blandford, who came up with this image. It's very exciting. I've never seen this before in my life. It is, as far as I can tell, a unique image from the Roman world. What we have here is a votive, a dagger that would be carried by a *secutor*, but it's not an actual weapon that would be carried in the arena. It's a votive; it's a dedication. What we have with this is the weapon of the *secutor* as a dedication, but if you look at the end of the hilt, you see the handle and the end of hilt actually are an image of Hercules. It combines those two public images of Commodus together here, one of the *secutor* with the shape and form of the weapon, and the other of Hercules. In this case, it's Hercules with his club raised over his head. It's Hercules *invictus*, Hercules unconquered, as a figure of power and of male achievement.

There are also letters on here, monograms, of VC. This could be the standard $2^{nd}$-century abbreviation for *vir clarissimus*, but it also actually might be a reference to Victor Commodus, so I think this is a particularly exciting find, which we're fortunate to show you. This is the first time this has been published, so you're seeing this here for the first time ever.

With these emperors, what we see very clearly is a need on the part of all of them—Caligula, Nero, Domitian, and Commodus—to distinguish themselves from previous emperors, and to create a new form of elite male achievement, much of it based on Greek achievement and part of it on the mythology of themselves as the sons of Jupiter, Hercules. The result of their behavior is that they are each one personally condemned for what they do. However, the long-term result is that what we see in Rome by the $2^{nd}$ and $3^{rd}$ centuries, certainly by the $3^{rd}$ century, is a successful redefinition of *virtus*, away from the battlefield to the very behaviors that these individual emperors show in their performances, most notably, wild animal hunting. We also see an expansion of the worship of Hercules and an appreciation of Greek culture in general.

All of these factors, through these transgressive behaviors, serve to change Roman culture and the very Roman notion of elite male achievement.

# Imperial Forums—Power and Policy in Rome

## Lecture 25



**The individual forums created by Julius Caesar, Augustus, Vespasian, Domitian, and Trajan created new public space in the crowded center of Rome. Each of these new forums provided law courts, temples, commercial and office space, and room for meetings and schools.**

All of the imperial forums, starting with Julius Caesar's, share a number of key components, indicating a standardized organization for these new public spaces. Each forum is largely axial and bilaterally symmetrical. Each is defined by a surrounding wall and a peripteral colonnade that surrounds each of the open areas of the forum. All of the forums are dominated by a temple and an open plaza that served multiple functions.

The first of the imperial forums was that of Julius Caesar, the Forum Iulium, dedicated in 46 B.C. The temple was dedicated to Venus Genetrix. It was designed to emulate the temple Pompey the Great built to Venus Victrix, meaning "Venus the guarantor of victory." Venus Genetrix means "Venus, founder of the family," as an allusion to the descent Caesar claimed from Aeneas, whose mother was Venus. The decorative scheme celebrated Caesar's ties to Venus as well as his military victories and beneficence. The forum contained a number of auxiliary buildings and hosted a variety of activities not directly related to Caesar and Venus.

The Forum Augustum, dedicated in 2 B.C., was also conceived as a victory complex. The temple was dedicated to Mars Ultor, Mars the Avenger, because Augustus vowed revenge on the eve of his battles against Caesar's assassins and their armies. The temple was the first of Mars built inside the city rather than outside its walls. The cult statue of Mars was joined by statues and reliefs of Venus and Caesar, emphasizing Augustus's legitimacy as ruler. The decorative scheme of the forum was complex, including statues of the *summi viri* (great men), art reflecting Greek greatness, and celebrations of Roman history, including the founding of the city. Auxiliary buildings and their uses were various, including religious meeting places and law courts. Most importantly, the forum became the location from which Roman generals would symbolically exit Rome for attacks and to which they would return to dedicate their military spoils and trophies.

The Flavian Forum Pacis, dedicated in A.D. 75, is the least understood of the forums because of limited excavation. The forum was paid for with the funds from the sack of Jerusalem. The forum, with a temple to Peace, was considered one of the three most beautiful buildings in Rome. The decorative scheme is unknown, but some of the auxiliary buildings and their uses are recorded by Roman authors. The smallest of all of the imperial forums was the Forum Transitorium, started by Domitian but dedicated in A.D. 97 by his successor, Nerva. The temple was dedicated to Minerva. The forum's major decoration emphasized female virtues, which Domitian promised to improve.

The largest of these forums was the Forum Traiani, dedicated in A.D. 113 by Trajan. It references the Forum Augustum but has unique visual elements. The Trajan forum was adjacent to Augustus's, and its imitates elements of the latter to draw comparisons between the emperors. The forecourt leading into the forum itself was dominated by Trajan's Column, Trajan's visual record of his great Dacian Wars. The complex hosted a wide variety of buildings and uses, including a basilica, the Atrium Libertatis, Trajan's Column, and a large open plaza.

Corel Stock Photo Library.

**Trajan's Column served as a visual history of his Dacian Wars.**

The decorative scheme throughout the forum was Trajan's victory in the Dacian campaigns. ■

## Suggested Reading

Anderson, *The Historical Topography of the Imperial Fora.*

La Rocca, *The Imperial Fora.*

## Questions to Consider

1. How do the decorative schemes of the imperial forums reflect the projected identity and values of the emperors who built them?

2. What changes occur over time in the motivation and form of these complexes? What stays consistent in their design?

# Imperial Forums—Power and Policy in Rome

## Lecture 25—Transcript

Welcome to this lecture on Roman imperial forums. In this lecture, we're going to be exploring the desperately needed spaces, the expansions to the old Forum Romanum undertaken under five different emperors. I say that word advisedly here because we're lumping Julius Caesar in with the imperial forums. Each one of these is one of the largest construction projects ever undertaken in the city of Rome. The final one is, in fact, *the* largest construction project ever undertaken in Rome. So they're phenomenal projects. Complex, they served a variety of functions. They fulfill a number of very practical needs, expanding the public space in the old Forum Romanum to allow for additional religious spaces, and law courts, and places for public, as well as private, interactions. But they're also superb opportunities for each of these individuals, the patrons of these complexes, to really create an enormous billboard to announce and celebrate imperial policy and personal identity. So we're going to look at these interesting complex spaces that are discretely organized and tailored to create new public space in Rome, as well as new images of each of these individuals.

When we're looking at all of these imperial forums, I think it best to start out by looking at them all together because all of them, each of the forums under Julius Caesar, Augustus, Vespasian, Domitian, and Trajan, have a number of common elements. We need to explore the common elements together, and then we will go chronologically through all of the forums as they were constructed.

Now in terms of common elements, we see them organizationally. It's like somebody has a blueprint in a cubbyhole somewhere in the imperial court that's labeled "Imperial Forum Blueprint," and they pull it out and that's what you do. So if we look at a plan, and we have a marvelous reconstruction plan that shows all five of these forums as they're all laid out together, we see a number of common elements in terms of organization of space and in terms of how the Romans are thinking about public space.

First, these are all organized axially. The entrances are all large rectangles, or in one case a large square. The entrances are always on the short side of those rectangles. On the short side, in the center, as far as we know we have formal entrances, and then directly across from those, on the opposite short end, is *the* major building in each of these forums, and that is a temple. For four of these it's an Italicstyle temple. That is, it has a small ground plan, but a tall podium and a tall *cella.* The temple itself stands up very tall, but it's small in size. These four that are standard Italic temples are to what we call traditional deities: Venus, Mars, Minerva, and one for personification: Peace. So we have a strong sense of axiality. The major buildings are along that central axis.

There is also a tremendous amount of bilateral symmetry in each of these. If it was possible and you could cut one of these forums down the center and fold it over, they're almost always identical. The only exception is the Forum of Augustus, which has a few buildings in the back-left corner of one side that it doesn't have in the backright corner. That's because Augustus couldn't buy the land in that backright corner. He didn't want to throw anybody off their land to build his forum, so he just relied on purchasing the property. You know how it is when you're building a school, or an airport runway, or something. There's always somebody who holds out, right? That was the case for Augustus's forum. Somebody held out and didn't want to sell, so Augustus's forum isn't symmetrical. But the others are bilaterally symmetrical.

Organizationally, as urban spaces, they're also organized around a central piazza, or a large central plaza. This is an open space, rectangular, that serves as a space for a variety of functions. Religious activities like sacrifice and procession would take place there. Law cases would be heard and argued out there. A rich variety of events would take place there.

These spaces are all defined by a surrounding wall, which makes each one a very discrete space in the urban environment. Inside that surrounding wall is a peripteral colonnade, that is, a colonnade that's roofed. It joins the outside wall on one side, but on the inside it's supported by a line of columns, and so what you have is a covered walkway that surrounds the open plaza and gives you a shaded area. It also covers a walkway for the subsidiary buildings that might be behind or into that surrounding wall. It also serves to create a frame for that temple, so when you step into that entryway looking across to the temple, that peripteral colonnade creates a surrounding framework for the temple. This is a Greek Hellenistic urban device.

The Romans, of course, had colonnades, but they used them in a different way in the republic. They used them in a linear fashion down streets to cover sidewalks so you could walk across all of Rome in the shade. They didn't use them in this way to define spaces. So this is really an interesting idea, and somebody is bringing a Greek notion directly into the heart of Rome.

All right, so we have all of these components that are common for all of them. There is axiality, the bilateral symmetry, the fact that they're dominated by a religious structure, a temple in all cases, the open plaza for multiple functions, and, of course, the peripteral colonnade.

What I would like to do now is explore each of these on the major buildings and the decorative program of each of these forums, starting with Julius Caesar's and then going through to the grandest: Trajan's.

When we look at this plan of the imperial forums, what I want you to note, in particular, is that it differs dramatically from previous manifestations of the forum, notably in the forum of Trajan. What we see here in this plan is that recent archaeological work has shown that we had the forum of Trajan backwards. Where we used to place the entrance to the forum is now known to be the spot for the temple of the deified Trajan. Whereas, on the far west side, where we used to place the temple is now know to be the entrance and forecourt into the entire forum complex itself. Some of the models we'll be viewing in this course don't reflect that.

The forum of Julius Caesar was defined by what Pompey the Great had done in his victory complex. In 52 B.C., Pompey dedicated a great victory complex out on the Campus Marcius, which included a theater, a temple to Venus, a peripteral colonnade, an open plaza, a senate house, and Rome's first public latrine—very exciting.

Caesar dedicated his Forum Iulium, the Forum of Julius Caesar, in 46 B.C., so very shortly after Pompey's great complex. If we see it, we see it is immediately adjacent to the Forum Romanum, and, in fact, designed deliberately to be an extension of the Roman Forum. It has virtually everything that Pompey's complex had. Pompey has a temple to Venus; Caesar has a temple to Venus. In Caesar's case, it's not Venus's Victrix, the Venus of Victory, the guarantor of victory, that Pompey used. In Caesar's case he's emulating Pompey, that is, he's trying to improve upon him, and he has a temple at the end of his forum to Venus Genetrix, Venus, the Founder of the Family, because Julius Caesar claims descent from Aeneas, the Trojan refugee who came to Italy and founded Rome, whose mother was, according to mythology, Venus. And so Julius Caesar is also descended from Venus, and he has this great temple to Venus, Genetrix, Venus, the Founder of the Family. It's a peripteral colonnade, shops along one side. The senate house, which had burned in the Roman Forum, is rebuilt by Caesar on a new orientation, directly oriented in the corner of his forum. Next to that—and it doesn't seem like the best location for it, but who am I to say—is Rome's second public latrine. So it's very clear that Caesar is competing directly with Pompey in terms of his public building program. The only thing missing from this is the theater, and Caesar started one on the opposite side of the Capitoline Hill from here, the Theater of Marcellus, which he didn't live to complete, but he did begin one, again, to compete with Pompey deliberately.

These are the buildings, but the decorative scheme is also something we need to think about. In a certain way it also competes with Pompey's great complex. The theater of Pompey and associated buildings had a number of Greek statues in it, and Julius Caesar also fills his forum with Greek statues and Greek paintings. There's a statue of him, of course, a statue of Cleopatra, but I think one of the most interesting things that he does because it actually establishes precedence, is that he puts on display under the colonnade a large collection of carved gems, large cameos, as well as intaglios, carved gems on display for the Roman people. This is important because it establishes the notion of imperial forums as museums for the first time here, and we'll see that continue on.

The forum, as I mentioned, has a number of auxiliary buildings, a tremendous number of mixed uses. I should mention that the front of the podium of the temple has no staircase on it, so it can serve as a tribunal so legal cases could be argued. The advocates would stand there and argue to the jury down in the forum below them, so it's very thoughtful the way they have designed this to incorporate a number of different types of activities.

The next of these great forums is the Forum Augustum, the Forum of Augustus, dedicated in 2 B.C., again, an extension of the Forum Romanum and an extension of Caesar's forum built immediately adjacent to it and just north of it. Augustus's forum, the Forum Augustum, has the same forum with the peripteral colonnade and a great Italic podium temple. In Augustus's case, the temple is dedicated as a votive to Mars Ultor. This is an aspect of Mars the Avenger, and Augustus really made this as a votive because he made a vow the night before the battles at Philippi when he's fighting against Caesar's assassins. He vowed that if he defeated them he would dedicate a temple to Mars the Avenger. He won those battles, came back, and did this. He built the first temple of Mars inside the walls of Rome. So it's really an unprecedented event to bring the worship of Mars inside the city for the first time.

The cult of Mars and this notion of piety are joined in the decorative program with a cult statue to Mars, and Mars is in the back of the *cella* as well as on the podium. But in each case, in the back of the *cella*, as well as up on the pediment above the podium in the front, Mars's image is flanked on the one side by Venus Genetrix, developed from Caesar's forum, and on the other side by the deified Julius Caesar himself. Augustus is making a statement here about identity and policy. Mars the Avenger establishes his piety, whereas the images of Venus Genetrix and Julius Caesar establish his dynasty, his descent from Julius Caesar and his legitimacy to rule, all there in that three-figure grouping. It's a significant visual statement about what he hopes to achieve here.

That notion of Mars and that notion of warfare continue as part of the decorative program throughout the forum. If we look at an image of the forum from a distance—this is actually taken from the Capitoline Hill looking down—we see the great wall behind where the Temple of Mars stood, the great surrounding wall that framed the forum. We zoom in and get a little closer. You can do this if you're fortunate. I've been fortunate to come down and examine the excavations down here on a tour with the archeologists. You have to wear a hard hat and arrange it years in advance, but it's worth it. It's really an extraordinary experience to come down and be here on the floor of the forum, which is not normally open.

What we see in this image is on the left are the surviving flanking columns from the Temple of Mars Ultor. And then, around the wall at the pedestrian level we see a number of large niches. These were part of the decorative program on the ground floor, extending that notion of the military because each of these niches held a life-size bronze statue, sadly no longer with us. Each statue had a plaque down below, and some of those are still with us, so we know who was here. These were images of the *summi viri. Summi viri* is Latin for the greatest men. This is Rome's idea of who the greatest men are. The greatest men in ancient Rome are those people who served the State as magistrates, but most importantly, as military leaders. This is appropriate to support a space dominated by a temple of Mars.

Who do we have down here among the *summi viri*? We have Pompey the Great. We have Marius, and Sulla, the great dictator of the 1st century. We have Scipio Africanus, and we have my personal favorite, Marcus Claudius Marcellus, the man who in the Second Punic War captured Syracuse, a great Roman general. This sort of Hall of Fame of Roman military leaders culminates in two statues on either side of the temple in great semi-circular *exedrae*. We have two statues that face one another across the forum and make a cross-axis with that temple of Mars. On one side we have Aeneas, and on the other one, Romulus, the two founders of Rome who face one another across the temple, and are also on axis with the statue of Augustus, who claims to have refounded the city of Rome. He's associating himself here, not just with Julius Caesar, but with Aeneas and Romulus on his two sides. That is a particularly powerful association that we have.

That's the major decoration down at the ground floor. In the attic story, the second story above the peripteral colonnade, we have another form of decoration that makes another statement. It has large panels with images of Zeus Ammon. Zeus in this aspect is the father of Alexander the Great. These are flanked by caryatids, ionic Greek columns that are in the form of women. These caryatids are direct copies taken from a temple on the Athenian Acropolis built in the 5th century B.C. There were caryatids here in the form of Augustus, and there were also caryatids down in the Pantheon built by

Augustus's right hand man, Marcus Agrippa. And so there is a statement here about classicism. Rome is the new Athens. There is a real statement about cultural transfer of what it means to be a classic capital.

In terms of use, we have religious functions, we have legal cases being heard here in the forum, but the most important use is military. The Forum of Augustus becomes the spot in Rome where Roman generals would make their formal ritual departures and returns. When they are departing to go to battle and when they're returning from battle, presumably successfully, they would do so here in front of the Temple of Mars Ultor. When they came back, successfully, and they made dedications, these under the republic, the arms, or armor, or military standards, would go in the atrium of the successful general, in the living room of his house.

Under the empire they come here and rest under the colonnades surrounding the Temple of Mars Ultor. So that museum function that the Forum of Julius Caesar had is extended in the Forum of Augustus. But here it's really defined. It is a museum to Roman military might. That's what the Forum of Augustus really becomes, and it serves as that for hundreds of years, as a museum of Roman military victory.

The next of the forums is the least understood. The Flavian Forum Pacis, or Forum of Peace. It's least understood because the space where it was is occupied today by a large Catholic church in Rome, and so excavations have only taken place in small areas around that church. But we do know a little bit about the Forum of Peace from literary references. The Forum Pacis was dedicated in A.D. 75 by the first of the Flavian emperors, Vespasian. It was part of an enormous complex. Vespasian came to power after a civil war, after the suicide of Nero in a brief civil war of A.D. 69. Vespasian becomes the victor of that civil war. What he does is something that I think is very shrewd, and that is, he builds a large public entertainment complex on the grounds of what had been Rome's most hated monument at that time, Nero's golden house. Nero had taken over the center of much of Rome for a private residence, and Vespasian effectively returns that to the Roman people. He builds the Forum Pacis. He builds a great bath complex, the Baths of Titus, and then adjacent to the Baths of Titus he builds the Colosseum. So we have the Flavian Amphitheater, or the Colosseum, the Baths of Titus, and the

Forum of Peace. The name of the Forum of Peace and the money to build all of this comes from the origin of the money, and that is from the great Jewish Revolt. When Nero was emperor there was a great Jewish revolt. This was the occasion of the great mass suicide at Masada, where the Jews, besieged by the Roman army generaled by Vespasian and his son, Titus, committed suicide rather than fall into the hands of the Romans and become slaves again.

With the destruction of the Jewish Revolt and, most particularly, with the destruction of the city of Jerusalem and the destruction of the Temple of Solomon, all of that wealth from the temple that had accumulated over hundreds of years is brought to Rome and used to build the Forum of Peace, celebrating the end of that revolt, as well as the end of the civil war, as well as the Colosseum and the Baths of Titus, and a number of small monuments in between as well.

We don't know much about the decorative scheme here, but we do know that there was a library, some city offices, the Temple of Peace itself, of course, at the rear office at the entrance to the forum. There are some fountains and some Greek statues. But we do know, most importantly, that the museum aspect of the forum that we saw with Augustus and Julius Caesar continues. A number of statues that Nero had in his golden house were brought out here and put on public display.

We also know from the historian, Josephus, that a number of the spoils from the temple in Jerusalem were brought here to Rome and put on display in the colonnades of the Forum of Peace. We see those illustrated on the relief panel from the Arch of Titus. The menorah from the temple, the temple table, and, according to Josephus, the Law, the Torah, was brought here as well.

The smallest of all the imperial forums is actually not much of a forum. The Romans called it the Forum Transitorium, which means Passageway Forum. It was started under Domitian, but dedicated by his successor, Nerva, in A.D. 97. What Domitian did was take a narrow street leading into the old Forum Romanum and formalized it. There wasn't room for a large peripteral colonnade on either side, so he has to align it in gauged columns on brackets down either side of the wall, and then the Temple of Minerva, Domitian's patron deity, is squeezed into one end. So it's a narrow, awkward space. Minerva is the Roman version of Athena, who was the patron deity not just of Domitian, but of Hercules. So I think this is an aspect of that association between Domitian and Hercules.

The decorative features of the forum exist in a series of reliefs that went all the way around the inside of that wall. Domitian, probably unwisely, forgot a lesson that the Romans, like us today, are constantly relearning, and that is you cannot legislate morality. You cannot pass laws and make people better. Domitian tried. He decorated the inside of the Forum Transitorium with a frieze which showed Roman women performing domestic tasks, things that they're supposed to do, most notably, tasks that involve making fabric, making cloth, weaving, and spinning, and things like that, the tasks that Minerva herself is the patron of. This is intended to model appropriate behavior for Roman women. You're supposed to stay inside and weave fabric all day long. This, of course, did not lead to any great changes in Roman culture, but it's Domitian's attempt.

The greatest of all of the forums in terms of size as well as complexity is the Forum of Trajan. Trajan's Forum is dedicated in A.D. 113, the Forum Traiani, and it's clearly designed with reference to the Forum of Augustus next door. It also has pairs of enormous semi-circular hemicycles, or *exedrae*, in the forum itself. The forum is fairly standard in terms of its organization. There's a large piazza. There's an entry forecourt. There's a library as we saw in the Forum of Peace, but there are some unique elements here to the Forum of Trajan. We need to take a look at those. I think those are the most important.

The forecourt leading into the forum itself, and you see it on the left of this reconstruction, is dominated by Trajan's Column, Trajan's visual record of his great Dacian War, his great Dacian campaigns, bringing what is in modern terms, Romania, into the Roman sphere.

There is also transverse of the Forum of Great Basilica, the Basilica Ulpia, named for Trajan's family name; he's an Ulpian. At the end of the Basilica Ulpia one of the great hemicycles, or semicircular areas down at the end, is the Atrium Libertatis, literally, the Hall of Liberty. This is the ceremonial spot where Roman slaves were freed. In a brief ceremony a slave would be freed by his master and put on a cap of liberty, and his name would be inscribed in the roll of Roman citizens, which was kept in the Basilica Ulpia in cabinets in the great Atrium Libertatis. And so it becomes an important spot for this very vital civic function, that is, the enrolling of new citizens. So we have the Basilica; we have the atrium; we've got Trajan's Column flanked there by two small libraries, Greek and Latin.

If we look from the other direction, that is, from the great piazza that dominates the size of the forum, I should mention that we're not going to look at the temple at the end of this forum because it no longer exists. But it was, quite notably, not a temple to any of the pagan deities. It was a temple to the deified Trajan himself. So this forum, completed by his successor, Hadrian, obviously, because Trajan is deified by that time, serves as a monument to the life of Trajan in a way that none of the other forums do.

The greatest monument here is Trajan's Column, and it still dominates the forum today. The column itself serves a number of purposes. The shaft is 100 Roman feet tall, and that shows how much of the hill behind was excavated out to make this tremendous flat area, over 600 Roman feet across, to have the area for this forum. It also serves as Trajan's burial marker. It's his tombstone. Trajan and his wife are cremated and their ashes placed in a golden urn under the Column.

The most remarkable thing about the column is the decoration. The entire exterior is one long, continuous relief done in a frieze that spirals up the shaft of the column, and this frieze is an account of the Dacian wars, apparently, from their beginning to their conclusion. This is quite a remarkable achievement. It's unprecedented in the Roman world as a visual monument of warfare. It's also unprecedented because this is the first time ever in Roman history that scenes of the actual prosecution of warfare are brought within the city walls. Instead of just celebrating triumph and showing images of victory, what we're seeing here is actual warfare taking place. We get snapshots, very circumstantial images, of that war. It's a marvelous scene here of Trajan as his men come back from battle holding up the heads of his enemies and presenting them to him. They're rich images of thousands of figures. To give you a sense, each of these relief panels is about three feet in height, so about three feet to work with here. We have Trajan leading his men in battle, the men cutting down trees to make palisades to build forts. We see marches. We see religious events. We see victorious moments with Dacians being captured and being brought to Trajan, just a range of all sorts of events taking place within the context of this war, from its origins down below, finally in the culmination and victory at the very top of the column. It's really an extraordinary monument.

It's difficult to see today, but in the ancient world it was all painted. There's a rich polychrome here that I think would have made all this stand out with realistic colors, so it would have been a lot more vibrant and a lot clearer. You're not looking at just white on white, but you'd see the full range of colors in this scene. It might look a little cartoony to us, but for the Romans it would have been visually stunning.

That theme of the active prosecution of war is not just here in these scenes on the column. We also see it in what is called "the Great Trajanic Frieze." This is an enormous frieze, well over life size, and the figures are over six feet tall. This frieze went along the inside walls of the forum, and so we have no idea what its original extent was. It could have been hundreds of feet long. It's the same themes that we see on the column, that is, the Dacian War. What we see here are, again, scenes that are richly ideological, scenes of Trajan accepting prisoners, Trajan in battle, Trajan being crowned by the goddess Victory in the Great Trajanic Frieze, all themes that celebrate the public aspects that Trajan wants to celebrate and wants to identify himself with.

What I think is perhaps the most important of all these scenes is a marvelous scene that shows Trajan on a rearing horse. On the left riding into battle is Trajan on a horse, a barbarian crumpled under the fore hooves of his horse as it seems to be rearing over that barbarian. Then in front facing Trajan is a kneeling barbarian chieftain who is kneeling before the emperor and holding out his own sword in surrender, while behind him, coming back from battle, that same motif we saw on the column, Trajan's men holding up the heads of his enemies by their hair. So it's a wonderful image of the triumphant general, of victorious Roman troops, of the defeated enemy, all put together in this one image of Rome's greatest emperor. Trajan is, in fact, the greatest of all Rome's emperors. He is the Optimus Princeps, the best of emperors, and that becomes his title after his death. He is declared to have been Optimus Princeps.

When we look at all of these forums together, we see a remarkable pattern of construction. It continues over 150 years, filling the center of Rome with Greek-inspired urban design, but more importantly, Roman temples and thematic decorations that announce and celebrate imperial identity and policy. So what we're seeing is an expansion of the practical areas of the old Forum Romanum into areas that are richly symbolic and serve the purposes and needs of each of these individual emperors as they celebrate their rule throughout the center of the city of Rome.

# Imperial Arches, Columns, and Monuments

## Lecture 26

**The large-scale building projects in the Forum Romanum created a public center in Rome, but monuments celebrating imperial policy actually lined the major streets and avenues of the city, from its gates into its forums and public spaces, including the Circus Maximus and Colosseum.**

Roman public monuments filled the city from gates to center and created an "armature of celebration," highlighting Roman foreign—and sometimes domestic—policy along every major avenue in the city. These monuments take a variety of forms, but perhaps the quintessential form is the arch. Many of the almost 100 arches that eventually filled the city were found along the route from the north that led into the city and directly to the Forum Romanum. These effectively extended victory imagery away from the triumphal route, spreading it along another key route in the city. They served to turn ephemeral events into eternal reminders for the Roman people.

The earliest of these monuments were not arches but much more modest forms. The earliest of the Roman triumphal monuments are actually markers to naval battles and take the form of decorated tribunals (speakers' platforms). The front of the tribunal was lined with *rostra*, the bronze rams off the prows of Carthaginian warships. The name was transferred to the platform, which became known as the *rostra* from that time on.

In addition to the tribunal, the earliest monuments were tall but slender columns, probably also erected for naval victories. These columns were placed around the open area of the forum and decorated with the bronze rams from captured ships. Some were also used to display military trophies such as captured arms and shields, which were attached to the columns along with plaques announcing the victory commemorated.

Arches were the characteristic triumphal monuments that eventually filled the city, placed along the triumphal route and clustered at significant locations.

Key arches were constructed at important locations such as the Circus Maximus, at each end of the Forum Romanum, and flanking important temples. The effect was to create a history of military victory through their dedicatory inscriptions and decorations. Hadrian's arch celebrated *pietas* through images of sacrifice and *virtus* through images of hunting. The Arch of Titus demonstrates extensive relief decoration used to portray the actual triumphal procession.

**The earliest monuments were tall but slender columns, probably also erected for naval victories.**

We see in the 2nd century A.D. a return to victory columns, a form that was popular in the middle and late republic, but on a different scale. The Column of Antoninus Pius (r. A.D. 138–161) is an example of Roman triumphal monuments extending outside the city walls. It extends the imagery of columns beyond the purely military and creates a more complex marker in the cityscape. The best-preserved and best-understood of these columns is the Column of Trajan. It is the central monument of the entrance piazza of his forum, and its 100-foot shaft is decorated with a continuous relief of the Dacian Wars. The Column of Marcus Aurelius is based in size, style, and decoration on Trajan's and commemorated his German campaigns. Its placement along the Via Lata, halfway between the gates and the Forum Romanum, created a new visual marker in the northern section of Rome.

The obelisks made their appearance in Rome when Augustus absorbed Egypt for the Roman people in 30 B.C. Augustus brought the first six to Rome from Egypt and placed them on bases, announcing that they were the gift of Augustus personally. Augustus's obelisks show us how flexible these triumphal monuments can be, not just in form but in how the Romans chose to define triumph. ■

## Suggested Reading

Brilliant, *The Arch of Septimus Severus in the Roman Forum.*

Kleiner, *The Arch of Nero in Rome.*

## Questions to Consider

1. How do the arches and columns redefine the topography of the city of Rome with military values and images?

2. In what ways do these extend the kinetic spectacles of triumphs and funerals into lasting monuments of imperial contributions to Rome?

# Imperial Arches, Columns, and Monuments

## Lecture 26—Transcript

Welcome to this lecture on Roman imperial arches, columns, and other victory monuments. In this lecture, what we're not going to do is look at the great building spaces inside the city of Rome, how Rome and the Roman emperors created urban spaces. Instead, we're going to look at the monuments that actually lined the major streets in Rome. What we're going to see is that these are large-scale monuments are really markers of Roman power. What they create is what I term "an armature of celebration." We see this armature of celebration from one wall of the city all the way across to the other, from gate to gate, and along all of the major roadways in Rome, as well as dominating a lot of the major public spaces. So we're not going to be looking at buildings, but instead looking at monuments that celebrate Roman imperial power, victory monuments in the forms of arches, columns, and a variety of forms of monuments that celebrate Roman imperial achievement, as well as displaying emperors acting in socially formative ways, that is, emperors as great generals.

Roman monuments filled the city from the center all the way out to the edges, so we need to think about the forms, where they're placed, and how this all works in an urban environment. What we see is what I term an armature of celebration, which celebrates Roman policies, in particular, foreign policies, but on occasion some domestic policies as well. These worked along every major avenue in the city, every major road in Rome would be lined with a number of these markers to Roman military success.

A word here about what this means. This may sound repetitive to us and redundant, a marker to Roman military success here, there, and everywhere else. In fact, I think it's not. For the Romans, that repetition serves a vital function. Think about our major cities. If you drive into a major American city today, you're going to see a very limited range of buildings that are among the largest, that celebrate the identity of that space. I'm not even talking about going to Washington, DC, where you can't throw a rock without hitting a monument to some dead politician or military leader. But no, just your average, everyday city. You're invariably going to find that the largest buildings there are celebrations of particular things that we as Americans value. In terms of office buildings, there are going to be financial institutions. Banks and insurance companies have large skyscrapers that dominate cities, from small cities like mine, Hamilton, Ohio, to great cities like—if you can call Cincinnati a great city—Cincinnati, New York, Indianapolis, with great skyscrapers. The largest buildings also are celebrating a narrow function of American values, and that is sports. The buildings and monuments with the greatest footprints are sports monuments.

There was a great book written several years ago called *Hoosier Temples*. It was an illustrated history of Indiana's high school basketball gymnasia. It was really a brilliant idea celebrating all the small towns in Indiana that build enormous gyms as their temples. These were defining the community. Again, it's both repetitive and redundant, and is echoed across the entire state. For the Romans, the value that defines them for most of Roman history is the value of military achievement, the value of *virtus*. And so we're going to look at those monuments of *virtus* here.

These monuments take a variety of forms. Perhaps the quintessential form is the arch, the great triumphal arch. We have an image here from the Forum Romanum dominated still today by the great arch of Arch of Septimius Severus. It's built along the west edge of the Roman Forum. I have counted several times, and I keep coming up with different numbers. Approximately 100 triumphal arches are built eventually within the city of Rome over its history, so it's one of about 100 arches that fill the city from, again, gate to gate, serving to frame the great avenues of Rome in this armature of celebration.

It effectively serves to literally petrify victory imagery in stone. The great triumphal processions that occur are petrified in the images that we find on these arches throughout Rome. So it serves to make permanent these ephemeral events and the great achievements that Romans themselves are supposed to be emulating.

As I mentioned, arches are perhaps the quintessential monument. We find them in the forum. We find them on all the major avenues. They, of course, are incorporated into a number of important spaces, the great imperial forum perhaps, but the best example is the Circus Maximus, where we see at one end of the Circus in the center of the great curve of the cavea, the seating area, is a great triumphal arch because the Circus Maximus itself is part of the triumphal procession route, and so there's an arch built there for the triumphal processions to pass through, and is a permanent marker of Roman military achievement.

If we look, however, at some of the earliest of these forms of displays of victory, what we find are actually much more modest forms, and forms that are not found later on. They're unusual, and they're forms that don't continue in later iconography.

The earliest of the Roman triumphal monuments, or victory markers, are actually markers to naval battles. This is something I thought about quite a bit because Roman military, that is, army success, or military victory, had been going on since the founding of Rome. When Romulus founds the city in 753 B.C., he marches out, apparently immediately, and begins conquering Rome's enemies. From 753 B.C. throughout the Regal and early republican period, we don't find large-scale victory monuments in Rome. It's only with the First Punic War, from 264 to 241 B.C. that we see the first great triumphal monuments, the first great victory monuments in Rome. I don't think this is just because Rome is facing an implacable foreign foe, but it's the type of victory because it's with the First Punic War that we see Rome's first large-scale naval victories. The first victory monuments that we have from ancient Rome in any scale are actually naval markers. They celebrate naval battles.

I'm not sure why this is. I've thought about it quite a bit. I suspect it is because for the Romans, military victory, that is, victory by the army, is pretty much taken for granted. The Roman army will continue to fight until they're successful. The Roman navy, on the other hand, has never had a leading role, and frankly, never won a major battle until the First Punic War. So perhaps it's surprise on the Romans' part, perhaps it's the unprecedented scale of the battles, or perhaps it's just because of naval victory. Whatever the event is, what we see during the First Punic War are these first grand triumphal monuments that are, in fact, naval, and they're not arches. In fact, the first one is a decoration of the speaker's platform, the tribunal in the Roman Forum.

What the Romans did after a great naval battle against the great Carthaginian fleet was to take the bronze battering rams from the front of the Carthaginian galleys. These are the big bronze beaks on the front of the ship, one of these great galleys with all the oars. You've got the rowers going fast, and you can ram enemy ships and actually split them in two if you're going fast enough. So these bronze rams are powerful symbols of the projection of power by that enemy force. So the Romans take those bronze rams off the fronts of those Carthaginian galleys and they nail them around the front and sides of the tribunal, the speaker's platform.

Those bronze rams are called "*rostra*." From those *rostra*, that name gets transferred to the speaker's platform. So from about 260 B.C. on, the tribunal in Rome is actually called "the *Rostra*," named for the rams that decorate it.

In addition to the *rostra* that we have—and I have to call it now from now on—there's a new form of dedication that we have in the Roman forum. These don't exist any more, but we have images on coins to show us what they look like, and we've got a reconstruction you can take a look at here. These are tall, slender columns that were put up in the Forum Romanum that are also decorated with these *rostra*. One of these columns is called "a *columna rostrata*," that is, a column with *rostra* on it. We can see a nice example here decorated with pairs of *rostra* on either side, along with anchors down the center. These forms of decorative columns, or dedicatory columns, actually become a very popular form of victory monument. We find them scattered throughout the city of Rome in public spaces. The most important is the Forum Romanum, but we find them throughout the city of Rome eventually, initially as naval victory monuments, but eventually also as military trophies, with captured arms and shields bound on, and always with a plaque or an inscription down at the base naming the victory and saying who has made this dedication. So there's an element of the didactic involved in this. The 10 percent of the people who can read are educated constantly about what this victory means, who made this possible, and so on. So it reinforces the elite status with these individuals. So we've got the columns and the *rostra*.

These forms of republican, or mid-republican victory monuments extend throughout the Roman Republic, but are never the most popular form of victory monument, and that is always the triumphal arch. The triumphal arch was originally the single passageway arch built initially all along the triumphal procession route. We have a nice map of the city of Rome which shows that triumphal procession route marked, starting down at the Campus Marcius down at the Circus Flaminius and making its way through a large portion of Rome, culminating at the Capitoline Hill. This route was eventually studded with arches, which again, would not just create a definition for the city of Rome, but actually would be engaged. Every time a triumphal procession came through they would pass under the passageway of that arch, reenacting the event that led to that arch being built or founded in the first place. So there's this wonderful notion of a self-referential monument in each one of these victory monuments. I think that's a particularly interesting and important aspect for the Romans.

Naturally, these are built in a number of spots, first along the triumphal procession route, but then eventually at key locations. I mentioned the Circus Maximus. We also find them at either end of the Forum Romanum, creating gateways into and out of the forum at prominent topographical spots, high and low places, places where the triumphal procession route made turns and things like that. You can trace that route today if you want. It's not hard. It's about a three mile walk. I do it when I go to Rome in the summer. It's a wonderful opportunity to reenact that event.

Let's take a look at some of these markers. Initially, these are all victory monuments. They all show images of victory, emperors, or Roman generals being crowned by Victory, things like that. But eventually, what we begin to see is a broadening of the imagery. I mentioned in my introduction that we see emperors acting, as I termed it, in socially formative ways. One of the best examples is the round reliefs from an arch of the emperor, Hadrian. Hadrian built a triumphal arch himself, which is no longer with us. It was actually disassembled in antiquity and the reliefs were placed on the Arch of Constantine. They're still there today, so if you go and take a look at the Arch of Constantine right next to the Colosseum, you'll see these rondels up in the attic story of the arch.

Here are two of the eight that we can see here. They show us the imagery of this monument of Hadrian. Although the monument was a triumphal arch, the imagery is not military. What we have are paired scenes that show Hadrian as a big game hunter displaying his *virtus* as a hunter paired with scenes of Hadrian sacrificing to gods. So he's celebrating his *virtus* in this new form of male achievement that we see under the emperors, combined with images of *pietas*, of Roman piety. So this is a nice combination there showing the expected male achievement and, of course, the achievements of the particular emperor. If we look closely at these, those people who know these very well can identify particular individuals at the court of Hadrian. They're very interesting monuments in that they serve a sort of documentary purpose for Hadrian's reign as well.

These are unusual. The more standard form is what we have in one of the best preserved examples, the Arch of Titus. The Arch of Titus was constructed by his successor and younger brother, Domitian, at one of the topographically significant points at the height of a hill, so it's one of the highest points at the triumphal procession route. It's a little peak between the Forum Romanum, which is in a low, swampy area on one side and on the other side the Colosseum. The Arch of Titus stands up between the two on a fairly high little hill, again, over the triumphal procession route.

The form of the Arch of Titus is very conservative and very traditional. It's a single passage arch, allowing people to pass through along the Sacra Via, the Sacred Way. In the spandrels of the arch, the little triangular spaces on either side of the archway opening, we see Victories with trophies, that is, Victories carrying military trophies. Above them is a small frieze that shows the actual triumphal procession taking place, and then culminating on the top of the attic is the dedicatory inscription, arguably the least important aspect, first because only 10 percent of the Romans could actually read it, and secondly, because these dedicatory inscriptions are formulaic. They don't actually say anything significant. They just give the official titles of the dedicators, so it's not a lot to work with there.

The great thing about the Arch of Titus is the relief decoration inside that passageway showing scenes from the actual triumphal procession. So again, there's that petrification of the event taking place here in this image that we have for you. You can see Titus in his chariot. Behind him, the personification of Victory is crowning him, and as he goes forward in that four-horse chariot, the chariot is being led by the personification of the city of Rome itself, Roma, the goddess. It's a wonderful image of that triumph.

When we go into the Roman Forum and back up, you can get a better sense of how the Arch of Titus dominates because it is up on a hill. You go down into the forum and it looms above everything and creates, again, this armature of celebration.

That sort of armature exists across the entire city of Rome. I don't think it's just the fact that the Romans ran out of space along the triumphal procession route. I don't think that's it at all. What I think we're seeing is a deliberate set of decisions to extend victory imagery outside of the narrow confines of that route into the new spaces that Roman emperors are creating throughout the city, both inside and outside its traditional walls. So when we look at imagery across the city, we see that in many cases some of the largest, most prominent, and best decorated of the monuments we see are victory monuments, arches like that of Titus on one side of the Roman Forum and Septimius Severus on the other.

Other monuments I think are unique, and that is led by the Column of Trajan. The Column of Trajan is also important for us because it gives us evidence for the missing component of Roman triumphal arches. We're seeing the triumphal arches as they exist in the marble form that we have, but each one of them would originally have been topped by a bronze group of sculptures, which would have added, in some cases, up to 10 feet to the height of the arch. The bronze statues, in some cases were gilded, so you've got these marvelous gold statues. These have all been pulled off and melted down to make canons, or doorknobs, or whatever in the Middle Ages in Rome. But we have images on the Column of Trajan. We can just see in one of the reliefs there's the fleet sailing into Ancona. The Arch of Trajan at Ancona is topped with a dynastic group: Trajan and his wife, and his sister, actually. So we've got this marvelous dynastic monument.

The best example extant of these large-scale statues isn't in Rome at all, but it's a reconstruction of a Roman triumphal arch in St. Petersburg. If you go to St. Petersburg in Russia you'll see this reconstruction of the Arch of Septimius Severus. It's those proportions in size, and it's topped with a great image of Victory. There's that chariot being driven by the personification of Victory herself. And then around the arch you see the dynastic statues as we would in a Roman triumphal arch. These, of course, in Rome are all gone, but we have this nice reconstruction to give us a sense of how they would have added to the entire experience of the arches, and add a personal image of these free-standing, life-sized, or colossal statues of emperors, their extended families, Victory, and so, augmenting this entire spectacular imagery.

Arches are by and large the most common and most popular form of triumphal monument that we have. As I say, there are approximately 100 of them eventually built, but they're not the only monument. We actually see in the 2$^{nd}$ century A.D. a return to victory columns, a form that was popular in the middle and late republic, but of a different form and, certainly, a different scale than we had previously.

One of these columns is the Column of Antoninus Pius. Antoninus Pius is one of the least appreciated of Roman emperors. He served as emperor from A.D. 138 to 161, longer than any emperor since Augustus, a period of tremendous peace in ancient Rome. The Column of Antoninus Pius is no longer with us. We don't have the actual column shaft, but we have the base of the Column of Antoninus Pius. What we see here is an extension of two things: Number one, of the context of these victory monuments because the Column of Antoninus Pius is not inside the walls of the old city of Rome, but actually outside in the Campus Marcius, and this is where we see an extension of those victory monuments outside the walls.

The second thing is an extension of imagery because with the Column of Antoninus Pius we don't see the replacement in military imagery, we see an augmentation, that is, new imagery, a new form of iconography is added to that military imagery. We see that on a relief that shows us what we can think of as the front of the base of the Column of Antoninus Pius. It's a scene of Apotheosis, that is, the ascent into heaven of Antoninus Pius and his wife, Faustina. They're on the back of this great personification figure. They're flanked by eagles, which are symbols of their spirits ascending up into heaven, and then down on the ground we have personifications. On the right is the city of Rome herself, Roma, the goddess, and she has her hand raised in farewell, saying, "So long." On the other side is a personification of the Campus Marcius. This is the area in which this monument is built. The Campus Marcius is particularly important here because he has indicated his attribute is an obelisk, another form of imperial victory monument that we see. And so for the Romans, this imperial victory monument, the obelisk, actually is being used to define the space outside the city of Rome. So it's a really interesting monument in that way. It serves to show us the extension of this imagery, as well as how important these monuments were for the Romans for defining their city.

Both of the flanking sides, the left and right sides of the base, show images of military maneuvers. What we have are infantry in the center on a ground line with standards, flanked by cavalry in a military maneuver. This is not a battle taking place. Antoninus Pius actually never fought any battles. He did overcome a potential invasion by the Parthians. The Parthians were all lined up on the Syrian border one time and Antoninus Pius got wind of it, and you'll never guess what he did. He wrote a letter to the Parthian king. That was it. He didn't send troops, just wrote him a letter. The Parthian king read the letter and called off the invasion; went home. That's great government. So [Antoninus Pius] never won a military victory, but has this military imagery on the base of this column and, again, extending that idea.

The best preserved and understood of these columns is the Column of Trajan. It's the centerpiece of Trajan's forum, and the Column of Trajan is a really remarkable monument with its 100 foot shaft, as I mentioned. It's decorated with a continuous relief of Trajan's Dacian War. In that we see these real scenes of the act of prosecution of warfare. The Romans march out and go forth and are conquering. It's a great image here in this continuous frieze of Romanization, with the Roman Empire expanding and new areas being brought into the Roman world.

When I took Roman art and architecture as an undergraduate, so this was a while ago, my professor railed against the Column of Trajan. He said it's terrible art, and you know it's terrible art, because no one could read these from the ground. You couldn't see all of these reliefs. We can't see them as well today as perhaps the Romans could have because we don't have the paint any more. He said you also know it's terrible art because it was never emulated. Nobody ever imitated the Column of Trajan and that's how you know it was unsuccessful.

It pains me to say it, but my undergraduate professor was, in fact, wrong. We have a tremendous imitation of the Column of Trajan, and that is the Column of Marcus Aurelius. Like the Column of Antoninus Pius, his predecessor, it's not built within the walls of Rome, but out in the Campus Marcius. The Column of Marcus Aurelius is based in size, and style, and decoration on Trajan's Column. It's exactly designed to imitate Trajan's Column. The imagery is of Marcus Aurelius's great German campaigns. It's placed out here along the Via Lata. By the way, Via Lata is literally Latin for Broadway. That's what it means—Broadway. The road is called Broadway out here. And so it does what Trajan's Column did. It celebrates military victory, but it extends that imagery here outside the walls.

The imagery that we have on the great Column of Marcus Aurelius is the same as we saw on Trajan's in a lot of ways. It's a continuous relief frieze spiraling up the shaft of the column, but the details are much different. What we see in the Column of Marcus Aurelius is fascinating in a lot of ways, and one we don't fully understand what the Romans thought of this. We're not just seeing the act of prosecution of warfare in the Column of Marcus Aurelius. We're actually seeing the horrors of war: captives being dragged to death, prisoners being executed and being driven into pits and killed. It's quite an extraordinary set of scenes, not just of war taking place, but of the horrors of war taking place. We don't know if this was a deliberate attempt to show what war was really like, to show what Marcus Aurelius thought about war, but we do see, again, an extension of the traditional triumphal imagery into a new form here; not the form of the column, but the form of the art that decorates it.

In addition to these columns, perhaps the quintessential imperial victory monument is the obelisk. We also saw on the base of the Column of Antoninus Pius that the Romans themselves used the obelisk as shorthand to define the Campus Marcius. Obelisks as victory monuments make their appearance in Rome under Augustus. When he captures Egypt for the Roman people in 30 B.C., he brings the first obelisk into the city. These serve as victory monuments. They're used out in the Campus Marcius initially. We see them flanking Augustus's tomb. We eventually see one along the *spina* of the great Circus of Gaius, the Circus of Caligula out of the Vatican. We see one in the center of the stadium of Domitian out in the Campus Marcius. It's still there today.

What we see are originally six Augustan obelisks that are brought to Rome and placed in key locations outside the walls of the city to establish this notion of Roman power over Egypt. The obelisk itself makes this statement, but it's helped by the inscription down on the base, and these all read about the same. I'll show you one of the best preserved. It tells us very clearly *The Imperator Caesar Augustus*, and then gives his titles: Chief priest, consul, tribune, and so on. At the end of the sentence it says, "The Imperator Caesar Augustus gave the gift of the sun to the Roman people." *Augustus dedit donum solis*, gave the gift of the sun. So here he's not emphasizing the military achievement. He's not emphasizing his great triumphal procession . He's emphasizing the outcome. This shows us how flexible these triumphal monuments can be, not just in form whether they're arches, columns, *rostra*, or obelisks, but in how the Romans choose to define triumph, in this case by the gift of the sun being brought to the Roman people.

To really appreciate the effect of all these, you need to go to Rome today, along the northern edge of Rome, to the Via Flaminia, where the Piazza del Popolo has been reconstructed as a Roman urban space, decorated with a range of these victory monuments. We see *rostrated* columns flanking the piazza in the foreground, an obelisk in the center, and in the background the entrance into the piazza del Popolo is designed as a triumphal arch. And so all three of the major forms—the column, the obelisk, and the arch—are all present here in this reconstructed Roman space. These serve to give us a sense of how the Romans used these monuments for, as I term it, an armature of celebration to expand the imagery of triumphal monuments throughout the entire city of Rome.

# Imperial Baths in Rome—Spas for the Masses

## Lecture 27

**These buildings—lined with marble; floored with mosaics; decorated with the finest statuary, fountains, gardens, and architectural details—provided a grand space for social and political interaction.**

Roman imperial baths were used by everyone and provide a great example of imperial beneficence. The evidence makes clear that all Romans visited the grand imperial bath complexes, sometimes on a daily basis. Baths provided everyone from the emperor down to slaves with a luxurious space for a variety of bathing and spa activities. The result of this was a shared experience among Romans of all social classes who, despite their shared nudity, interacted in ways that reinforced rather than eliminated the distinctions between them. Imperial beneficence began with the building of these vast complexes but extended also to providing free admission, amenities, and maintenance.

Baths reinforced Roman cultural values in terms of the political, social, and philosophical. The very notion of these complexes relies on the Roman ideal of *mens sana in corpore sano*, "a sound mind in a sound body." Roman patricians met at the baths to discuss politics and business, using the space as a setting for valuable networking and reinforcing their elite status. Lower-class Romans used the baths to gain favors from Roman patricians such as dinner invitations, which were considered an obligation of the upper classes. Social interactions included romantic encounters and assignations in the luxurious and relaxed surroundings.

Activities in the baths were broad and comprehensive of both physical and intellectual options. The actual bathing itself involved a sequence of rooms whose decor and comfort reinforced the notion that it's good to be a Roman. Bathers would undress in an *apodyterium*, a changing room with lockers for their belongings. Generally adjacent to this was the *frigidarium* (cold water room), usually containing only a cold plunge. In more elaborate bathing complexes, a *natatio* (outdoor swimming pool) was also an option for bathing outside the climate-controlled sequence of baths. A *tepidarium* (warm water room) and a *caldarium* (hot water room) completed the basic group of bathing rooms that were at the core of the bathing sequence. In addition, some baths offered special rooms such as a *sudatorium* (steam room) and a *laconicum* (dry sauna).

In addition to actual bathing, the complexes provided other ways to take care of your body and mind. Various forms of exercise were common in baths, including wrestling, ball games, running and walking, and some weight work. Food and drink vendors were integral to the complexes, given the amount of time Romans spent there. Health and body care also included options for haircuts, massage, and visits to doctors, all within the baths. Intellectual and cultural aspects of the baths included lectures, concerts, debates, and philosophers teaching in the rooms of the complex.

**The complexes provided other ways to take care of your body and mind.**

All of these activities were conducted in surroundings of the greatest luxury and grandeur. The main blocks of the bath buildings were designed to evoke a sense of wonder, appreciation for the benefits of Rome, and cultural superiority. Architecturally the buildings were enormous, with walls rising more than 100 feet to great coffered ceilings and windows with glass panes, all elements missing from the homes of even the wealthiest Roman citizens. All of the interior surfaces were covered with expensive or vividly colored materials, such as imported marbles, painted stucco plaster, or mosaic floors. The decorative schemes were often aquatic in theme, including mythological water creatures, consistent with the bath complex. Large-scale statuary filled the baths as well, with the majority from Greece or of Greek mythological subjects, celebrating Roman cultural superiority through this captive Greek material. The effect served to reinforce the Roman political, social, and class system, so that every time a citizen entered, he would be reminded of his place in the Roman world. ■

## Suggested Reading

Fagan, *Bathing in Public in the Roman World.*

Yegül, *Baths and Bathing in Classical Antiquity.*

## Questions to Consider

1. How did the baths differ from other spectacular offerings such as games in providing Romans the benefits of imperial rule?

2. What aspects of Roman culture are further reinforced in the design, decoration, and activities of the bathing establishments?

# Imperial Baths in Rome—Spas for the Masses

## Lecture 27—Transcript

Welcome to this lecture on Roman imperial bath complexes. What we're going to do here is take a look at these grand complexes that emperors built successively throughout the urban fabric of the city of Rome. Now when I say bath, I don't want you to think about your bathtub or your bathroom at home. These are really spas. I need to say a word about that word as well.

I don't know about your neighborhood, but in my town, it seems that everybody with an emery board and a tabletop fountain is opening what they call a "spa." We have lines of these down my main street, little nail salons all termed "spa." These are great little buildings, and great little businesses, and I go to one myself, but that's not what we're talking about here. When I say "spa," I want you to think about not that little nail salon down on the corner, but a luxurious resort. That's what we're thinking about, so spa here equals grand resort. I've never attended one myself, but I have an idea of what they might be like thanks to Roman imperial bath complexes.

These complexes are a very important topic for us to look at because for the average Roman they're not going to be going out and seeing newly conquered territory. They're not going to be in a triumphal procession themselves, and they're certainly never going to be a member of the senate. So a lot of the institutions that define Rome are off-limits to the vast majority of Romans. That's not the case for the baths. The baths are open to everybody. They are the great example of imperial beneficence. We're going to look at the building forms, we're going to look at the types of activities, and we're also going to look at these analytically: how the buildings, the fact of imperial construction, and the activities all serve to reinforce Roman social and cultural values. So quite a bit to get in here.

The first thing to keep in mind is the buildings themselves. What we have here are tremendous buildings. We have a nice cutaway to give you a sense of the size and scale of these. They're enormous structures that provided everyone in Rome with the tangible benefits of empire, and grand, lavish spaces that act to reinforce those cultural values. So there's a social role involved here in bathing.

The evidence makes it clear that the Romans would use these baths on a daily basis. We need to think about a culture here, the Roman culture, without the Protestant work ethic or without a capitalist economy. There's no moral imperative or economic incentive to work constantly. The Romans see no problem with spending hours a day at these spa resorts, at the imperial bath complexes, and in fact, we know that they did. Sometimes on a daily basis Romans would go down and just spend hours down here. That's something to keep in mind in terms of the use.

We also know that the baths were used by everyone, and I mean everybody, from slaves all the way up to the emperor. All classes attend the baths together. A number of people, scholars who write on the baths, think that this means that because everybody is in here together that somehow this shared experience, particularly the fact that everybody is in here naked together, somehow removes, with your clothing, all of the class and social distinctions that exist in ancient Rome. I think this is not, in fact, the case. Social and class distinctions are, in fact, reinforced in the baths. Just because the emperor is in here naked doesn't mean he is just like everybody else. Anecdotes from the ancient world make this very clear. One of my favorites—I have favorite bathing anecdotes, how sad is that? One of my favorites is from the life of Hadrian. Hadrian, of course, is emperor, and there's an account of him going to a bath complex. As he walks through with his retinue he sees an old soldier, a veteran, up against the wall rubbing his back on the marble wall because he's got nobody to rub his back for him. So Hadrian gives the man a slave so he has somebody to massage his back.

The next time Hadrian went to the baths he saw a whole line of men up against the wall rubbing their backs on the wall waiting to get a free slave. Hadrian went up to them and turned them around so they could rub each other's backs. It's a great example of his sense of humor, but for our purposes it's also an important example of the notion that when the emperor is in the baths, he's still the emperor and everybody knows it. So class and social distinctions don't disappear with your clothing. I think that's important to realize as well.

Something else to keep in mind about the baths is that they exist because of imperial beneficence, because of the emperors as patrons deciding to build these baths. emperors successively, starting with Augustus, built large-scale bath complexes. Augustus, Nero, Titus, Trajan, all through the imperial period they built these grand complexes.

The complex itself is part of the benefit, having this grand, luxurious space. But the benefit actually starts with the construction because these building programs are actually jobs programs as well. As emperors begin to build these, they're putting people to work. We have a marvelous anecdote that tells us about this from the life of Vespasian. A man comes to the Emperor Vespasian with a device, probably some kind of pulley, which enables him to lift heavy stones that would take many men to lift, but he could do it by himself. Vespasian thanks the man for his invention, pays him for it, but says, "I can't use it because what would my people do for bread?" It's a very powerful anecdote because it tells us the emperors are thinking about these building programs not just in terms of their legacy, or their propaganda, or settling the plebs, but in terms of giving people jobs. It's a great jobs program, so I think that's something to keep in mind as well.

So they're vast public works programs, bringing employment to thousands of Romans, but once again, reinforcing the role of the emperor in their construction, as well as in their maintenance. Many people—emperors—leave gifts of money so that you cannot just have the bath complex, but you can attend it free. Sometimes there's free olive oil given out, and the Romans used olive oil as an emollient, as a skin lotion. They used that in the baths. There's free hardwood to run the furnaces that heat the buildings, and so there's a lot of maintenance in one of these buildings and the emperors take care of that so that it's all available to people.

We have a marvelous cutaway here of an interior reconstruction of the baths to give you a sense of what we're talking about with the grandeur and luxury. When we think about the baths, we need to think about how they operate in reinforcing Roman cultural values. I think that's significant. The foundational value that we need to be aware of is a phrase. It's a Roman phrase in Latin, "*mens sana in corpore sano*," that is, "a sound mind in a sound body." That encapsulates the purpose of the baths because it's not just bathing. It's not just coming in and getting clean, and it's not just doing things with your body, that is, massage, and exercise, and all of these regular activities you might find at a spa or a gym or things like that. But the idea is to really have a space in which you can exercise the entire body and mind together. When you look at a marvelous reconstruction of the baths like we have here, you should be struck, I think as most people are, at just how little of the space is given over to bathing. Very little of the ground here is actually pools of water. Much of the space is given over to large rooms and outdoor spaces where a variety of activities are taking place, again, *mens sana in corpore sano.*

So we have social events taking place at the baths. Roman Patricians will meet here and use this public space to discuss politics and business. It's an opportunity for networking, to reinforce their social and political connections with one another.

Lower-class Romans came to the baths all the time. As I said, probably on a daily basis. One of the things that they came for, and we have a number of references to this in the ancient literature, is they came for favors. They sought out elite Romans who they could recognize even without their clothing. They sought out favors, in particular, dinner invitations. It was a social requirement of upper-class Romans to invite lower-class Romans over for dinner, and the lower classes showed up asking for these or making a nuisance of themselves until finally they were invited over for a lavish banquet in somebody's house. So again, all these activities reinforced the social and class roles that we have.

There are also the more, what we might term, informal social interactions, the romantic encounters and assignations that take place in these luxurious and very relaxed settings. The fact that people are coming to the baths to pick up girls tells us that there is mixed-sex bathing going on. It also tells us something a little more subtle, perhaps, than that, and that is that the baths are an appropriate place to meet people because Roman science is governed by the notion of the four humors. For the Romans, blood is associated with heat, and so when people come to the baths and get physically hot, they are sexually hot in the way we use the term. So for the Romans, the baths become an appropriate venue for sexual expression because of their understanding of science at the time, and those great four elements of earth, air, fire, and water, which are connected to the four humors. So the baths reinforce this notion of science as well as they do the political, social, and class roles.

We need to talk more about the more formal activities that take place; the broad and comprehensive physical and intellectual options that one can undertake in the baths. One of the best ways to do this is to think about the variety of events and the variety of spaces. We'll go through the baths and talk about some of these spaces and then what's going on in them.

First, I want you to contrast in your mind what we've got here with the baths. We have a nice reconstruction of the interior of a bath, of people bathing, and sitting around playing games, and so on, the great high ceilings, and the rich light pouring in, and the decoration. Contrast that with the living conditions for your average, everyday Roman. The vast majority of Romans are living in what we would term slums, that is, tenement rooms, small rooms, no climate control, poor lighting, no heat. Coming here every day to these grand spaces is going to reinforce your connection to the entire Roman world, your social and political connections, but more than that it's going to reinforce the notion that it's good to be a Roman. It's a tremendous benefit, and a tangible one, to being a Roman. So that is something to start with when we're thinking about these things.

The baths are laid out in large blocks of rooms, and they're pretty much organized all the same way, although there are a number of these. We have a plan here of the baths of Trajan. In the center you can see a large block of buildings surrounded by blank space, which is the gardens, and then there's a surrounding wall around that. The main rooms run up that central axis in the middle of that block of buildings. The Romans are famous for their construction based on axiality and symmetry, so when you run up that central axis you hit mainly all of the main rooms in the bath.

The first of these rooms is an *apodyterium*, the changing room. You might see an example of this in a marvelous reconstruction painting. This is the changing room that contained lockers. People would come in, take off their street clothes, and put their clothing in a locker. There are benches and things for people to sit on. And then from this they would go into a variety of rooms. These rooms are all climate-controlled with different forms of heat, or cold water, as well as different humidities. So you can experience a rich range of atmospheres as you move through. Generally adjacent to the *apodyterium* we have the *frigidarium*, the cold room. This is very simply a plunge, usually just a large round basin in the floor with cold water in it. It was fed by aqueducts, so it's just a standard groundwater temperature room, and so you have a cold plunge. I must tell you that the order of these rooms I'm giving is in the order of the architecture. We don't know what order people would participate in these. We don't know how people would go back and forth. There might have been a prescriptive order or there might not, but we'll just take them from the architectural standpoint.

Next to the *apodyterium* is the *frigidarium*. In more elaborate bath complexes like the imperial ones that we know of, there is always an outdoor *natatio*, or swimming pool. It's an open-air swimming pool, out in the open, where people would swim. That's fairly standard as well.

In terms of the indoor rooms, the next room that we generally have in the sequence is the *tepidarium*. That is, as the name suggests, a warm water room. That's followed by the *caldarium*. This is the root of our word to "scald." "Scald" comes from "*caldarium*." And that's the hot water room, which is usually heated all the way around with radiant heat. The furnaces that heat the bath complex are actually chimneyed out under the floors and around the walls of the *caldarium* so that heat radiates out of the floor and out of the walls. So you walk into this room and you get this marvelous baking heat.

This may not sound good if you've been to Italy recently, and we almost always go in the summer. You go to Italy in the summer and it's 98 degrees and you think, what were they thinking? When you go back to Italy in December, and my family has done this, it's cold there. It's amazing. So if you're living on the 5th floor of a tenement and there's no heat, and you walk down here into the *caldarium* on a December day, you just stand there and absorb this baking heat. That would be really tremendous. Then at one end of the *caldarium* you're going to have a hot water plunge. It's set into the floor and heated just like the walls and the floor are. Then at the opposite end you're going to have a cold water basin, so you can go back and forth between these. Sit down there in that hot water, get out, splash some cold water on your face, and go back and forth and control your own experience throughout the baths—hot, warm, cold—all the way through these rooms. It's an extraordinary experience.

There are also some specialty rooms. We know that there are some special rooms such as a *sudatorium*, which is a sweating room. This seems to be a room with both heat and high humidity where people would just go and take the steam.

There is also a room called a *laconicum*, which is a hot baking room. It's even warmer than the *caldarium*, but it's a dry heat. This is a dry sauna where people would go and take that baking heat in the dry sauna. As I say, people would spend hours here, moving back and forth between these rooms, chatting, networking, picking up a dinner invitation, all this sort of thing. This really gives you a sense of the luxury involved. And it's free. Anybody can come in and anybody does.

In addition to the actual bathing, or the saunas and the steams and such, the complexes provide a lot of other ways to take care of both the mind and the body. We'll stay with the body for just a minute. There are a lot of forms of exercise taking place in these bath complexes. We know this from the descriptions, from the spaces, and also from the decorations. Many of the baths are decorated appropriately and effectively in self-referential ways so that the decoration in the bath reflects the activities taking place.

I've got a couple of mosaic images here that I've taken from a bath complex, which show us athletics taking place in the bath. They're not actually in the bath rooms, but in the complex outside in the open areas around the main building block. And so we have a variety of events taking place in these mosaics. We see boxers, wrestlers, people doing all the standard sort of things that we refer to as "track and field." In addition to boxing and wrestling, we see evidence of javelin and discus throwing, people throwing a shot put—just a whole range of the standard sort of traditional athletic events taking place.

We also see evidence, from these mosaics and from literary accounts in the ancient world, of trainers. This mosaic shows a boxer exercising in the nude, as was appropriate. Right next to him is an older man with a beard, and he's a little shorter, and he's got a wrap around himself. He's not naked. He's the trainer. This is the older man telling the young man what to do. If you've seen *Rocky* you can get a sense of this. In fact, I think the older guy here looks a lot like Burgess Meredith, so go watch *Rocky* and you'll get a good sense of what that is like.

So we've got all of these forms of exercise: running and track and field events. People are, again, spending hours here at the baths, so there are also food and drink vendors. There is a lot of evidence of that from poets who tell us that baths and wine go together, so it's not just all exercise and health. There are a lot of people here just loitering around, playing games, sipping wine, having snacks, and things like that.

There is also the sort of what we might term auxiliary health events taking place. You've come to the bath to get a haircut. You've come to the bath to take a massage. You would also come to the baths to see a doctor. There is evidence that doctors actually saw patients here, and very often would prescribe the baths for their patients. So there is a rich array of these activities taking place as well.

These are all the physical activities and we have excellent evidence for all of these. There is a particularly good letter from the philosopher, Seneca, talking about living above a bath complex and listening to the sounds of a fat man getting a massage, or somebody getting their armpit hair plucked out, the screams and things like that. It's a good time.

But there are also the intellectual and cultural activities. Again, it's a sound mind in a sound body, and we need to turn our attention to those as well. There are a lot of intellectual activities taking place in the baths. It seems curious to us, in terms of going to the gym or going to a resort, to go and listen to a lecture there, but that, in fact, is what the Romans would do. Philosophers would hold school in bath complexes. There are lecture rooms. There are concert halls. There are debates. There are all sorts of intellectual activities taking place in the baths, so it's a whole range of events.

One of the other surprising things, I think, is the fact that there's evidence—again, from the baths of Trajan—for a library at the bath complex. You could come here into this very pleasant urban space and just sit and read, maybe sip a cup of wine, attend a philosophical debate. This probably isn't our idea of a spa activity, but it is for the Romans. It's a much more well-rounded idea of what is involved here than I think that we have.

Now I have emphasized a lot of the physical, as well as a little bit of the mental here, but I want us to think also in terms of the context for all of this. I've mentioned the living space for your average Roman up in his 5th-floor tenement, but that's not everybody, of course. The Romans who are living in these spaces are well aware that the upper classes have their own grand spaces, their own grand buildings, their own grand villas, with their own formal gardens. So what we're seeing in the baths is an opportunity for the whole of the Roman population to have the same experience as the upper classes. I'm not suggesting, again, that there is a violation of the class distinction. I think they're still there, but this is an opportunity for everybody to become one of the exploiters of empire as opposed to the exploited.

What I mean by that is in the grounds of the baths. The baths themselves are not just large, but they're luxuriously appointed. If we look at the baths of Caracalla, I've got a nice scene of it from recent years, you can see how tremendous the scale is. Architecturally, the buildings are vast. I think the upper ceilings at the baths of Caracalla are just over 100 feet tall. There's none of this Frank Lloyd Wright, human-scaled architecture stuff. No, that's not it. The notion is to evoke a sense of wonder, of greatness, that you are part of something bigger and greater than your life, and it is right here in the baths. So it's not just scale, but it's also the decorations. You walk into these spaces; everything on the inside is going to be richly decorated. The walls will be clad in either sheets or marble or, beyond a certain height, painted plaster, so they're all stuccoed and painted lavish colors.

The floors are also marble. I know we talk a lot about how practical the Romans are, but it's not all about practicality. Anybody who has ever renovated their kitchen will tell you that marble is a lot more expensive than, say, stainless steel. The Romans know this as well. What we see from the baths of Caracalla is an example of just the enormous spaces that are covered with marble mosaic floors, patterned mosaics. If you look at these colors, I think you get a sense of just the epic achievement involved here. If you look at an image here of the floor of the baths of Caracalla you see four colors: red, white, yellow, and green marble. The white marble is Italian marble, but the yellow marble comes from North Africa. The red is from Egypt, and the green is from Greece. This is the emperor making, I think, a very clear statement about bringing the benefits of this entire Roman Empire into the city of Rome for everybody.

Again, think about importing stone from central Greece where there are no good roads and no good waterways. That stone for these mosaics is quarried out in large blocks, put on the back of carts, carted out about 100 miles before they could get to a good port, then sailed here, and then brought to the baths of Caracalla, where the floor is laid out. So if you walk across this, you get that sense that, wow, everything works. My government is working on my behalf and it's good to be a Roman. So everything is expensive; it's vividly colored; it is imported, and you get a great sense of the decorative features here.

A lot of the decorative schemes are aquatic in theme and we see a lot of images of Neptune and Nereid and things like that, but we also have tremendous large-scale statues. I want to show you a couple of these, also from the baths of Caracalla to give you a sense of what we have here.

We have sculpture that is thematic to the baths. Once again, it's self-referential. We know the Romans were particularly concerned about having appropriate decoration in appropriate spaces because we have a marvelous series of letters from Cicero. Cicero is trying to decorate his villa and he's writing to a friend in Greece asking for sculptures to decorate his own little academy, his own library and philosophical hall, and his friend sends him athletic sculptures. Cicero writes back and says what am I going to do with all these? I'm not decorating a gymnasium. I'm decorating a philosophical hall here. Send me busts of philosophers, send me something thoughtful. So it's very clear that the Romans are concerned deeply about having the appropriate decoration to reference the activities taking place.

In the baths of Caracalla here we have two excellent examples of this. We have large-scale statues, once again, vast in scale. The achievement of bringing these here is something we should not underestimate. One of these is a large sculpture of the punishment of Dirce. It's a scene from Greek mythology, and I think it's marvelous because it not only decorates this, but also reinforces that notion of culture. There is no label on this. You're supposed to know what it is. We know that upper-class Romans at least would recognize this story. It's also in itself a tremendous achievement that's supposed to evoke wonder because this statue is nine feet on a side. It's nine feet tall and nine feet square, carved out of a solid block of marble, and imported here into the baths. I don't know about your bathroom at home, but mine doesn't have enough room for a nine-foot-tall statue in the center of it. Caracalla's, of course, did, and it's placed so that people could walk around it and see it from all sides and really get a tremendous sense of the wonder of this.

The other sculpture I wanted you to take a look at from the baths of Caracalla is a much more famous one. This is the Farnese Hercules. Images of Hercules, along with athletes and other burly hero-types are fairly standard in bath complexes, again, reinforcing the activities in the space. The Farnese Hercules here is like the punishment of Dirce. It's about eight feet tall. It's carved out of a solid block of marble by a Greek sculptor, carved probably in Greece, and then shipped here into Rome and imported into the baths of Caracalla. It may be contemporary with the baths, but we think it's actually older, so it's brought here deliberately. The idea is that this gives you a sense of the activities as well as the cultural aspect that you are undergoing here in the baths.

So when we think about these baths, I want you to think about and take away with you a couple of key ideas. The first is that it's not just bathing. We're not just coming here to get clean, although there is certainly that aspect of it. This is a spa. It's a resort in the center of the city of Rome with formal gardens, walkways, exercise rooms, bathing facilities, and also all the cultural aspects of lecture halls, and musical concerts, and things like that all taking place in this space open to everybody.

That brings me to the second point, and that is beneficiaries of empire. Everybody who comes in here becomes a beneficiary of the Roman system, and directly and tangibly benefits from the work and patronage of the particular emperor who has endowed these baths.

The other thing I want you to think about is the cultural aspect; that the baths serve, by their existence, as well as the activities, to reinforce the Roman political, social, and class system so that every time you come in here, just as you did when you enter the Colosseum—I think the Colosseum is our best example—you're reinforcing your place in the Roman world. You're all naked together, but that doesn't eliminate these important class, social, and political distinctions. So you can really take advantage of these activities on a daily basis and by doing so, you're effectively putting yourself in your place in the Roman world.

# Roman Engineering—Linking the World

## Lecture 28

**The entire Roman Empire was linked by a tremendous series of roads, tunnels, aqueducts, canals, and bridges unmatched until the 20th century.**

Roman civil engineering has been interpreted as the ultimate expression of Roman practicality but seems to have served significant symbolic purposes as well. Roman emperors used the ability to create vast engineering marvels to indicate Roman power to both Romans and non-Romans. Caesar's bridge over the Rhine during his Gallic campaign was considered a wonderful achievement, extending Roman power into Germany for the first time, a fact he celebrated in a detailed description in his history of the war. Trajan's Column features his great bridge over the Danube during the Dacian Wars, a feat considered the greatest architectural achievement of his age.

The creation of these wonders also celebrated Roman power over nature. Trajan's cut through a coastal cliff for the new Via Appia was marked with numbers, recording the 110-foot hand-chiseled road cut for all who traveled along it to appreciate the achievement. An arch on Domitian's new road from the Via Appia to Cumae marked where it passed through the cut in the ridge that had isolated Cumae from the interior of Campania for centuries. Every mile of a Roman road was marked with a milestone inscribed with the mile number, the emperor responsible, and the army unit that built the road, allowing all those literate in Latin (mainly Romans) to appreciate this benefit of their government and military. Roman aqueducts and bridges were also marked with large dedicatory inscriptions announcing the identity of those responsible for them; in the case of bridges, the inscriptions could be read by those sailing under them, suggesting that the fact of bridging a river was more remarkable than the crossing of it.

Canals and bridges seem to have been considered assaults on the realm of the sea from the land. Caligula commanding the army to literally assault the sea shows this mind-set at work. Nero's inauguration of his canal in Greece began with a trumpet blast, as did military maneuvers, in this case with the Praetorian Guard standing by. These engineering marvels were also intended to provoke a sense of wonder. Caesar's and Claudius's plans for canals in Italy were motivated by a desire to defeat the storms that threatened the grain fleet and achieve an awe-inspiring, but ultimately impossible, engineering feat. On his column, Trajan's bridge over the Danube was illustrated as a conquest over the personified god of the river.

**Every mile of a Roman road was marked with a milestone inscribed with the mile number, the emperor responsible, and the army unit that built the road, allowing all those literate in Latin (mainly Romans) to appreciate this benefit of their government and military.**

The long, straight lines of roads, aqueducts, and tunnels differed dramatically from the systems of pre- and non-Roman people and served to mark the landscape as Roman, so that the famous phrase "all roads lead to Rome" seems true. These engineering works dominate the rural landscape leading up to the Roman cities, especially Rome itself. Those approaching Rome on the Via Appia, for example, would find the last several miles of their trip paralleled by the Aqua Claudia, Claudius's aqueduct into the city. From the north, the Via Flaminia cuts across formerly Latin and Etruscan territory to run straight into Rome, terminating at the Capitoline Hill and effectively projecting the capital of Rome straight out into captive territory.

Augustus's establishment of a golden milestone in the Forum Romanum created the notion that Rome was centrally located in the world. This idea borrows from the Greek notion of the *omphalos* (navel) of the world, which was supposedly at the sanctuary of Apollo at Delphi. Rome now succeeded to that position. The centrality of Rome in the empire is clearly symbolic rather than actual, making this visual statement more important than the actual geography of Roman rule. ■

## Suggested Reading

O'Connor, *Roman Bridges*.

Sitwell, *Roman Roads of Europe*.

## Questions to Consider

1. In what ways did the engineering feats of imperial Rome serve to create or mark territory as specifically Roman?

2. How did Roman emperors use the creation of bridges, roads, and canals to establish their command of nature and their control over the empire?

# Roman Engineering—Linking the World

## Lecture 28—Transcript

Welcome to this lecture on Roman engineering. I would like to particularly thank you for getting past the title. I realize titling a lecture "Roman Engineering" is probably not the sexiest thing and is not going to get everybody to immediately flip open into it, but this is great material. I think it's particularly relevant for us as Americans who have such a tremendous infrastructure in our world. Think about those of us who live in North America, and in the United States and Canada with our tremendous dams, and highway systems, and bridges everywhere. We really are beneficiaries of a powerful system of infrastructure that makes our society possible and, I think, makes it possible for us to relate to the Romans.

I have to tell you that this material has a fond place in my heart because my father is a civil engineer. And if you're like me, and I suspect you're not, we would drive down the road, and he would point out dams, and roadways, and things like that as we went along, and give little lectures about the civil engineering involved. The culmination of all this was one time we went on a family vacation and went on a tour of a sewage treatment plant as part of the vacation, probably an experience most of you have not had. But it was good because it gave me an appreciation for not just the fact of infrastructure, of roads and bridges and so on, but really the achievement involved.

That, coupled with my 10, 12 years of college, has also given me a sense of the symbolic aspect of this study, and the fact that these works that we're going to be looking at aren't just achievements, and aren't just practical applications, but they're really the way the Romans imposed their society on the world, the creating, through these public works, a topography of power, which spread out from Rome across the entire Roman Empire, and so I think that these roads, and bridges, and canals, and so on really deserve quite a bit of thought and attention, not just for what they are and what they achieve, but for what they symbolize as well.

The Roman emperors, of course, were well aware of this. They used the ability to create vast engineering marvels as components of their public visual programs. They didn't just build bridges, but they showed themselves building bridges. Case in point: Julius Caesar in his great Gallic campaign. One of his great achievements was building a bridge over the Rhine River. We have a marvelous reconstruction of this so you can get a sense of what this was like.

This also brings up an interesting notion in the fact that in all of these monuments, as in so much of Roman art, there are a couple of key audiences we need to have in mind: the Roman and the nonRoman. For the Romans, this is a tremendous engineering achievement, being able to build a bridge over this fast-moving, powerful river, spanning from land to water to land, all the way across. For them it's a projection of power.

For the Germans on the other side of the river it's going to be a completely different message, of course. For them as an audience it's really going to say that their world as they knew it with that protective boundary of the Rhine is over, and the Romans now have entered it.

So we've got those two audiences, and I think these monuments are made with those two in mind. Bridges are one of the most important of these engineering achievements. Caesar doesn't just build a bridge over the Rhine, but tells us about it in his commentary. He makes a big point about writing that commentary home to the people in Rome and telling them about this achievement.

Caligula does the same thing. He holds a great sort of pageant where he builds a great bridge over the Bay of Baiae and rides back and forth, one day dressed as Alexander the Great and the next day as a charioteer driving a chariot over dry land that he has created. That notion of dry land where once there was water is part of this symbolism.

We see how important the symbolic aspect of these engineering achievements is with an image from the column of Trajan. At the very bottom, at the initial stages of the Dacian campaign, we see a bridge that Trajan had constructed over the Danube River. In the image that we have on the column, we see the personification of the river, the river god hemmed in by this bridge as it just goes over his head, and he's powerless to do anything about it. That's important for two things: Number one, the fact that this bridge over the Danube was at the time considered to be the greatest architectural achievement of the age, more so than the column itself, more than the markets, or the great Forum of Trajan, or anything else that you could name. It was that bridge that everybody comments on as the greatest architectural achievement.

The other thing that I think is particularly notable about this is that, once again, the symbolism is critical. For the Romans, what they're doing is projecting their power on nature. In this case, we have a symbolic projection of power much the same way that the Romans did with their animal hunts, bringing in wild animals from the edges of their empire to show control over those areas. Here, it's clearly control over that personified god, effectively. That's a pretty pretentious statement, but for the Romans it's one that I think is very important. They're defining the world in their terms, and so these engineering marvels are more than just practical aspects. They are making powerful ideological statements.

One of my favorite of all of these statements is one, again, under Trajan. Trajan, who was a great builder, really built a lot of infrastructure improvements throughout Italy and the Roman Empire, decided to re-route the Via Appia. It passed through Campania on the inland side, and he re-routes it to be a coastal road, so it runs through a number of coastal communities, including Terracina. There was a mountain in the way, so Trajan had it taken down. What we're looking at here on this slide doesn't look like much. It's a cliff face, but it's an artificial cliff face. This is the cutting for the Via Appia where Trajan had the road re-routed. There was a mountain in the way, so he just had it taken down, and here's the cutting. The important and amazing thing about it is, if you look in a close-up of this cutting, you will see a couple of things: Number one, the fact that all of the tool marks are still there. This mountain, over 115 feet of solid rock, was all cut away by guys using hammers and chisels. It's all hand tools. I can't even imagine that, approaching a mountain with a group of people and somebody saying, "Boys, cut it all away."

The second remarkable thing about this is that in order to really display the marvel here, the achievement is that if you look carefully here you'll see all the way down the cliff base. Every 10 Roman feet there's a little plaque called the "*tabula ansata*," and in there are Roman numerals, and you can follow them down. I've done this down the cliff face. It's a little dangerous at times, but you can go down the cliff face and count down as the Romans carved all the way down until at the very bottom they get to 110 feet. In this slide you can see 80 and 90 and then just behind the trees down at the bottom is 100. So it's not just a matter of making this available to the Roman people, but celebrating it and making the announcement of what this achievement is.

We see this with Trajan's cutting here in the Via Appia. This is the same sort of thing with a different form of monumentalization a little farther south. The Via Appia, even as Trajan routed it, still went inland when it got down to "inner Campania" as we call it, that is, it passes through Capua in the middle of Campania. This isolated the city of Cumae, a Roman colony on the coast. It's actually the first Greek colony in southern Italy. It was founded back in 775 B.C., and it was always isolated because there's an enormous solid rock ridge that separates the territory of Cumae from the rest of Italy. This, of course, is initially defensive, but then it becomes a burden for trade, and economy, and so on, so the Emperor Domitian has a new spur road for the Via Appia punched off the Via Appia straight through that ridge, and puts in an enormous cutting and a road all the way down to Cumae, for the first time in 800 years, linking the city of Cumae by road, by major highway in the ancient terms, to the rest of the Roman system.

If you go down there today you can see, as we have in an image here, the actual road that Domitian had put in. It's still there with the original pavement and he has monumentalized the achievement of that cutting through the ridge with an arch in the form of a triumphal arch because this is a triumph, called in modern Italian, the Arco Felice, the fortunate arch. You can see the arch here in this shot and then some openings in the attic story. Those originally held statues of Domitian and his family, so it was a dynastic monument as well. It really makes a statement about bringing the benefits of his rule directly to these individuals.

We see the same thing on a smaller scale pretty much everywhere that Roman roads go as well. We've got these cuttings, and we've talked about bridges. We need to talk about the roads themselves as well. Every mile of a Roman road was marked with a milestone. I have an example that you can take a look at here, and it has fairly standard forms. It has the names of the emperors on top. There you can see on the third line Macrinus. Macrinus is a 3rd-century emperor in the Severan dynasty, and then there are all the other names and offices. And then down at the very bottom you can see the Roman numerals "LVI." This is a milestone that's constructed as the road was built. It's the 56th mile of this road under Macrinus.

This tells very clearly who the authority is, who made this road possible. We do this to a certain extent in our highway projects. If you go on a highway today and you see all the orange barrels and you slow down, you'll see a sign out there that says this highway improvement project is 30 percent state and 70 percent federal, or something along those lines. Most of us don't read those signs; we're too busy cursing those orange barrels. But what those signs do is what the Roman milestones did, and that is, they tell you that your government is working for you, that the infrastructure is being improved, and that it's making a difference in your life. This isn't tremendously sexy, I appreciate, but it does give people, to a great extent, what they want from government, and that is, they want things to work. They want infrastructure, and roads, and bridges that they can drive across and not fall down. It's not a large-scale bath complex, but on a smaller scale, it makes the Roman system work. So these milestones are part of that ideological display as we see with the Arco Felice and with Trajan's cutting.

We also see the same thing in Roman bridges and aqueducts, and we have a nice shot here of a Roman bridge. This is in the city of Rome, connecting Rome with the island in the middle of the Tiber River. That island, by the way, never had a name. It's just called "island" in Latin, *insula*, the way the Tiber is just the Latin word for river. The Romans are, in a lot of cases, not the most creative people in the world. If they have an island, it's called "island." If they have a river, it's called "river." In any case, what we have here is a marvelous bridge that dates to 73 B.C., and if you walk over the bridge you don't see a dedicatory inscription. It's only if you're sailing up or down the Tiber. What you see in this image in the right-hand arch in that white stone that makes up the decorative span of the arch, there's an inscription there with the name of the man who's responsible for building this in 73 B.C. What I think is interesting about this is where this dedicatory inscription is because for the Romans, it's not a matter of crossing the river that I think is the most important thing. What it is, it's a matter of celebrating the bridge itself, so that when somebody goes up and down the river they see that bridge above them, and it's a celebration of that achievement of the bridge. It's not a celebration of being able to cross over. I'm not sure if that entirely makes sense, but I think the perspective here is one of being able to appreciate the achievement from where you are down below. That is the significant aspect here, and that's the remarkable part of it.

Roman engineering and all of the civil engineering projects, whether they're bridges, roads, canals, aqueducts, or whatever, are manifestations of that Roman ability, or at least the Roman desire, to conquer nature. I think that's the key. This is the same notion that we see in Latin poetry and in Roman wall paintings where the Romans create a great landscape. Unlike in the Greek world where they will just have a landscape and put some people in it, a Roman landscape always has Roman buildings in it. The Romans are defining the landscape by what they impose on it. So when we see, for example, outside the city of Rome the great arches of the Aqua Claudia, the great aqueduct passing along, what the Romans are doing is imposing themselves upon the landscape. We see this with aqueducts, canals, and bridges.

The Emperor Caligula, for example, shows us this mindset at work with his assault on the sea when he lined up the army and marched them out to the seaside to collect shells. This is a whimsical event denigrating the military, as I have mentioned, but it's also an assault on the realm of water. That's really what these works are, canals and bridges in particular.

We see an excellent example of how the Romans are viewing these engineering marvels in Nero's inauguration of a canal in Greece. He tried to put the first canal across at what is called "the Isthmus of Corinth." There is a canal there today, although it wasn't built until the early 1900s. But Nero tried first to dig a great canal across there to make commerce and just all sorts of shipboard travel easier so you could cut through at Corinth rather than sailing around the dangerous Peloponnese of Greece. When he did this, he went out for the ceremonial inauguration of this cutting and he had the military with him. They blew a great trumpet blast just as they did when they were setting out on a great military maneuver or starting a battle, and Nero gathers up the first basket of earth and carries it away, flanked by the Praetorian Guard, his military honor guard. So it's very clear that he's viewing this is a campaign against nature. That's really the Roman perspective on all of this. Everything here is something that needs to be subdued. So the sea, the land, all of these hostile forces need to be subdued. We see that in very symbolic events from Caligula and Nero in particular.

The other thing that I think is important about these grand engineering projects that we often don't think about is the sense of wonder. We don't really emphasize a sense of wonder any more the way the Romans did. We're somewhat more cynical, or perhaps just more practical of mindset. I was trying to look up modern notions of wonder, and came up with the Wonder Bra. It's just not the same. But the ancients had a tremendous sense of wonder. They're the ones who gave us those first lists of the Seven Wonders of the Ancient World and things like that. They are supposed to be human activities, human achievements that just evoke a sense of awe. That's it. You're not supposed to understand them and unpack them, just to appreciate them with that sense of open awe and wonder.

That is one of the goals of these engineering feats. It's partly a symbolic attack on nature, partly an expression of that notion of wonder. With that notion of wonder you're supposed to associate it directly with each of the emperors who makes it possible. So if, for example, Julius Caesar's and then afterwards, Claudius's, plans to excavate great canals up the west coast of Italy had taken place, you would approach these with a tremendous sense of wonder. The plan was fairly simple and straightforward in its design, but audacious in its scale. We're going to start a canal—and you can still see the cuttings today—down on the Bay of Naples, and cut that canal all the way up the Italian peninsula to Rome so that ships that came down into Italy would actually enter the harbor down on the Bay of Naples and then sail inland from the Bay of Naples all the way to Rome, bypassing that dangerous western coast. It's a brilliant idea. Of course, the scale made it impossible, but the idea was to evoke this sense of wonder.

Caesar and Claudius eventually did something smaller, but nonetheless, almost as grand. Caesar planned and Claudius built the large harbor complex at Portus at Ostia down at the mouth of the Tiber River. So they didn't get that canal done, but they got the harbor done.

Trajan's bridge over the Danube is supposed to be a great achievement that evokes a sense of wonder. We know this because the Romans themselves are not analyzing this achievement based on the engineering. We don't see schematics or anything like that. We just see that caged god. That's what we're supposed to be thinking about.

That's what we should also think about when we think about these aqueducts. In many cases we want to appreciate them for a practical application. Aqueducts are really a tremendous achievement. Think about this. How do you get water from hundreds of miles away through the city of Rome with no pumps, all gravity-fed? Water moves through those aqueducts at a steady rate, and then into Roman houses, baths, fountains, and fountain houses—formal, elaborate fountains, as well as just small fountains where people go and get their water—all of it is constantly moving and eventually passing through the city of Rome through a sewer system, never stopping.

This is a tremendous achievement because the Romans had a better per capita water supply than any city up to the 20th century in London and New York. So imperial Rome, in the 2nd century, had a better water infrastructure than we see up to the 20th century. There's a great practical aspect, but there is also that sense of wonder.

If you look at something like the Pont du Gard in southern France, and you see this Roman aqueduct, I think you have to appreciate that the Romans know that what they're doing by bridging this great river valley is imposing order on the natural landscape. We see that with the aqueducts and the bridges, but perhaps the best manifestation of all of this is the road system. I want to contrast Roman roads with what came before and non-Roman roads at the same time.

When we look at walls and roads of non-Roman people or pre-Roman people, or Greeks, to give us a good example, we see excellent construction, but what we see are roads and walls that follow the natural topography. We've got a nice wall here where you can see it following the natural course of the topographical line of the top of a hill. The Romans rejected this notion of following the natural boundaries of nature in their aqueducts, canals, bridges, and roads. Instead, what we get is the quintessential straight Roman road.

There are many of these still extant and if you go overseas, I urge you to take some time and walk on one of them because it's really quite amazing to think about these being constructed out of nothing and against the notions of nature. I think we don't have an appreciation for this because we have our interstate highway system, which does the exact same thing. But for the Roman system, they're working in a non-technological, non-industrial world, all done by hand.

We have examples of the road at Ostia punching straight from Ostia, the port city of Rome, all the way up to the capital. Here's another example of a road that I shot a picture of here at Cassino, the Roman colony of Cassinum, on the base of what is today Monte Cassino. It's a famous Italian monastery on the top of a mountain. The Romans cut through the base of that mountain, so on one side you have the cutting of the cliff face and this road going right down the edge of it. You can still see the ancient tire ruts going down this road. It's still there; it's still serviceable; it's still used today.

These roads don't just serve to link particular areas. They also define particular communities. One of the best examples of this is at the Roman colony of Saepinum. Saepinum is in the middle of Italy in the foothills of the Apennine Range. There, the Romans built an enormous straight nature-destroying road right down the edge of the colony of Saepinum, heading across the peninsula of Italy. So that road itself links the colony, but it also serves to define it because it shapes the edge of that.

The best examples of this, of course, are leading into Rome itself. If you have the opportunity and you go to Rome today, go out the Via Appia south of the city of Rome. You can go out about five miles outside the city. I walked out there one day and walked back. I sent my mother out there one time. I said, "You've got to go see the Via Appia." She almost killed me when she got back. I think it was about a 14 mile walk. We're still speaking, but it's close.

If you get out there, about five miles outside the city of Rome, you will see the remains of the Aqua Claudia. It's a long line of aqueduct that comes into the city all the way across the Great Plain of Latium, and it's paralleled by the Via Appia itself. It runs alongside it. So you've got these two enormous lines coming all the way into the city. What these do is establish the Roman dominance over the landscape here. If you walk along the Via Appia as you can in certain sections where it still has the ancient pavement, what you also see is the Romans have imposed not just their engineering, but their entire culture on this landscape because the Via Appia out here is lined with Roman tombs. This is about three miles outside the city of Rome and it's studded with large-scale Roman family tombs all along here.

What the Romans have done is to impose a linear definition on the landscape. This is not just on the south side of Rome, that wonderful reflection between the Aqua Claudia and the Via Appia, but it's in all directions. Heading north out of Rome we get the great Via Flaminia, which cuts, at the time, across what was enemy territory, across northern Latium occupied by the Latin people that at the time, the Romans were still struggling with. And then of course eventually across Etruria, modern-day Tuscany, the homeland of the Etruscans, we get this great imposition of Roman power and projection of control right across enemy territory. It's a marvelous statement about what the Romans are trying to achieve.

These don't stop at the boundaries of Rome, but come into the city. So when you pass into Rome what you see is a reflection within of what is going on outside. We can follow the lines of aqueducts as they pass into Rome today. The lines of the ancient roads of the Via Appia and the Via Flaminia are still there today. If you start up north in Rome at the Piazza del Popolo and walk down Via del Corso, you are walking along the Via Flaminia. If you start on the south side of the gates of Rome and walk in past the tomb of the Scipio families, and the baths of Caracalla and the Circus Maximus where you can pass today, you're walking up the beginnings of the Via Appia. As you walk along you'll see these lines of the aqueducts along with you.

We see in the city of Rome itself that Augustus builds a wonderful monument in the Roman Forum right next to the *rostra*, the speaker's platform. This is a golden milestone in the forum. It establishes the idea that Rome is centrally located in the world, which of course, is not the case. Again, the Romans have redefined the geography of their world around their symbolic notions as opposed to the reality. So Augustus erects a golden milestone, much like one of those cylindrical milestones I showed you before, but again, gilt. This idea borrows from the Greek notion of the *omphalos*, or the navel of the world, which the Greeks placed at Delphi. And so the Romans are taking a Greek idea and updating it into not just a stone that is a symbolic naval, but into their practical engineering terms, this golden milestone, and from there distances are measured around the Roman world from that golden milestone. And so it's not the actual center of the Roman world, but it's the symbolic center of the Roman world, and for that rather pretentious idea I think we see the importance of this idea, this symbolic notion. It's valid and it's powerful. It's more powerful, arguably, than the reality itself because it gives a sense of the importance of this entire system to the Roman world.

It's also from that golden milestone where we get the notion that all roads lead to Rome because, in fact, not all roads do lead to Rome. But all roads are measured from Rome and that's what Augustus has, in fact, imposed upon this system. So when we analyze these civil engineering projects from the Roman world, whether it's bridges, or canals, or roads, or aqueducts, we need to look past the modern assumptions of practical Romans.

There is, of course, a tremendous practical application to every one of these works, but there's something more here. These are symbolic manifestations of Roman imperialism, of their powers over nature, and of the abilities of particular emperors—Nero, Caligula, Domitian, and Trajan, in particular—to defy the physical limits of their worlds, and to bring the benefits of their rule directly to the inhabitants across the entire Roman Empire. The result of all of these engineering works, therefore, is to rewrite the topography of the world into the topography of Rome.

# Roman Military Forts and Fortifications

## Lecture 29

**The placement, form, and embellishment of Roman forts seem to have been chosen with their visual as well as military impact in mind.**

Roman forts and fortifications were clearly designed for a military purpose, but they also served a tremendously symbolic purpose. Hadrian's Wall in Britain is perhaps the most famous and best preserved of all Roman fortifications. It functioned not just as a wall but as a military complex. The wall itself crossed the entire island from east to west and was 74 miles long; it was constructed of a combination of stone and turf and varied in height from 11 to 20 feet.

Milecastles, named for their planned placement every Roman mile, were small forts positioned along the length of the wall. Turrets for observation and signaling were built in pairs between each milecastle. Approximately 17 major forts were built at intervals behind the wall and were manned by units of 500–1,000 Roman auxiliaries.

Hadrian's Wall in Britain, a military complex as well as a fortification.

The Antonine Wall replaced Hadrian's for a time, moving the boundary of Roman Britain further north. Built under Antoninus Pius (A.D. 138–161) it moved the Roman frontier 100 miles north of Hadrian's Wall. The total length of the fort was less than 40 miles, but it also stretched from coast to coast at the narrowest point of the island. The wall was less than 15 feet high and was backed by a total of 19 forts along its length.

The German forts, the *limes Germanicus*, comprised a more extensive and complex system that separated Roman Germany from the unsubdued areas to the north and east. Construction began under Augustus, and development continued until the 3rd century. The entire system eventually measured almost 400 miles in length. Much of the boundary was composed of timber palisade fencing. Additional boundaries were found in the east and south. The *limes Arabicus* screened Roman territory across the desert of what is today Syria, and the *limes Tripolitania* separated Roman areas of North Africa from the Sahara Desert.

**Roman fort. These structures were manned by Roman auxiliary units that defended land within the empire.**

Despite their widely divergent geographies, dates, and building sponsors, the fortifications have a number of key consistencies that mark them as Roman. The use of quarried and squared stone blocks distinguishes boundaries of Roman fortification from native construction. The use of straight lines for walls and roads also created key distinctions from previous native practice. Traditionally, walls and roads followed natural features across the landscape, such as rivers and ridges. The Roman system involved the establishment of roads that often ignored geography in favor of point-to-point correspondence or orientation to cardinal points.

Although it seems contrary to their purpose, many Roman fortifications seem to have been largely or mostly symbolic in the Roman tradition of marking boundaries. The large and frequent gates in the walls suggest purposes to their construction other than military, as these would create weaknesses. It seems that these gates, large and clearly marked, were not fortified to withstand attacks as we know the gates of Rome, for example, were. They were instead constructed to direct access and attention and to extend Roman culture. This pattern of elaborating and marking the borders of Roman territory is traditional, and the elaboration of these spaces and finds suggests the projection of Roman identity as a primary motivation.

Symbolic elements were integral components of such fortified zones and created displays for Romans and non-Romans alike. Altars and statues of current and past emperors were regular features of barracks and forts, creating a Roman religious space and display. Each of the forts along the *limes* had special rooms to store and display the military standards of the units stationed there. Archaeological finds of parade armor and other materials indicate that the units made ceremonial presentations along the borders as well. ■

## Suggested Reading

Breeze, *Roman Frontiers in Britain.*

Whittaker, *Frontiers of the Roman Empire.*

## Questions to Consider

1. What evidence suggests that the symbolic aspects of Roman border fortifications might have been more important than their military aspects?

2. In what ways did Roman fortifications differ from the native architectural antecedents in the frontier territories?

# Roman Military Forts and Fortifications

## Lecture 29—Transcript

Welcome to this lecture on Roman forts and fortifications. In a previous lecture, we looked at Roman infrastructure projects that served to link the Roman Empire together—the bridges, the canals, the roads, and the aqueducts that served as armatures, creating a linkage across the Roman Empire.

What we're going to look at here are the liminal monuments, the forts and fortifications that were developed by the Romans on the very frontiers of the Roman world to create entrance monuments around the edges of Roman territory and space. And so this is effectively the converse of those linking monuments. These are very liminal structures, which are designed for a military purpose, but more than that, they also serve a tremendously symbolic purpose. In many cases, and I'll make this point later on, they seem to be used to project the image of Roman power as much as to serve for platforms for military activities. They are used in a lot of cases as far as we can tell to control access and to pronounce Roman power as much as they are as bastions of Roman defense. So here we're going to look at the full range of Roman monuments with those symbolic and what we might term "theoretical" aspects in mind.

The first thing I want to mention is how we know what we know about this material. We're fortunate to have a tremendous number of forts and fortifications that have been excavated and are still extant in some form, generally in foundations.

I also want to mention the tremendous service of the Column of Trajan, which has been sort of a touchstone throughout this course for the rich variety of reliefs and evidence that it gives us. We see on the Column of Trajan a fort building. We see the army marching forth in those Dacian campaigns, constructing forts as they go along. We get a great sense of what this was like, how the forts were constructed, the types of stone that were used, the way the military was organized. Every time they stop somewhere on a march for the night, they build a fortification, and then as they go through, they build permanent stone forts. On the column these are always carefully distinguished from the native architecture around them, and so the Romans are keenly aware of the fact as they construct Roman-style fortifications, Roman forts and Roman smaller bastions of defense, in these new territories, they're making a clear distinction between what is Roman and what was there previously. We'll take an in depth look at some of these now.

One of the best examples of all Roman forts and fortifications is Hadrian's Wall in Britain. Hadrian's Wall is the best preserved of all Roman fortifications and it's the most famous. We have an image here that is fairly iconic. You see it stretching across northern England here. It's also significant as the northernmost projection of Roman power. I argue that this is one reason why it is such an elaborate barrier. It's because it does represent the very limits of Roman power, and it's a liminal monument. The Romans made it as grand as possible. We'll go into how they did that in just a bit.

We're going to look at a number of elements that make up the Wall because the Wall isn't just a wall. It's really a military complex. The Wall itself crosses the entire island of Britain from east to west, and it's altogether about 74 miles long. It's constructed by military units who were stationed in local areas, and so the construction is not consistent all the way across. In each area the local unit used local materials, so we don't have large-scale importation of imported marble and things like that, but using local materials. Sometimes they're quarrying stone, other times they're using turf. They're just cutting out sod and stacking it up. So the Wall is inconsistent across its length.

The Wall varies in height from 11 to 20 feet, and as I say, each section shows us, in the final result, the evidence of individual construction by units. It also shows us that what the Romans are doing here is projecting not just military power, but in fact, their culture. When we look at the entire complex of what we term Hadrian's Wall, we see the Wall, but we also see a lot of Roman civilization behind it. One of the best examples of this is found at the ruined temple in one of the Roman forts directly behind the Wall, and this is a temple to Mithras, a Persian deity. In fact, his name is old. The name Mithras appears in Vedic text. Going all the way back to India we see the name Mithras appears. It travels over into Persia, and the worship of Mithras as this sort of young male creator deity spreads throughout the Roman world starting in the 1$^{st}$ century B.C., starting in the Near East in what is today Iran, Iraq, and then into Syria and then eventually throughout the entire Roman world.

Up here in northern England, the very borders of the Roman world, we see a cult site to Mithras, to this Persian deity, with dedications. It's a marvelous reconstruction of what this little shrine to Mithras would have looked like. We've got a standard iconography of the worship of Mithras in the back, reclining couches for a ritual meal to take place, so the Romans are not just bringing with them their army. They're bringing their entire culture. What that means is Latin literature, Roman dress, religion, and social organization. It's all coming along here, so it's really a projection of the entire Roman system as we have up here on the Wall.

Let's take a look at that Wall and some of the components. I've got a marvelous reconstruction here of one of the milecastles. These were, as the name suggests, placed about every mile along the Wall. These are small forts that are placed along the Wall, each one of which has an entrance across the Wall. So if you're looking at the reconstruction, the north is on the right hand side. That's barbarian territory. So the fort actually doesn't project into barbarian territory. It's built behind the Wall in Roman territory. It has a gate in the back and then a gate into enemy territory. I'm particularly fond of this reconstruction because it shows you what the Wall probably looked like because there's very good evidence that the Wall itself, along with these forts, were all whitewashed. This tells us how symbolic they were, that the Romans are not just throwing up a wall, but they're actually creating a marker in the landscape. This would have really stood out in the ancient world as they build this 74-mile long Wall, and then whitewash the entire thing. So you get this great white stripe across northern England, demarking Roman territory. Hadrian does this to a great extent for the first time in Rome, establishing formal boundaries across what is Roman and what is not. This is a great example of the symbolic aspect of the Wall. So we have these milecastles placed about every mile along the Wall.

These are supported in between, we have a milecastle a mile apart, and in between each milecastle are two small garrisons, called "turrets." These turrets are for observation and signaling purposes. They're tiny in size. They altogether are about 72 square feet. This is smaller in its ground plan than my bathroom. I went home and measured as I was thinking about this. Sadly, it's not smaller than my office. My office is about the same size as one of these, but as I say, it's smaller than my bathroom. So what we have here is not at all a useful fighting platform or a garrison location. These turrets make the point that what the Romans are doing is projecting power through their presence because these are not useful military stations. They might be used for signaling or observation, but they're not going to be used for combat. There's just no way you could fight a determined enemy from this small space, not with any sort of garrison. So what the Romans have thrown up across the north in the A.D. 120s is, in many cases, as much a symbolic boundary as it is an actual bastion of defense.

The actual military forces that we find in the North are behind the Wall in Roman territory. We have a marvelous reconstruction here of a fort at Chesters, on the east side of Hadrian's Wall. Altogether there were probably about 17 of these forts that stretched across the entire length of the Wall. They were manned by units of somewhere between 500 and 1,000 Roman auxiliaries placed in these forts. These are the real military forces, and they're not actually visible from the Wall itself. So the forces are behind. They're stationed back, presumably so they can be rapid response forces to go anywhere you need them to be. But the point is that they're not actually projecting Roman power the way you might think of a forward military base doing.

The other thing that I think is significant about these forts is their consistency. The layout of the forts is remarkably consistent. We can always find the commander's headquarters building. It's right in the center. There are always these large rectangles with crossing roads. There are a lot of straight lines involved. As I mentioned with the lecture on Roman roads, the Romans are very deliberately imposing their power on this landscape, building for the first time enormous, straight roads that come straight through these forts and intersect the Wall in the north at a right angle. So you get a sense of consistency wherever you go. These are the forts along the Wall and, as I say, they're remarkably consistent.

I mentioned that Hadrian's Wall is the northernmost projection of Roman power, and that's generally the case. But actually, Hadrian's Wall was abandoned for about 40 years. After Hadrian's death, Antoninus Pius attempted to move the boundary even further north, building a second wall, the Antonine Wall, up in what is today Scotland in an abandoned attempt at northern expansion into Britain. The Antonine Wall is about 100 miles north of Hadrian's Wall, and it actually crosses the island at its narrowest point. So the Antonine Wall is altogether not quite 40 miles long, to give you a sense of how narrow Britain is at that point. The wall is, again, as much symbolic as it is military. It's less than 15 feet tall, so a determined enemy in a conservative attack could easily overwhelm a wall like that. Fifteen feet is just not a great barrier.

It's also backed by about 19 forts along its entire length, so that concentration gives us a sense of perhaps the instability. You have 19 forts backing a wall that's less than 40 miles long, as opposed to 17 forts across the 74-mile Wall. We have a nice reconstruction of one of the forts behind the Antonine Wall, again, a consistency in Roman design and construction. We've got this wonderful rectangular walled fort with the Commander's building in the center, the gates on the center of each of the four walls, and roads running through—standard Roman layout. It's as though somebody is carrying—and I believe they did—a blueprint with them, and laying out a fort just as the military did.

Hadrian's Wall may be the best preserved of all the fortification systems that we have, but it was never the largest. The largest is actually is the *limes Germanicus*, the German fortification system that we find through Germany. It's the most extensive and complex of the fortification systems that we have. It was designed to separate Roman Germany from the unsubdued areas to the north and east. We have a nice reconstruction that shows us an early version of this.

The *limes Germanicus* was developed over a long period of time, about 300 years. It began to be constructed under Augustus, and then gradually is improved through the 3rd century. The entire system is about 400 miles long, so think about that. Hadrian's Wall is 74 miles long, but the German *limes* is 400 miles of fortification backed by military forts and garrisons, and so on. It's a tremendous work. There are over 60 forts and over 350 watchtowers. It's really a remarkable achievement.

The boundary itself, however, is actually fairly modest. If we look at this reconstruction we can get a sense of two critical things. The first is that it's a timber palisade. If you've ever looked at frontier forts along the old Northwest Territory in the United States throughout Ohio, for example, they look a lot like this. They're timber forts, log forts, and that's what we have here, a timber palisade.

The other thing that I want you to note besides the fact that it's just a timber curtain wall is the elaboration of the gateway. This is a characteristic Roman pattern that we'll return to in just a bit, but the gateway here is elaborated. So we have, eventually, fortification systems across northern England, across central Europe, across the Rhine, and the Danube. We also have boundaries, eventually, throughout the 2nd century, being constructed in the Near East. There's a set of *limes*, the *limes Arabicus* that goes through what is today Syria. We have a reconstruction of one of the forts. Again, it looks exactly like the forts that we've seen elsewhere, the same layout, the same organizational scheme, the same use of curtain walls and bastions. It's instantly recognizable. There's another set in Tripolitania, what is today North Africa, separating the rich, fertile areas of North Africa from the Sahara Desert south of them.

Hadrian is responsible for much of this construction, effectively formalizing the boundaries of the Roman world. These forts celebrate territory as Roman and mark it as Roman with a number of key consistencies in their design. One of these is the use of quarried stone, ashlar masonry, large blocks of masonry like we saw on Trajan's Column with the military tearing up and building their fort up. In many cases, these forts represent the first use of ashlar masonry in these local areas, and so people would recognize the building form here as characteristically Roman. Most people and non-Romans at the same time, would build with rubble walls, just dry stone as we see with dry stone fencing today and things like that. Rubble construction can be very strong, but it's characteristically not Roman. Romans quarry out blocks, lay them in courses, and create a very smooth rectangular outline. This becomes instantly recognizable, and I believe that was actually a feature of the architecture. It creates a distinction for these forts that when you see them at a distance they're Roman.

We also see the great height of some of these. I mentioned a 15-foot palisade or a 15-foot wall is not perhaps going to stop a determined foe, but nonetheless, it is in fact a large-scale monument compared to what was found in the areas otherwise. So they do represent a dramatic change in the landscape.

We also see an imposition of straight lines in an organic world. The non-Romans built their fortifications along natural defensible lines. The Roman, by and large, ignored the topography to impose their own straight lines in these forts. The walls, the roads coming up to them, the forts themselves, are always rectangular forts, and so they're not making use of the local topography. They're shaping the topography to their needs. This creates a sense of imposition of Roman power.

One thing to keep in mind, and I mentioned this in the reconstruction of the *limes Germanicus* is the symbolic aspect that we have of these forts. That is, in the gateways. For the Romans, we see a tremendous amount of effort being given over to formalizing gateways. Here's an example of a Roman gate with two of the characteristic components: crenellations, the little saw tooth that you see at the top of the wall; and bastions, the projecting bastions out from the sides of the opening in the gate. These are, again, characteristically Roman, repeatable phenomena, and consistent throughout Roman military architecture. I firmly believe that the notion is that wherever you go in the Roman world in these liminal monuments entering Roman space, you would see these and know instantly this is Roman territory. We see this even when there's no practical use for it. The elaboration of gateways is something that's characteristically Roman and designed to formalize your entry into the Roman world. This is consistent with the Roman notions of what one does at the boundaries of your territory. I've talked in other context about the Roman *pomerium* ceremony where you're laying out a Roman colony or the city of Rome itself, and how priests go out and plow a furrow in the ground to lay out those walls, creating a sacred boundary.

Boundaries are very important in the Roman world, and defining those boundaries is essential to knowing what is Roman. These gateways do this because they are weaknesses, not just in terms of military, but actually in terms of the religious, the symbolic boundary. So wherever you put a gate in one of these symbolic religious boundaries, you're creating a zone of religious conflict. And so gates are often heavily ornamented and, in fact, lavishly decorated. We have a marvelous example here of the Porta Maggiore, which is an interesting Roman gateway in that it actually doesn't have any gates. It's a formalized, elaborated structure made of white stone, which is heavily rusticated. The stones themselves are cut so that they project out from the courses. There are projecting columns and pairs holding up little aedicular roofs in between the actual openings. The wall on both sides is brick, but the gate itself is projected, and it's really emphasized.

What we see with these gates are entrances that are not going to withstand an attack. Instead, we see entrances that are used to direct access, to direct attention as you come toward these fortifications. A case in point is here made at the colony in Saepinum in central Italy. When this colony was founded it was enemy territory. It's deep in the Samnite heartland. In fact, it used to be the Samnite capital before the Romans wiped it out and put a colony down here. So this is, in fact, a military foundation in this colony in the center of what was then Samnite enemy territory. When we approach the gate at Saepinum we see just how important the symbolic projection of Roman power is and how they speak both to the Romans and to the non-Romans.

As you come up to the gate at Saepinum, we see in the central part of the gateway a great arch of standard Roman architectural form. Above, on the keystone of that arch, we see a *protome*, that is, a projecting bust. We don't know exactly who this is, but these projecting busts serve an apotropaic purpose, that is, they keep away evil, the same way as on the pediments above Greek temples. You'd have a face of Gorgon Medusa. It keeps evil away. And so this bust is designed to keep evil out of this sacred boundary of the city of Saepinum.

Above that, in the attic above the archway, we have a dedicatory inscription in Latin. So as you're walking up here, if you're a Roman citizen or somebody who speaks Latin, you see something that speaks to you. You see this apotropaic figure, which reinforces your Roman religion because it works within the context of your religion, and you see a dedicatory inscription. If you look at that dedicatory inscription, in the last line, the third line, there are two words you can make out: *murum* and *portas*. It tells us that the dedication is for the wall, as well as the gates. So this tells you who is responsible for this.

If you back up a bit and take a look at the sides, you see another image. What we see flanking that dedicatory inscription on either side, I think is intended not just for a Roman audience, but for a non-Roman audience because what we see on either side of the gate of Saepinum is a bound barbarian captive. So this truly non-military fortification is a symbolic gateway. Yes, it's in the middle of enemy territory, but it's constructed out of concrete. It's not really a heavy ashlar construction. Instead, it's projecting Roman power much the way I think many of these fortifications are designed to do through the elaborated gateway, through the architecture, and through the imagery that we have here of the captive barbarian.

The reason I make this distinction between projections of Roman power and actual bastions of defense is that when we contrast what we see in the fortifications along the edges of the Roman world with what surrounds the city of Rome itself, we see a dramatic difference. Here, in this image, what we have is one of the gates on the wall that's actually protecting the city of Rome. This is not some turf wall 11 to 20 feet tall, with a nice whitewashed exterior. No, this is in fact clearly Roman military architecture. We see crenellations. We see the projecting bastions. But the entire thing is closer to 60 feet tall. It's an enormous construction. This is serious military architecture. It's three stories tall. We have opening for archers and for military equipment. On top of each of those bastions, on the sides of the gateway, we have platforms for siege equipment, large *ballista* and things like that. This is an earnest military boundary around the city of Rome.

Could the Romans have built this around the frontiers? Of course they could have. They had the means, but they didn't have the will because it wasn't the goal to create an impenetrable boundary around the Roman world. It was to create a projection of Roman power with controlled access. That, I think, is the key to understand these liminal monuments.

When we look at the liminal monuments, we also see that there is a rich symbolic aspect in what we might call "the associated markers" that are along with these. In addition to the wall itself, we have a tremendous number of—let's take Hadrian's Wall, for example—markers of Roman culture. I mentioned that the little shrines of Mithras that we find throughout Roman Britain, but we also find a tremendous number of Latin inscriptions, which are clearly designed to be read by the garrisons themselves, inscriptions that give us, like milestones do, the authority. Who constructed this? Who is responsible for it? We see a number of these across the entire Roman frontiers, naming not just the emperors, but the actual military units who were responsible for the construction.

Not only do we find those, but we find something else that I think is tremendously exciting. We find those inscriptions of dedications and foundational inscriptions along the forts and along the wall and things like that, but we also see Roman communities springing up. This is another piece of evidence that suggests to us that these forts and military boundaries are not purely defensive because we have civilian communities growing around these military forts. Case in point, we have a marvelous funerary stele here from a deceased soldier, Gaius Decius, who was in charge of feeding the animals of the 20$^{th}$ Legion. He tells us about himself. His name there, Gaius Decius. He tells us how long he served, that he was a *miles* in the 20$^{th}$ Legion, and how long he lived. He lived, as I read this, 35 years. He served 16. These tombstones to soldiers and to sailors are actually found outside the fortifications. These people are dying and having their monuments placed here where they served in the civilian communities that grow up around these military forts.

What they're doing here is contributing to the Romanization of these areas. As they move here, as they serve here, if they die in service like Gaius Decius, or if they retire—many of these Roman soldiers retire here—what they do when they put their tombs here and bring in Latin inscriptions and Roman buildings is to Romanize this entire area. They are projecting Roman power, and then they're changing the very culture around that fort.

Perhaps one of the best and most vibrant examples we have of this is in the forts themselves. There are tremendous symbolic elements that are integral to all of the forts along the *limes* on all sides. We have altars and statues throughout the forts of current and past emperors. These are a regular feature that we find of military barracks and forts across the Roman world. We find plaques to the military units, but what we find are shrines that enable or require the soldiers to reinforce their connection to the Roman world. In every one of these forts there is a small shrine area where we would have the military standards of the legions on display, and in front of them are statues of the emperors. All of the soldiers would come in here on New Year's Day every year and re-swear their loyalty to the emperors and to the military, creating this wonderful symbolic ritual, but also bringing with them all components of Roman culture.

We also find finds that are scattered, but finds of parade armor and all sorts of materials that suggest that there are ceremonial presentations going on along these boundaries. So when we think about Roman military forts and fortifications, I want us to think about the practical aspects, the men who were serving here and what these stand for in terms of projections of Roman power.

We also should think about the symbolic, what these mean in terms of the Romans bringing Roman culture into these new areas for the first time. Creating zones of Romanization and access and control points across the entire Roman world, creating a frontier system around the Roman world through these liminal monuments.

# Images of Warfare—Roman Military Monuments

## Lecture 30

**While the city of Rome became increasingly full of triumphal monuments and images celebrating military victory, these forms and images were different in the empire at large. The use of images of active warfare and captives throughout the Roman world as scenes that reinforced control and power both to Romans and to subject peoples.**

Roman monuments across the empire resembled those within the city of Rome, but the monuments in the city were geared solely toward Romans. The continuous frieze on the Column of Trajan represents for the first time in Rome the portrayal of actual war. The column depicts Trajan in a variety of roles: military commander, priest, and chief engineer. The cumulative effect of the column is that Trajan personifies Rome itself.

The arch of Titus represents more traditional imagery. The major relief decoration on the exterior includes personifications of victory and the triumph itself. The spoils of war were given equal prominence with Titus, indicating the importance of victory more than the war itself.

The last major victory monument in the Forum Romanum was the Arch of Septimius Severus (r. A.D. 193–211), celebrating his Parthian wars. Once again we can see images of active warfare. On the ground level are life-sized reliefs of captive prisoners so that Romans can essentially reenact their procession through Rome and along the triumphal route.

We now move on to the monuments that were established in areas beyond the city of Rome. In addition to his column, Trajan erected a victory monument in Dacia, the ancient Tropaeum Traiani. The monument was in the form of a large victory trophy slightly more than 120 feet tall and on a base 120 feet in diameter. Topped with a great trophy display of captive Dacian arms, the monument was a tremendous visual marker of Roman conquest and the captivity of Dacia to the local inhabitants. Large Latin inscriptions carried the message of victory to the Romans who witnessed the monument, while the imagery did so to the native Dacians, who would see themselves in the figures subdued. Along the exterior of the base were 54 carved relief panels, each more than 4 feet tall and portraying Roman soldiers attacking or capturing Dacians, recognizable by their characteristic hair, dress, and arms.

Roman soldiers' tombstones in Britain reflect the same imagery, with consistent scenes of the conquest and capture of local Celts. The standard scene was of a Roman horseman trampling a Celtic warrior beneath the hooves of his horse. The Celts were portrayed in a stereotypical way, so that their identity is clear even to those who could not read the epitaph with its service details.

**On the ground level are life-sized reliefs of captive prisoners so that Romans can essentially reenact their procession through Rome and along the triumphal route.**

Images of emperors and their symbolic conquest of peoples are also found across the Roman world, so that even distant people could see the inevitability of Roman conquest of resisting populations. A statue of the emperor Hadrian found on Crete shows the type of the conquering emperor in its developed form. Hadrian wears a laurel crown with a central medallion, consistent with an imperator. He is dressed in military garb, including a cuirass decorated with Romulus and Remus. Under his left foot is a typical personification of a subjugated barbarian shown in female form, symbolizing the weakness of those who resist Rome.

The most extensive version of this imagery is found in the Sebastaeion, the site for the worship of the imperial cult, at Aphrodisias in modern Turkey. Augustus, founder of the dynasty, is shown as ruler over land and sea, both portrayed as female personifications. An image of Claudius as conqueror of Britain shows him subduing a female who lies under his feet along the groundline of the relief. Nero, in a slightly later relief, subdues Armenia as another seminude female figure unable to resist Roman power.

Another category of military monument includes images of triumph rather than conquest outside of Rome, thus extending the imagery and audience of triumph away from the capital and into the provinces. The most extensive version of this theme is found on the Arch of Septimius Severus at his birthplace at Leptis Magna in modern Libya. Another Severan military monument is the triumphal arch found at Orange, France.

The major reliefs on the arch are piles of Celtic arms and armor, commemorating the Severan campaigns against the Celtic inhabitants of Britain. Added to these are a set of naval reliefs that seem to show the naval component of the British and Parthian campaigns. ■

## Suggested Reading

Dillon and Welch, *Representations of War in Ancient Rome.*

Lepper, Cichorius, and Frere, *Trajan's Column.*

## Questions to Consider

1. How do the differing images on military monuments from Rome and the rest of the empire suggest differing messages and audiences for the monuments?

2. What does the extension of triumphal imagery outside of Rome mean for the Roman relationship to the capital and its place in the Rome of the high empire? Is its importance diminished?

# Images of Warfare—Roman Military Monuments
## Lecture 30—Transcript

Welcome to this lecture on images of warfare. In this lecture, we're going to look at Roman imperial monuments of the military across the Roman Empire. We already, in another lecture, looked at images of triumphal monuments across the city of Rome, and we'll touch on those at the beginning just to establish where we are. But what I want to explore here is going beyond the boundaries of the city of Rome throughout the entire empire to see how the Romans project images of warfare across the entire Roman world. When we do so we see a set of images and monuments that are based on what we find in Rome, but with a keen awareness of two very important but disparate audiences: Romans on the one hand and non-Romans on the other. And so when we look at these monuments we need to firmly keep those two audiences clearly in mind.

When we take a look at monuments inside the city of Rome to establish our foundation, the greatest of these, of course, is the Column of Trajan. We've seen the Column of Trajan before, and on the column we see, as I mentioned, for the first time in the city of Rome, actual warfare on a military monument. Prior to this, in the tradition, we saw images of triumph, images of victory, not images of the actual warfare. But it's on the great continuous relief that goes all the way around and up this 100-foot tall shaft of Trajan's Column. It's where we see the active prosecution of warfare taking place inside the city of Rome for the first time. We see a number of scenes, all of which are designed for a Roman audience. I believe—although I don't have good evidence for this—it's designed for a Roman audience with the notion of Roman citizens keenly in mind. Remember, this monument is immediately before the Atrium Libertatis, the Hall of Liberty where Roman citizens are created. I think they're walking past this monument, and what they are seeing here is Roman power in success as Trajan's Dacian campaigns take place and Trajan himself takes a prominent role. In the details we see in the center of this frieze Trajan himself directing battle, that is, pointing out where forces should go. We see him in a variety of roles: Trajan standing up addressing troops, telling them what to do, presumably giving them a little pep talk to the troops.

We also see him accepting Dacian prisoners. He is seated on his curial chair with kneeling Dacians in front of him. Trajan is flanked by the military standards, showing his authority in the military world that he represents.

We also see him in what we would term non-military capacities: sacrificing, for example, to the gods, and he presides over sacrifices as the Pontifex Maximus, the chief priest of the Romans. We see him again accepting offerings from Dacians. And finally, just a whole range of things: Trajan directing the construction of Roman military fortifications, telling people where to build forts, and how to do it, and things like that.

The theme of all of this is Trajan personifying Rome itself, personifying the Roman military, personifying power, and also the religious. We see him sacrificing and in a variety of roles, not just in his *cuirass*, his breastplate as a general, but wearing his toga, for example, in that civilian dress, so a variety of things, multiple times, doing all the things an emperor should do to project Roman power.

This, of course, is different than what we might term the traditional imagery of Roman triumph that we've seen, for example, on the Arch of Titus, a very standard single-passage arch that flanks one edge of the Roman Forum along the east edge with the inscription above the attic giving the dedication by the senate, Victories on the outside, and then on the inside of the passageway we have two reliefs. On the one side Titus in his triumphal procession, and on the other side, the spoils from the temple in Jerusalem being carried. Notably what we see is that the spoils are given equal prominence with Titus. In this traditional form of triumphal imagery we're seeing the importance of triumph as opposed to the actual warfare itself for the Romans. That changes over time.

We can get a good sense of how much that change has occurred when we look at the last of the great triumphal arches that's ever constructed in the Forum Romanum, and that is the Arch of Septimius Severus. Septimius Severus was emperor from A.D. 193 to 211, and he fought a number of wars, most notably a great Parthian campaign. At this time Parthians controlled the areas of what are today Iran and Iraq, and so Mesopotamia, the central

Mesopotamian area and what we just generally term the Middle East. If you think in terms or Iran and Iraq, that's the territory we're talking about.

Septimius Severus launched an invasion of Parthian territory and fought a series of enormously successful battles leading up to the culmination, the sacking, of the great Parthian capital. He came back to Rome and built a great triumphal arch, which was dedicated, I believe, in A.D. 197, although it's a little difficult to tell because the inscription has been defaced, but about A.D. 197.

We see here a continuation of what we saw on the Column of Trajan. It's a traditional style of arch, but with that new form, showing us in the reliefs the active prosecution of warfare. We have a nice detail here of a recently cleaned relief on the arch of Septimius Severus. If you can't make out the action on this, it is not your eyesight. This thing is a Rorschach test. The relief has been so badly damaged by air pollution that it has kind of melted. But what we're seeing here is one of the great battles of the Parthian war.

These reliefs cover the outside of the arch from the second story on up, but on the ground floor, what we might call the pedestrian level, we see a different form of imagery, a different iconography, and that is that of captives, Parthian captives being led in the triumphal procession. This is interesting because these are not quite life size, but quite large reliefs that are carved down here on the base of the supports for the free-standing columns on each side of the arch. They are walking down the road so that if you pass through the arch as you do today as a pedestrian, you pass along with these prisoners. It creates a monument that requires you to engage with it. You can either look at this and engage with the prisoner, or you can look at it and engage with the Roman captor who is walking along behind him. By the way, it's a really interesting notion to create this monument of engagement. So those pedestrian level reliefs of captives, combined with scenes of actual warfare, give us a great sense of the range of types and subjects that we have in triumphal monuments.

From there I want to move outside the city of Rome and think about what's going on with these monuments we have established in other areas.

I would like to start with another monument constructed by the emperor, Trajan. His great Dacian campaigns took place and were completed by A.D. 113. He's got the column in Rome for our Roman audience to celebrate, but out in Dacia itself, modern day Romania, at the site of Adamclisi we see a monument. The monument is at a site that is given the ancient name "Tropaeum Traiani," that is, the Trophy of Trajan, or Trajan's Trophy. Trajan created this enormous victory monument on the very edges of what was then hostile territory on the frontiers of Roman space. It's very clear that he is cognizant of the different audience that he has here, contrasted with that in Rome.

To give you a sense, we have a tremendous round monument. It's a great trophy with a large round concrete base that's about 120 feet in diameter. Originally, the entire monument was 120 feet tall as well. We have a nice reconstruction model from the local museum there to give you a sense of what this looked like. So the base is a large round drum. On top of that is a roof, and projecting above that is a large Roman military trophy, a large support, covered with Dacian arms and armor. Then on either side of the intermediate element above the drum and below the trophy are large Latin inscriptions. Think about this for just a minute. This thing is as tall as a 10-story building. It's actually taller than Trajan's Column. It's a tremendous monument. Out here in the middle of Dacia there would have been nothing of this scale ever before, and so what Trajan is doing here is creating a monument celebrating the remarkable achievement of this military victory, and he's doing it in a way that I believe is designed to speak to the people here directly.

First, he decorates it with Dacian arms and armor. That tremendous trophy at the top is designed to reflect the local arms and armor. There's no way the local people would not recognize this. This is the equivalent today of somebody creating a military monument and using their enemy's flag, or their enemy's tanks, or military uniforms as the base for it. It would be instantly recognizable to these people as a monument of subjugation. It's a powerful example of this awareness of audience.

We do have the large Latin inscriptions, which carry a message of victory as well, but I think these are designed for the Romans. For the Romans we have the Latin inscriptions; for the Dacians we have the trophy on top.

We have a nice reconstruction to show you a portion of it. Along that base is a series of 54 large-scale reliefs. These are tremendously large relief panels, all surrounded by very classicizing frieze decoration, and these figural relief panels—54 of them all the way around the circumference of this—all show images of battle and of the aftermath of battle. What is particularly notable about these reliefs is that unlike the friezes around them, the figural reliefs are carved in a local style.

If you look at the frieze decoration around it, it's heavily classicizing. These are elements out of Greek architecture, acanthus and engaged Corinthian pilasters, and that marvelous plant, acanthus, frieze down below. It looks like it's taken right off the Temple of Apollo or the Ara Pacis in Rome, contrasted with that are the figures in the panels. They're carved in a very frontal, flat, bold style, very abstracted in style. As I say, this is a local style of carving. It's not that Trajan couldn't afford the finest Greek sculptors to come here and carve a monument. He's obviously done that with the surrounding material. But he had the local style used for the figures, and I think this is a deliberate attempt to make sure the Dacians recognized themselves in this monument. They see in this style the characteristic Dacian captives. They see the Romans portrayed in their local style.

Here we have a marvelous relief showing the Romans carrying their military standards. The message here is very clear. It's a projection of Roman propaganda under Trajan directly to the Dacian people. It shows us the distinction between monuments in the provinces and monuments at Rome.

We see the same thing in Britain. If we go to Britain, there are a number of Roman soldiers' tombstones, having consistent scenes that show the subjugation of local people. In the case of Britain, we see local Celts in one of the standard motifs of a Roman cavalryman riding over a Celtic warrior, a British warrior under the hooves of his horse. The Celts are always shown in a very stereotypical way with long, flowing hair and large mustaches, and Celtic-style arms, much the way the Dacians are. It seems, again, that these are designed to speak to two audiences. The Latin inscriptions on the tombstones speak to the Romans, but the image of the Celt in the local style designed stereotypically as a local Celt, I think is designed to reference the local people. It projects that Roman power through that imagery.

Images of emperors and their symbolic conquests of peoples are found across the Roman world, so that even distant people can see the inevitability of Roman military success, that is, resistance is futile. If you resist, you will be destroyed.

The standard motif that we see of this projection of Roman power is in a statue of Hadrian found on the island of Crete. Hadrian didn't have much military success. In fact, he seems to have provoked the only war that he fought. He decided after the Temple of Jerusalem was destroyed by Vespasian and Titus in the Jewish Revolt that he was going to rebuild the city of Jerusalem, and this is some 50 years later when Hadrian is emperor, but he's going to rename it after himself, his family name, Aelia Capitolina. And then he is going to rebuild the Temple of Solomon as a temple of Jupiter. As you can imagine, this didn't go over terribly well. It led to the second great Jewish Revolt, which Hadrian then had to subdue; put down brutally, as a matter of fact.

In this image we see Hadrian not as an insecure emperor or a poor diplomat, but as a military conqueror. Hadrian is dressed in a very imperial way. He's wearing not just a laurel wreath, but a *diadem*. He has a laurel wreath with a great gem in the center of it, and he's dressed as a successful Roman general. He has on a *cuirass*, which has victories crowning a statue of Athena, and then down below that figure we see Romulus and Remus and the she-wolf. So it's a statement of Roman military victory. Then, below his raised left foot, he has a small-scale crushed barbarian. He's standing on the back of a subjugated barbarian here. This barbarian is the personification of an entire ethnic group. This was a standard motif for the Romans to portray an entire ethnic group through one individual, almost invariably a female, to show the weakness of the entire group. So Hadrian's monument here, this statue we find in Crete, where there were no wars taking place, is designed to project this image of Roman military dominance to a population to show them what the inevitable result is going to be of resistance to the Romans, and that is Roman success.

This is just one image. We have an extensive version of this imagery found at the site of Aphrodisias in what is today Turkey, and then the province of Asia, but really in the middle of what today we think of as Turkey.

At the site of Aphrodisias we have a very well-preserved Sebastaeion. "Sebastaeion" is the Greek word for a shrine to the cult of Augustus, that is, the cult of the emperors. It's a site for the worship of the entire imperial cult. What we have here is a large, open plaza. It's a rectangular plaza flanked on two sides by a colonnade that was three stories tall, with relief panels in all three stories. All the way up, at the far end of the colonnade, we have on the short end a temple to the imperial cult. We don't have much of a temple left, and the formal entryway, which is where we're standing in this image, is largely gone, but we have a lot of the relief panels and tremendous large-scale imperial reliefs. These are significant because they're not put up by the emperors. As far as we can tell, the Sebastaeion is an example of the imitation of Roman imperial art by local individuals. Local individuals have seen what Roman imperial art is and have adopted it.

I want to show you three of these reliefs because they're really quite extraordinary. One of the earliest ones that we can see here is of Augustus, the founder of the dynasty. Here he is in a very symbolic way. He is heroically nude, as is appropriate for a deity. We believe this is after his death. Here he is the conqueror over both land and sea. In the lower left, just below the cornucopia that he's holding is the personification of all the lands. On the right, just below the rudder that he's holding in his other hand, is a personification of the sea, again female personifications. There's a very strong image here of Roman male, masculine military power subjecting feminine foreign power. And then he's got his cloak billowing around him in a very heroic Greek way.

We also have reliefs that were added to that Augustus relief under later emperors. We believe these were probably done in their lifetimes. We have an image, for example, of the emperor, Claudius, again with a flowing cloak behind him, almost heroically nude. He's wearing a helmet and the cloak, and here he's subduing a female who is lying on the ground, and he has his knee in the small of her back. This is the personification of Britannia, or the island of Britain. He's got one hand in her hair and a knee in her back, and he's subduing Britain here in this image.

The third one I want to show you—and again there is a strong element of gender politics here as the masculine, naked Romans are subduing these foreign female figures. They're all slumped over and are very passive. This is a very heroic Nero. Nero, as I am confident never looked in his entire life, is subjecting the province of Armenia, and there you can see her *Frigian* cap that she's wearing, a standard sort of eastern form. This Nero is, again, heroically nude with the exception of the baldric and the cloak, subduing the province of Armenia, which in fact, he did send a military expedition to conquer while he was emperor, just as Claudius had conquered Britain, or at least had begun the conquest of Britain.

Once again, it's important to realize that these monuments seem not to have been part of imperial beneficence. The emperors didn't send these out or request them to be made. These are being made by local officials celebrating Roman power in the subjects and motifs that they see projected from Roman imperial monuments. This is a very interestingly nuanced monument because we're seeing a communication taking place, somebody looking at what the emperors are doing and saying, "Oh, that's what it is, okay," and then making their own. And so we see these local civic officials creating these.

I want to show you here is sort of a companion for the arch of Septimius Severus in the Forum Romanum. I showed you the final triumphal arch that we have in the Forum Romanum. What we see here is something actually pretty extraordinary, and that is, the extension of Roman triumphal imagery and triumphal processions outside the city of Rome into a place where they have no business being. A triumphal procession, quite technically and legally, as voted by the senate, only takes place at that prescribed route in Rome, culminating at the Capitoline Hill at the Temple of Jupiter. It is a Roman ceremony celebrating a Roman military victory. What we see here at the site of Leptis Magna, the birthplace of Septimius Severus, is a translation of Roman triumphal imagery from the city of Rome to Leptis Magna.

This is an incredibly powerful set of markers and monuments and actually a powerful set of acts because what Septimius Severus is doing by holding a mock triumph here at Leptis Magna is equating his birthplace with Rome, something that had never been done before, and actually one of the things that got Mark Antony in trouble. One of the things that allowed Augustus to move against Antony and Cleopatra and crush them was Antony's equation of Alexandria with Rome. But here we are, some 200 years later, and this is apparently successful.

Here at Leptis Magna we see a great tetrapylon arch. It's a four-way arch as we see it in its extant form, and I want to show it to you in a model because you can see that there are four passageways. This arch is built not just as an armature over one roadway, but actually over an intersection so that we have two roads crossing at right angles underneath the arch. So it projects four instead of two faces. You can get a good sense of that here in this corner view.

The tetrapylon arch here is lavishly decorated with sculpture on the inside of the passageways, as well as on the exteriors. We see a whole range of subjects of reliefs. In the inside passageways we have a series of relief panels that are almost exact copies of the battle panels that we saw in the arch of Septimius Severus in the Forum Romanum. They are, sadly, in bad condition, so I'm not going to show them to you because they don't look like anything. Again, they're pretty much a Rorschach test. But we know what they were. They're scenes of the great Parthian battles that Septimius Severus undertook, and so we have those in the passageways down below.

In the attic story, on the other hand, we have four large panels, one relief panel on each side. These reliefs show the major stages in that triumphal procession that Septimius Severus and his entire family held here at Leptis Magna when he came and visited the city during his reign, probably in the year 197 as far as we can tell.

I'm going to show you one of these because this is the best of them, and we want to see the best. It shows this triumphal arch very clearly, once again, outside the city of Rome, where it has no place being, combined with that imagery of the active prosecution of war. In this relief we see Septimius Severus in a chariot drawn by four horses, standard triumphal imagery. He's flanked in the chariot by his sons, on the one side Caracalla, on the other Geta, showing us his interest in dynasty. This is consistent with the practice in Rome where young sons of triumphant generals would ride in the chariot with their fathers.

So far we have the Roman officials behind him, we have Roman officials in front of him, and it looks like a standard triumphal procession scene, but if you move your eye just past the center point on the right you see a monument that gives architectural context to this entire scene. That's the lighthouse here at Leptis Magna, rebuilt by Septimius Severus in the harbor. So it's recognizable to us as it would have been to them, and that gives the context. This tells us where we are. We're not at Rome. We are, in fact, in Leptis Magna and that lighthouse tells us this.

Well, so what? We've got the emperor coming in in a chariot, we've got the lighthouse. Why isn't this just an *adventis* scene, an entrance or an exit scene? If you go even further over to the right on the right extant edge, you see the captive Parthians. These are the captive barbarians in two registers here, and then down below, about four figures from the right edge, you see a young boy trying to break away from the captors. He's wearing the *Frigian* cap, and he's dressed just as one of these barbarians is. It's a little boy barbarian Parthian captive.

This makes it very clear that what Septimius Severus is doing is holding a triumphal procession in Leptis Magna, effectively reducing the status of the city of Rome in favor of this provincial city. So he is not just moving the imagery of military victory outside of Rome, but moving the celebration of military victory outside of Rome for the first time ever in Rome's, at this point, 900 years of history. So this is a momentous monument.

I want to show you one last Severan arch. The Severans were big arch builders, and that's here at the site of Orange in southern France. This Severan triumphal arch is like the arch of Septimius Severus in the Forum Romanum. It's a triple passageway arch with a large central passage and two small pedestrian passages on either side. Like the arch in the forum, it is richly decorated with reliefs.

This one is different, however, because it is not a celebration of the Parthian war. We can tell from the arms and armor that decorate it that this is a celebration of Septimius Severus and his sons' campaigns in Britain because the arms and armor that decorate this are all Celtic. There are piles of Celtic arms and armor. You can see characteristic Celtic shields, and swords, and dedicatory material here that's instantly recognizable.

In addition to the military imagery, we have naval imagery celebrating the fleet and the naval component of the British campaign in particular. This is remarkable because he has chosen to place in a Celtic area a monument to subduing a Celtic people in Britain. I can't believe this is a coincidence. He's placed here in modern day France, in Gaul, a monument showing the subjugation of Celtic or Gallic peoples in Britain. This shows us the awareness of these disparate audiences in this projection of Roman imperial power through these monuments across the entire world.

We see in these notable patterns of the spread of this material into the provinces a systematic attempt by the Romans, with awareness of the two key audiences, to spread the imagery of Roman military success, the images of real warfare, outside the city of Rome throughout the entire Roman Empire. We also see its emulation as we did at Aphrodisias by local officials who take this material up and spread the themes and subjects around so that they are effectively buying into this entire system so that as you pass through the Roman world from one edge to the other, you would see a Roman world defined by images of warfare with the inevitable idea that resistance to Roman power is futile.

# Roman Colonies—Small Romes

## Lecture 31

**From early in its history, Rome sent out colonies that were self-consciously designed as small versions of the capital itself.**

The city of Rome had a set of key features that were critical to Roman identity and were repeated in colonies across the empire. The major civic space of the Forum Romanum, with its categories of civic, religious, commercial, and legal buildings, was deliberately replicated across the Roman world. The curia, or senate house, was reproduced for the local city council, which emulated the senate. Its members were called *decuriones*. Basilicas as legal and commercial spaces were invariably found in colonial forums, generally situated close to the curia.

The most important religious space in Rome was the Temple of Jupiter Optimus Maximus on the Capitoline Hill, reproduced in every colony as the major indicator of Roman culture. The Temple of Capitoline Jupiter was instantly recognizable because it had three *cellas*, the interior chambers that housed the cult statues—one each for Jupiter, Juno, and Minerva, who were all worshipped here. The Temple of Capitoline Jupiter became the *capitolium*, the characteristic temple that dominated the forum of virtually every Roman colony.

The characteristic Roman entertainment buildings , including baths, amphitheaters, and theaters, were also found almost invariably in Roman colonies. The placement of these buildings at Rome was away from the Forum Romanum, generally on the edges of the city or in a cleared space, whereas in the colonies they were often more central and therefore visible. In the colonies, these buildings were emulated as constructions of common Roman culture and values.

The layout of a colony represented an ideal Rome; the  of the city did not directly reflect Rome itself, which grew organically. Each colony was laid out generally with a square or rectangular  invariably surrounded by walls. Cross-streets were laid out in strict orthogonal form. The major north-south street, or *cardo*, established the central line. Other north-south streets were laid out at regular intervals. The major east-west road, the *decumanus*, was surveyed to intersect the major *cardo* at the exact center of the community. The secondary east-west roads were laid out at regular intervals, creating rectangular blocks in a form of orthogonal town planning adopted from Greek models.

The colony's forum was placed in a central location where the *cardo maximus* and *decumanus maximus* intersected, representing its importance in the colony. The forum was generally a rectangular space laid out parallel to the major streets but, like the Forum Romanum, arranged with a central open area flanked by key buildings. The *capitolium* dominated the center of one of the short ends of the rectangle and visually established the space as Roman with its tall podium temple. The civic and legal buildings were always found in the forum, often grouped together with archives halls and perhaps a place for citizen assemblies. Markets and other commercial spaces were the final element that was invariably found in the forum. On occasion, baths were placed adjacent to the forum, making them a central colonial element and also a statement of Roman cultural identity.

Examining case studies confirms the development of the Roman colonial foundation and how it served to create this integrated Roman urban world. Ostia, the earliest Roman colony, is an example of a colony established at a preexisting community, with Roman order imposed on already-accepted traffic patterns. The earliest walls of Ostia show the Roman emphasis on orthogonal planning from the beginning of colonization. The forum represents a developed type, with a curia, basilica, and *capitolium* grouped together at one end, establishing a key connection between these buildings. Adjacent to the forum was a large bath complex, while just down the *decumanus* was a theater.

The colony of Paestum, established in 273 B.C. at the site of a Greek settlement, displays the integration of some previous elements with the imposition of important Roman buildings. Although some were almost indistinguishable from Roman forms, the Greek political buildings were all destroyed and the civic center of the forum moved to a new area when the Roman colony was founded. The forum contained a *capitolium*, curia, and basilica with a bath complex and amphitheater adjacent, all part of what might be termed the standard buildings. Paestum also demonstrates the redirection of architecture and worship in forums, with the addition of cult spaces for the worship of emperors.

Pompeii, founded as a colony in 80 B.C., shows the same pattern of colony establishment on a previous community. The forum provides the best-preserved assemblage of colonial public buildings in Italy, with an early basilica, curia, and *capitolium*. Pompeii exemplifies the key roles of entertainment venues in Roman colonies, with the erection of an amphitheater and baths and with the renovation of the theater just after the colony was established. The forum of Pompeii has decorative elements such as statues and reliefs that mirror those found in Rome itself.

One of the last of the Roman military colonies, Timgad—founded by Trajan in A.D. 100—was a new foundation that exemplifies Roman urban planning and the creation of an ideal community. Because it was founded on new territory, Timgad is actually the best example of an ideal colonial form, with its square , regular *cardo* and *decumanus*, and walled exterior to define but not defend the community. Entertainment buildings reinforce the idea that the Romans brought every part of Roman culture with them when they colonized. ■

## Suggested Reading

Bradley and Wilson, *Greek and Roman Colonization.*

Salmon, *Roman Colonization under the Republic.*

## Questions to Consider

1. What insights into Roman urban planning and organization of space do colonies provide that the city of Rome does not? How can you account for that?

2. In what ways are Roman colonies conceived of as small Romes?

# Roman Colonies—Small Romes

## Lecture 31—Transcript

Welcome to this lecture on Roman colonization. What I want to achieve here by the time the lecture is over is an understanding of the processes of Roman colonization through case studies. We're going to look at four Roman colonies: where they're built, how they're designed, and how they operate. For the Romans, their world is an urban world, to an extent not seen anywhere else in the ancient world. To us, we think about cities all the time, and cities are how we've defined a lot of communities. Prior to the Romans, that wasn't the case. It was really the Romans who create this notion of an urban world, and so we owe them our way of looking at our own world.

The Romans do this through creating colonies. Many of these colonies, in fact the vast majority, are, in fact, little Romes. They contain aspects, key elements of the city of Rome, and they're spread throughout the Roman world, so that what they serve to do is to project the benefits, the stability, and the integration of the entire Roman state throughout the entire Roman Empire. In order to understand those elements, what we're going to look at first are where these occur in the city of Rome, and then we'll move out through our case studies.

If you look at a plan of the city of Rome in a reconstruction of the Roman Forum, we see down in the Forum Romanum a major civic space, in fact, arguably, the major civic space in the city of Rome, with a number of categories of civic, religious, commercial, recreational, and religious buildings. Among these we see a core that are effectively immutable. They don't change, and we see those replicated across the Roman world.

The major building among this core is the curia, or the senate house. We've talked about this in other lectures, how the senate house is constructed under the republic and then rebuilt by Julius Caesar. If we look at our reconstruction we see the senate house there transitionally between the Forum of Caesar and the old Forum Romanum. It's still there today. If you go into the Roman Forum it's right there on the ground plan where Caesar built it.

No other colonies have a senate, but they have a curia, and instead of a senate they have local city councils. Those city councilors call themselves "*decuriones*," men of the curia. And so that becomes an identifiable building that serves to create Roman identity in these new colonies that are founded. The other buildings around it, and if you'll look at the plan on either side of the open space of the forum, we see long colonnaded buildings called "basilicas." These are multiple-use structures that serve as law courts and places for people to meet and conduct business and things like that. Basilicas, generally clustered around the curia, go also throughout the colony, so they have the curia and the basilicas. Along with those there is a variety of subsidiary buildings, the temples, the altars, and things like that, and we'll see some of those as well that serve deliberately to link colonial identity to Roman identity.

But among the religious buildings, the most important is not down there in the forum. Arguably, the most significant religious space in Rome is up on the Capitoline Hill, most importantly, the Temple of Jupiter Optimus Maximus, Jupiter Best and Greatest, the Capitoline Temple of Jupiter constructed under the last of the kings. This is always the most important religious space. It's the terminal space for Roman triumphs, for example, and it's richly decorated. It's instantly identifiable as this large podium temple up on the Capitoline Hill, and we recognize the form of the Temple of Capitoline Jupiter because it has three *cellas*, are three interior divisions in the room inside because Jupiter is not the only god worshiped here. Jupiter is in the center and he's flanked on one side by Juno and on the other by Minerva. That Capitoline triad is the core of Roman religious observance in these spaces. We'll see this again replicated.

We want to see a plan of the *cella* to get a sense of what that looks like. We've got a good example for you here with this tripartite *cella*, or Jupiter, Juno, and Minerva. This temple type, the Temple of Jupiter Capitolinus, becomes the *capitolium*, and the *capitolium* is the major Roman religious building that we find replicated in colonies across the Roman world. We've got a nice example here from North Africa from the Roman colony of Dougga. We have this small—compared to the Temple of Jupiter Capitolinus—podium temple, but it's on a high podium, so it's actually pretty imposing as you approach it. It has four columns across the front, so it has three entrances in between those columns. Those lead back into the tripartite *cella.* In the back wall, what you see are three niches; a larger one for a statue of Jupiter, and then flanking ones for Juno and Minerva. This houses these cult statues and becomes a core of Roman worship. This also gets translated into colonies.

We also find the characteristic Roman entertainment buildings, things that are particularly Roman: Roman-style theaters with stage buildings, the amphitheater forum, and things like that, and we'll see those replicated as well when we go throughout colonies.

I need to point out that in Rome these entertainment buildings are not placed around the forum for reasons of space or for decisions of patronage. These large entertainment structures are generally placed outside of the forum area. If you think about the major amphitheater in Rome, the Colosseum, it's not right on the forum. It's actually about a 10-minute walk away. The theaters are down on the Campus Marcius area and so on. These forums are so characteristically Roman, whether it's an amphitheater, a bath complex, or a theater, that in colonies we often find these actually attached to the forum. They become part of that set of monuments that are brought by the Romans to define this space as Roman.

In addition to the monument set, or the building set, a curia, basilicas, *capitolium*, and entertainment buildings, what we also have is urban design. This does not come from the city of Rome itself. The historian, Livy, has a marvelous description of Rome. He says, "Rome looks like it was occupied, not planned." He's right. Rome grew what we might term agglutinatively, and that is, space is added on, Rome expands throughout the centuries. And so it doesn't represent the Romans' very notion of what is ideal in the urban environment. Instead, for that we go out to the colonies. It's in the colonies where we see an ideal Rome, the outline of the city, and how Romans decide to organize their urban space. So if we take a look at it, and we have a marvelous plan of a colony for you to take a look at here, what we see is that each colony—and this is standard—is laid out with a square or a rectangle surrounded by walls. These walls are not fortified zones. These, in fact, mark the religious or sacred boundaries of the community. This is the *pomerium*, that great sacred boundary that demarks urban space from suburban space.

When we look at a colony we see the establishment of the walls, and that's always the first thing that seems to occur within this rectangle. And then we see a series of streets, north-south streets, in the singular, a "*cardo*." A north-south street is known as a *cardo*. And then east-west roads, the "*decumanus*," or "*decumani*" in the plural. And so we see a major *cardo*, north-south street, that runs from the center of the colony, and then a *decumanus* that runs from the center all the way across, creating a cross in the center. It's in the center of that colony where those two roads cross each other at right angles, where we see the major public buildings, generally the forum, and then associated with that forum, entertainment buildings.

Evenly spaced from the *cardo maximus* and *decumanus maximus* in the center, we see other roads—north-south and east-west—that come off. This is orthogonal planning. What it creates is a series of regular blocks, either square or rectangular. So what the Romans do in their colonies is they subdivide all of the space first, creating an ideal form with these regular rectangular blocks, orthogonal planning. This is a Greek idea. It comes to the Romans from the Greeks. It goes all the way back to the Middle Kingdom of ancient Egypt, although I haven't been able to see that the Greeks adapted it directly from Egypt. But nonetheless, it's very clear that the Romans adapted it directly from the Greeks.

They create this orthogonal planning, and then lay out the entire city within the walls very ideally. We've got public buildings in the center, we have neighborhood baths around the edges, and then we have a rich variety of community activities throughout the entire urban fabric. The Romans are not like us in that they don't have strict zoning rules as far as I can tell. We have rich and poor living together, we have industrial zones next to large houses, all sorts of things in a Roman city. But what we invariably have is that forum in the center of town, generally a square or a rectangle, an area that's laid out and open with a *capitolium*, that temple to Jupiter, Juno, and Minerva, at one end as a prominent marker of Roman religious identity. Although the plan that we're looking at now, Timgad, shows the capital on a rise, just outside the city, as is seen in other colonies like Cosa.

Generally at the opposite end from the *capitolium* we'll find a number of civic buildings, of curia, that is, the local city council, basilicas, archives, things like that, all of the sorts of buildings that we would put in a downtown today, the courthouse and all the buildings around that. We also find markets and commercial spaces, and a number of entertainment buildings make their appearances on the edge of these colonial forums: theaters, baths, and so on. And so this makes up the core of the community and helps to identify it to those who come in as a particularly Roman urban space.

What I want to do now that we have established the outline of what a colony is and how it's established, is to go through our four case studies, starting with the earliest, the city of Ostia, and take a look at the development of the Roman colonial foundation and how it serves to create this integrated Roman urban world.

If we look at Ostia, what we see is something that on the surface appears to violate everything I've just told you about how you establish a colony. Ostia, I want to point out, is special in a couple of ways. First, it's the earliest Roman colony. It's traditionally dated to 338 B.C., but we really just should say 4th century B.C. because that firm date is a little unsubstantiated. So it's very early in terms of the development of colonies.

The other thing about Ostia is that it's built on a pre-existing community, so it's not built just on clear ground. The Romans are adapting previous structure.

Ostia itself is built as the harbor city, or port city, of Rome down on the mouth of the Tiber River, so it also is built along the edge of the Tiber. If you look at our plan, you'll see the ancient river course going along the city of Ostia.

Nevertheless, what the Romans do is impose Roman notions of urban space and Roman identity onto this pre-existing community. If you look carefully at the plan what you can see is, particularly where the crossroads occur, orthogonal planning. The Romans imposed blocks. They imposed a very strong *decumanus maximus* through the center of this community. They have a forum and other public buildings around that, so it really does have all of the elements of a colony. It just doesn't take on the normal rectangular form.

When we look at the details from Ostia we see that everything we expect is there. Looking at an image, for example, of the forum we see at one end of it the *capitolium*, the great Temple of Jupiter, Juno, and Minerva. This is one of the highest of the *capitolia*. I sometimes take students to Ostia in the summers and we race up the steps and every once in a while somebody needs oxygen. It's a really intense run up the steps, and it's deliberately designed to be an imposing monument, projecting Roman religious authority into this preexisting community. So we've got the *capitolium* at one end of the forum.

Here, and somewhat unusually, on one side we have the curia and on the other side we have a basilica. So the civic buildings are actually in Ostia right next to the *capitolium*. On the opposite end of the forum where we might expect to have the civic buildings, what we have is a large bath complex. In this bath complex, the forum baths at Ostia, is a large complex laid out right adjacent to the forum. So this violates the Roman notion that we see in the city of Rome of where you place baths, but it's perfectly consistent with colonial practice, where all of these recognizable and characteristic public buildings are placed together.

We also have another characteristic Roman entertainment venue, and that's a theater. This is a very standard Roman-style theater. The seating area is semi-circular. It has a stage and a stage building behind it, so it's recognizable as a Roman theater rather than a Greek one, and it's also recognizable because if you look at the seating area you see those first few rows are much broader and deeper than the other seats. So what the Romans have brought here is their class structure. The seating area in the theater reflects the requirements of Roman class structure, that the local members of the *decuriones*, the local magistrates, are sitting down there in front, themselves on display as well. And so the Romans are imposing and bringing their entire culture with them: public bathing, theaters, and so on, all here at Ostia. Again, this is a very early colony and it's all here.

When we move on—and we'll continue on chronologically to another colony—we'll see this same idea. If we look at the colony of Paestum, we see a remarkably similar set of monuments. Paestum was founded in 273 B.C. Paestum and Cosa were both founded as maritime colonies to establish

Roman dominance along the west coast of Italy, Paestum in the south and Cosa in the north. Paestum is actually down in Lucanian territory, what is the area of the Lucani, people that the Romans were subduing at the time. It's a beautiful site. You should visit it at some point. I had the privilege to excavate here for some years, and it's really a tremendous opportunity to come and visit.

Like Ostia, Paestum is a pre-existing community. It was actually a Greek colony first. The Greek colony was founded here about 600 B.C., and then when the Romans took over this area they imposed, again, Roman identity onto it. When the Romans came here in 273, there were a lot of Greek buildings still here. This was still an active community. It hadn't been abandoned or anything. There were Greek religious structures. There were all of the Greek civic structures around what for the Greeks is a forum. They call it an "*agora*." The Romans deliberately chose to bury the Greek *agora* to cover up their civic buildings, even though in form a Greek curia building is virtually indistinguishable from a Roman one. But that's not the point. The Romans covered up the *agora*, buried all the civic buildings, maintained the religious ones, which is why we have these tremendous Greek temples still here today, and moved the forum over, establishing their own tremendous, large rectangular forum.

This is of a standard type. The proportions are 5-to-1, so it's five blocks altogether, lined up. If you look at a plan of Paestum, the orthogonal planning, the forum is at a crossroads, the major crossing of the *cardo* and *decumanus*. If you look down you'll see the blocks of houses spread out from there.

Around the forum we have all of the standards buildings: on one end, the *capitolium*, at the sides, on the long sides, we have the civic buildings. We have a curia, we have a basilica, we have a place for the market to meet. We also have a bath complex as at Ostia. There's a set of baths here at Paestum.

What we also see at Paestum, and this is particularly significant and shows the development of colonies, is a redirection of worship. The *capitolium* is at one end, at the sides what we see starting in the 1$^{st}$ century A.D. are little shrines—or little *sacella* we call them—to the imperial cult. These are interesting because what the Paestums did, they took market stalls, little shops, knocked down walls in between to join them together, and then built out into the area of the forum. So these small shrines to the imperial cult are the only things that actually violate that open rectangle in the center, which you want to keep open for public meetings.

Also unlike Rome, Paestum has an amphitheater right next to the forum. This is something we don't see in Rome where the amphitheaters are all out on the edges. And so the Paestums are projecting a very strong form of Roman identity by putting every characteristic Roman-style building in this new area of the forum: the bath, the capitolium, the basilica, and the amphitheater all here together to say this is now Roman territory. And the Paestum people apparently were aware of that.

There's a marvelous story about the old Greek inhabitants after they had been occupied. They have one Greek festival left, and every year they gather for their Greek religious festival. They sing some songs in Greek, everybody bursts into tears, and they go home, and that's the end of their Greek identity. The Romans are here, and they've imposed their identity on this. And I think it's a very deliberate decision on their part.

The best preserved of all of the colonies we have is Pompeii. Pompeii was founded as a Roman colony in 80 B.C. by the dictator, Sulla. Like Paestum and Ostia, it is also imposed on a pre-existing community. At this point, just after the Great Social War as we call it, the civil war between the Romans, mainly, and the Samnites, the Romans imposed this community, this colony, onto the city of Pompeii. When they do so, they follow the pattern we've looked at already, bringing with them all of these buildings that we've taken a look at.

I've got a marvelous view for you here of the city of Pompeii as it's laid out, and you can just see it goes on, seemingly forever. When we look in detail at the city of Pompeii, we see that the Romans have followed the same plan that they did at Paestum. They lay out a forum here in the center of the community. It's one of these long, rectangular fora. At one end there's the capitolium. On the opposite end we have all of the major civic buildings. There's a large basilica laid out. You can see very clearly a large columned hall. There are three small buildings along that short south end of the forum, and these are the curia and other office buildings for government. In between, there are markets and religious spaces all laid out here, all the standard Roman forums.

Also, the Romans are very careful, and I think deliberately so, to bring their entertainment venues with them. We see when the colony is imposed here in 80 B.C. that what the Romans do is they bring with them the amphitheater. Pompeii's first amphitheater, and it's the oldest one we have extant in the Roman world, dates exactly to 80 B.C. This is not a coincidence. When the Romans found their colony they lay out the forum, they put in a capitolium, a basilica, all of the major government buildings, but they also bring the amphitheater as a characteristically Roman entertainment venue with them.

If you look at a drawing of the city of Pompeii, you see that here they have placed this amphitheater out on the edge the city. Remember, this is a pre-existing community, and so there's no space in the center for them to put this amphitheater. So they put it out on the edge, and then at this time they build a wall around it, and so they enclose it within the urban space to make a statement that this is, in fact, part of the community. So the amphitheater is out there on the edge, on the far southeast edge of the city.

Next to it is a *palestra*. It's a large exercise ground. This, arguably, also has some symbolic aspects as far as we can tell. It's thought that this was an area for military units to exercise. I'm not convinced on that I must tell you, but nonetheless, there's every possibility that that's the case. In addition to the amphitheater, what we see is another entertainment area, what we may call "a theater district" in Pompeii. Pompeii already had a Greek theater, the standard Greek type built into a hillside with more than semi-circular seating, and an orchestra area for the performance. The Romans adapt that very rapidly after 80 B.C. into a Roman-style theater. They cut off the seating area into a semi-circle, they build a stage and a stage building, and then they renovate the seating area so it reflects Roman class distinctions. So it's all very clear that the Romans are here, not just occupying, but bringing their entire culture.

Next to the open air theater, they also built a small closed theater, a roofed theater building. This is called an "*odeon*." We don't see many of these survive. There's one in here at Pompeii and one in Athens down in the old Agoran. The Romans built one down there. This is a building for Roman-style theatrical entertainment, particularly mimes. These occur down in a smaller space of the *odeon.* In addition to these we also see Roman—style baths because public bathing is a characteristic Roman event. If you look at this marvelous reconstruction drawing that we see, there are some cloudy areas throughout the city, and those are indicative of the smoke and steam coming out of these bath complexes. The Romans imposed these neighborhood bath complexes across Pompeii and we'll talk more about those in another lecture.

So far we've looked at a number of colonies that are established to impose Roman power on pre-existing communities. We've got some great images from Pompeii that show you how the Romans are doing that. If you look at the capitolium down there at the base of Mount Vesuvius you get a good sense of how the Romans are using topography here to create this image of power. They're bringing in their own style monuments.

We don't have any of the statues from the forum, but what we do have are the statue bases. There are a lavish number of these. There are dedications by the local *decuriones*, as well members of the imperial family because here at Pompeii, as at Paestum, we see that redirection of worship. This is a little shrine, or a little cult site, to the imperial cult in the back of the market because the imperial family is responsible for the prosperity of the State. So when you come and pick up your vegetables or your meat, you come and you make an offering to the imperial cult because they make this possible.

The final one of these colonies I want to show you is Timgad. This is the plan of Timgad. It's the one I started with. It's really an extraordinary example of Roman colonial planning. Timgad was founded in A.D. 100. My students always love it when I put Timgad on a test because they can remember that date; 100 is easy. It's founded by the Roman emperor, Trajan, and it's one of the last of all of the Roman colonies.

Timgad is a marvelous example because unlike the other ones I've selected for you, it is in new territory. It's not built on a pre-existing community, so it's laid out completely on new space. There were pre-existing roads in the area, and if you look at the southern part of the plan, you'll see a road coming in at a non-Roman angle. It's coming in at a sharp diagonal because actually Timgad is placed here because there were six major roads here that intersect. I should tell you where here is in case you want to visit. It's just on the north side of the Atlas Mountains in what is modern day Algeria, which is not the vacation spot you might hope for. We would hope that eventually they'll settle their civil war and we can all go to Algeria. I have not yet been able to go.

Timgad exists as a marvelous example of an ideal Roman colony. It has the surrounding walls, which again, are not fortifications. They're just really to reflect where that boundary is, establishing city from non-city. It shows a tremendous example of orthogonal planning with a strong demarcation of *cardo* and *decumanus*. Interestingly, what they do at Timgad is vary the normal plan. We see the forum not at the direct intersection of the *cardo maximus* and *decumanus maximus*, but off just half a block, so it parallels the major *cardo*. And immediately adjacent to that we see the theater.

The other thing I think is important to take a look at about the plan of Timgad is that we see how rapidly the city expanded. We can't tell dates, of course, from the plan, but take my word for it. There's a lot of construction outside the walls of this city. This is exciting because it shows the success of this community. The Romans have come here into North Africa, what was at the time disputed territory, imposed this Roman-style community, and it grew beyond even their plans. So we've got this marvelous organic construction around Timgad. I didn't realize it kind of looks barnacle-like hanging on the outside, but it represents the success of this form.

If we look at a couple of images that we have of Timgad you can get a sense of this site. Timgad is a UNESCO world heritage site, and I think deservedly so because it was abandoned by the 6th century and so much of the city is preserved, at least up to about three feet of stone. The lower areas of walls were stone, and then above those are largely mud brick, and so we have all this stone here. You can just walk through a Roman city here. It's really extraordinary. You can do much the same thing, of course, at Ostia now. If you get a chance you should do that.

At Timgad we get a great sense of urban design, urban organization, and Roman culture because it's not just imposing urban organization on an area, it's bringing all of Roman culture with them. In this image from Timgad we see the theater in the foreground, and then behind that we see two key buildings: one, the remains of the capitolium. They've brought Jupiter, Juno, and Minerva with them. And then beyond that, on the very edges of the city, we see a triumphal arch. Trajan has brought triumphal imagery all the way out here to the very edges of Roman territory, much as he has done in Dacia and all the way through the city of Rome.

But it's the theater in the foreground I want to leave you with. This is our touchstone for Roman culture. When the Romans bring with them these colonies it's not just a matter of establishing military presence. It's really bringing everything that it means to be Roman together. When you look at that seating area of the theater, with its sharp divisions into upper-, middle-, and lower-class seating, this tells you everything you need to know. The Romans are bringing their own form of entertainment, their own buildings, but they're bringing with them everything it means to be Roman. That really is the essence of colonization.

# Local Baths and Roman Bathing Culture

## Lecture 32

**Outside of Rome, bathing in public served to create communal identity, to reinforce political power, to provide an outlet for generosity, and to define one as a Roman.**

Local bathing in the Roman world served many of the same purposes as bathing in Rome in terms of political, social, and cultural values and interactions. Baths and bathing facilities were an integral part of local political systems. Baths were enormously complex structures that cost a great amount of money to build, improve, and maintain. Therefore, wealthy elites and local magistrates were frequently the sponsors. Elites with less money would underwrite admission fees or maintenance, such as the cost of water or firewood for heating the water. Baths in local communities became civic social centers because of the Roman habit of daily bathing. Bathing establishments were spots for networking and social engagement in the small towns of the Roman Empire. In a society without office buildings, baths played a central role in the political and social business of the community. Local baths, like those in Pompeii and Ostia, projected the same cultural values as found in the large imperial establishments at Rome. The wall decorations emphasized Greek mythological subjects and scenes. Floors were covered with mosaics, a Greek form, often in styles that directly emulated Greek practice.

The facilities differed markedly from those in Rome and from each other in terms of size, scale, amenities, and expectations. At their best, the local baths imitated Roman models but on a smaller scale, suggesting a cognizance of expectations. The forum baths at Cumae and Ostia are virtually identical in design and decoration, with the same use of imported marbles and extensive heating systems. The local baths often featured two full suites of bathing rooms, one for men and one for women, ensuring fully separate bathing experiences. Unlike Rome, where the same facilities were used by men and women together or at different times, local baths often featured separate entrances and facilities. The one common room was often the latrine, where apparently men and women both used the facilities. Some of the baths were used therapeutically, with doctorprescribed regimens.

Despite their restricted size, these baths were signs of local beneficence and were designed to evoke a sense of luxury. Amenities were provided by local officials across the Roman Empire. At the forum baths at Pompeii, for example, we see benches and basins with dedicatory inscriptions from local benefactors.

**In a society without office buildings, baths played a central role in the political and social business of the community.**

Lavishly painted and stuccoed walls created relief decoration and panel paintings in the bathing, dressing, and lounging rooms, surrounding the bathers with appropriate imagery. Scenes of nudity were as common in the decor as they were in the baths themselves. The themes of Dionysiac imagery reflected the sense of abandon and drinking of wine that were described as integral to bathing enjoyment. ■

## Suggested Reading

Fagan, *Bathing in Public in the Roman World.*

Yegül, *Baths and Bathing in Classical Antiquity.*

Zanker, *Pompeii: Public and Private Life.*

## Questions to Consider

1. How do local Roman baths reflect the luxury available at Rome but on a smaller scale and reduced budget?

2. In what ways do local baths and bathing culture display continuity with the cultural and political expectations of imperial baths in Rome itself?

# Local Baths and Roman Bathing Culture

## Lecture 32—Transcript

Welcome to this lecture on local baths and Roman bathing culture. In another lecture, we looked at the enormous and extraordinary bath complexes of the city of Rome, the great imperial complexes built under and by particular emperors to serve the city of Rome. Small towns across the entire Roman Empire didn't have access to those tremendous bathing structures. Nonetheless, Roman bathing culture is spread throughout the empire.

What I want to do here is take a look at that culture of Roman bathing, how it persists throughout Roman space, how it's adapted, and how it serves the local communities because, in fact, it does. It serves a number of the same ways that we saw in the city of Rome itself. It serves to create a sense of community, a sense of Roman identity, but it also serves to reinforce political power, with the role of the emperor being played by local political elites here, and it provides an outlet for generosity and for, in the Greek sense, evergetism, that is, beneficence at the local level. So there's really a lot that bathing does for the Romans.

Local bathing in the Roman world, as I say, is paralleled by what we saw in the city of Rome to a certain extent. We'll look at some of the variations in just a bit. Bathing and the facilities that are necessary are an integral part of Roman urban space, and we see everywhere the Romans go, whether it's their colonies or their smaller communities, municipalities as they're called, or military attachments, forts and fortifications. We see bathing areas up on Hadrian's Wall, for example. The Romans take what we might call their bathing habit with them. This, I think, is an important component of what it really means to be a Roman to the Romans.

In local terms, baths would be built, would be maintained, improved, or augmented largely by those who were in the political elite. We see through the dedicatory inscriptions that we find that there was a strong correlation between those who were making bequests to baths or constructing them, and those who were serving in local office. So it seems as though this is a requirement or an expectation of those who were serving the local community, that they also give back, in particular, related to bath buildings.

Those with less money than the actual elites could do other things. They could underwrite admission fees or pay for wood. We think that buying a rick of wood doesn't sound like a great thing, however, baths and the climate control that they allow, was all based on burning hardwood, lots of hardwood. And so those people who gave a certain amount of hardwood per year get a nice dedicatory inscription and thanks from the local community. And so there is a lot of opportunity here to give back to the community.

Baths, in addition to those practical and political aspects, were also social centers. If you think about the Roman world, we're in a society not just with no office buildings, but with actually no identifiable offices. You wonder, where do people meet? Where are the lawyers meeting with their clients and all these other professionals who we know of and who the Romans had as well: architects, and doctors, and lawyers, and so on, but there are no office buildings anywhere. Well, the answer, of course, is the baths. People are spending hours a day, perhaps, at these local bath buildings, and this is where, in fact, a lot of the social and professional networking is very clearly taking place. And so the baths serve the function not just of cleanliness, but of creating a social center for the entire community.

Local baths also serve in a number of ways to project community values. Rome, as I've made the point before, is very much an inclusive culture and so the decoration that we see in the baths is largely Greek decoration.

When we look at the baths, I think it helps to take a look at particular baths and explore them in detail. We have a marvelous drawing here of the so-called "Stabian baths" in Pompeii. This is the name we give to them because they're on a road that led out to Stabiae, the Via Stabia, so the Stabian baths. What the Romans called them we have no idea. But we have a great reconstruction drawing of the Stabian baths that we will be returning to many times, and it's an excellent example of local bathing culture. We'll get a sense of what this looks like and we'll look at some of the components here as well.

Although the local community doesn't have tremendous building forms that the Romans do in the city of Rome in terms of the imperial bath complexes, that doesn't mean they're not cognizant of the bathing culture and have a certain level of expectation. Their bathing facility, although it's modest in scale, is also going to be luxurious, lavishly decorated, and to reflect what the expectations are in Rome for elite bathing facilities. Case in point, the decoration at the Stabian baths in Pompeii. If we look at one of the walls around the open courtyard, the *palestra* in the center of the Stabian baths, and we've got a nice shot of it here for you, what we see is a stucco wall. It's very faded now, but it was originally richly painted. This stucco decoration that we see here, if you look at it carefully, actually makes a number of key points about this elite identity because what we have in the stucco, that is, carved in plaster here, is a Roman stage building. It's a multi-level stage building that has elements that both project forward and recede back just as a Roman stage building did, and so it's all a very theatrical display here in the stucco. It's lavishly illustrated to give you this rich sense of theatricality. There are figures in here as well, both human and mythological. However, this isn't just a generic stage building. The form of this decoration is actually firmly datable. We know that in Pompeii there was a massive earthquake in A.D. 62, and this bath decoration post dates that. We know this because after 62, particularly after the fire of 64 in Rome, Nero built a series of palaces, which he had decorated. The final one, the Domus Aurea, the Golden House, we still have, and the Golden House revolutionized Roman interior decoration because it introduced this forum of theatrical wall painting.

What the people here in Pompeii have done after the earthquake of 62 and they have all recovered and everything, is redecorate their bath in the latest style. It's a style that doesn't reflect just Roman decoration. It reflects the palace decoration of Nero. So it's perhaps, to a certain extent, pretentious, but it's a pretention toward the very finest of Roman interior decoration. I think that shows an awareness of that, and appreciation of it, and an expectation of what we have here, which is that elite decoration.

We see that when we look inside the bath as well. There's more of this rich stucco, and we're very fortunate to have Pompeii with us because it provides these examples that we don't have preserved elsewhere. This is inside one of the changing rooms, the *apodyterium*. You can see here in this illustration the little lockers in the wall where you placed your street clothes before you went in to bathe. Above that you see a line of the decorative stucco work, a frieze here. The whole register is divided into small squares, which are figural. They're richly decorated with elements here from Greek architectural decoration, as well as Greek mythological figures. So again, it shows that cultural inclusiveness. For the Romans, high culture is Greek culture, and in this case it's Greek culture based on the way the emperor decorates the inside of his house.

There's another illustration that I think makes this point even better. This is a detail on the inside of the stucco on the interior of the Stabian baths. There are three small elements here that I want you to take a look at. On the left is a little cupid hanging on the back of a dolphin as he's riding through the water, which, in fact, doesn't exist here, but that's okay. Just go with it. On the right underneath a sort of a pergola area, a little formal framework, is a nude statue. This reflects the decoration of baths with these statues. In between, hanging on the wall, are copies of small-scale shields of a type that we see in Roman interior decoration. This notion of placing a shield with a portrait in the center of it—and these are these shield portraits that we see in Roman villas—comes to Roman elite decoration, that is, Roman villa decoration, from Greek palace decoration.

And so in the baths here at Pompeii, what we're seeing are a number of trends of decoration coming together. We see elements that reflect the activities. The dolphin reflects the water, of course, the nude figure reflects the luxury and casualness here. But these figures in the center reflect the notions of Roman elite decoration that are in this space being made available to everybody. That is part of the essence of the bathing establishments. They bring the luxuries that would normally be in the private elite dwellings, the houses of Roman patricians and senators, out to everybody.

We also see, in addition to the walls, the floors of baths are richly decorated, mainly with mosaic work. We see a tremendous number of mosaics. The most common are these Italic black-and-white figural mosaics, cut pieces of marble, cut into small cubes and laid out into patterns that show us scenes of black-and-white figures, usually black figures on a white background.

I selected two of these that are particularly fine examples, but they are, trust me, characteristic. One is from a set of baths at Ostia. What you see here is a set of figures in this black-and-white figural style that go around the faux architecture in the center. So the architecture in the center actually reflects the ceiling architecture above you, what's holding up the roof. We've got a great vault system laid out in the mosaic. And then the figures around are in two registers. The outer register contains all nautical themes. They're all aquatic themes. We have Neptune riding a chariot being drawn by seahorses. We have also Nereid and Triton figures, and we also just have swimmers, men swimming. So the decoration reflects the activities here. The inner register, the upper one that we see around the central element, is all men in mule carts. This bath is actually a bath that was paid for, apparently, by a local guild in Ostia, the Guild of the Muleteers, the men who drove the mule carts supplying the city in from the harbor. They paid for this and so they're incorporated into the decoration as well. That's unusual, but the rest of it is fairly characteristic. We see at Ostia that water theme decoration. We see the same thing in a black-and-white figural mosaic from a room at Herculaneum in the baths inside the city of Herculaneum.

We see again this aquatic theme. We can see a Triton figure in the center with this forked snaky tail. He's got an oar over one shoulder, and he's surrounded by sea creatures. I can't make them all out. I see a squid and an octopus. There are a couple of dolphins up at the top. But this notion that the decoration is self-referential of the activities, or of the atmosphere, of the baths is something that we find throughout the Roman world. So these local baths reflect a keen awareness of Roman bathing culture, about the expectations, and they project that. They emulate what's going on in Rome and serve to spread that Roman culture throughout the entire Roman world.

We also see baths that I think are not just different than the facilities that we see at Rome, but actually show evidence of a remarkable amount of comparability, and that is, in particular two of the baths that I have studied in person and analyzed. The forum baths at Ostia, which I mentioned, and the forum baths at Cumae—I have a shot for you here of the forum baths at Ostia—are identical, and I mean absolutely identical down to the types of marble used to decorate the inside. It's really an interesting idea. We don't know how this happened because both of these are built by local individuals. But somebody has a plan of what should be a bath complex next to a forum as we see at Cumae and at Ostia, and has built these together. What we see here is this notion of emulation of the emperors. The emperors built enormous bath complexes in Rome. People in the colonies or in the smaller towns build smaller-scale baths, on their own level, at their own scale, luxurious, with imported marbles, with heating systems throughout and things like that. But here at these two we have a notable example of just how imitative these are, in that they have the exact same forms.

Now I would like to return to the Stabian baths at Pompeii and spend some time analyzing the Stabian baths. This is our best example of what's going on in a local bath because we understand the rooms, we know what's happening here, and we can get a sense not just of the extent, but also of the limitations, of Roman bathing culture and the local adaptations of it.

If we look at this wonderful reconstruction of the Stabian baths, what we see is a block of rooms on three sides around an open courtyard. We'll just look at the reconstruction and talk about the parts for just a minute. The open courtyard is the *palestra*, or the exercise ground. Just above that you see a *natatio*, an open air swimming pool where people are swimming. The wall that I showed you earlier with the stucco theatrical decoration is to the left of that. If you go through the *palestra*, the entrance into the baths is on the left hand side of the *palestra*, where we see a little gabled roof. We go through that *palestra* to the very back of the complex to the rooms that are along the far side. On the axis with the entrance we see a latrine. Beyond that there are service rooms. We see a large open cistern of water and that's where the aqueduct delivers water into the baths, and that cistern is high up to maintain the gravity flow, which is what feeds the baths.

All of this area in there, the *palestra*, the *natatio*, and the latrine, is common area. I say common area because this bath is actually different than any bath that we have in the city of Rome in that it has separate suites for men and women. But all the area that we have there is common. As far as we can tell, it's all area that both genders would use.

I need to say a word here about gender divisions in baths. In Rome, the major bath buildings, the great imperial complexes, generally have one large suite of bathing rooms that runs down the center of a block of the main bath building along the axis. We can't tell if they are coed facilities. They're either used by men and women together, or they're used alternately. We don't have two sets of suites of rooms. So they're either using the baths together, and there's strong evidence for that from the literary accounts, or they're alternating, and there's some evidence for that in legal cases. Emperors are occasionally passing edicts saying men use the baths at one time of day, women at the other.

That's not the case here [at the Stabian baths]. Here, we have a common area and then the separate suites. In that common area, surprisingly, is the latrine, and this seems to be of common use for men and women. I think this is a surprise to us, but it's standard for the Romans. We never see men's rooms and women's rooms for using the toilet. There's always just one latrine. And so although they're bathing separately, they're using the bathroom, so-to-speak, together, and this is somcthing that points out the differentiation in cultures.

The other thing that's common besides the exercise ground and the swimming pool, which are standard, is that there is a small hallway adjacent to the latrine. In that small hallway is a series of small chambers. On this plan it just shows you the lateral hallway and a series of divisions. Each of those little chambers has just enough room for one bathtub, and in each one was found an amphora, a large storage container which usually holds liquids. So we have, in this case, five of these small individual bathtubs. At another set of baths outside the city of Pompeii there were seven of these, all in a row, small chambers with what looks like a bathtub just like you would find in your house today.

Scholars have debated what these are used for because Roman bathing practice is public bathing. Everybody gets together and bathes. It's the community that bathes together, stays together sort of thing. So the purpose of these has been a source of a great amount of speculation throughout the scholarship. A lot of that speculation revolves around prostitution. We know that prostitutes used the baths as a base just as doctors, and people who gave haircuts, and so on did, and so a lot of speculation is that these individual chambers were used by the prostitutes.

I have to disagree with this. I think is probably very unlikely. In one brothel that we have from the ancient world, the little chambers that the prostitutes used have beds in them, grotty little beds with stone mattresses and pillows, but beds nonetheless.

What we have here, I think, is a set of therapeutic baths. I mention that doctors are at the baths, and doctors are not just in the baths, but they're prescribing baths to their patients, and there's ample evidence of people coming to the baths on the advice of their doctors. Doctors will advise a cold plunge, or hot baths, along with a certain diet and exercise in order to regulate the humors. But when somebody had a serious infection, doctors might recommend therapeutic bathing besides just heated or cold water.

We know that in Rome there were baths that had special waters on tap, that is, salt water, sea water that you could bathe in for certain skin conditions, a whole variety of mineral waters. Nowadays we have this phrase, "taking the waters," and that means people are going to spas at Baden-Baden in Germany, or Bath in England, or Harrogate in England. They have a lot of these in England, don't they? They're taking these waters. They're either drinking or they're soaking in these therapeutic types of mineral waters. The Romans did the same thing, but rather than traveling to the spas, sometimes they had the water brought to them.

I think what we're seeing here at the Stabian baths are therapeutic rooms. Each one has a bathtub and an amphora to either soak in or drink the particular form of water, and so I think it's very likely that what we have here is one bathtub and amphora that had sea water in it, one that had sulfur water, one that has a particular kind of mineral water, and then so on. As I say, there are four or five of these, depending on how you count them. We can easily count the number of special mineral baths that the Romans used here. So what I think we're seeing there is a suite for that.

So that's all common area in the baths, but if you look down into the lower area of the reconstruction now, return back to that, what we see in the center of the main block of baths is the infrastructure for the bath here in the Stabian baths, and that is the furnace and the cisterns that are heated up by the furnace. That's in the center and you see three round cisterns of water. Those represent the boilers that are heating up water.

On either side of those we have the suites of rooms. We believe that the men's rooms are on the left, men's bathing suite, and the women's are on the right. These are mirror image suites. If we take the rooms on either side of the furnace, what we believe we have there on either side is the *caldarium*, the hot room. Remember, the furnace is being fed under the floor, and the smoke and heat are all passing under the floors of those rooms immediately adjacent, and then chimneying out through the walls around them so that heat radiates from the floor and the walls of those rooms. There is also in each one of those rooms an inset bath at one end, set into the floor so it's heated from all sides. So we've got hot water in a hot room, and then at the far end of each of those rooms, the end nearest the *palestra*, we have a standing basin of cold water. Next to those we have the *tepidaria*, rooms with just warm water farther away from the furnace, and then farthest away from the furnace of all are the *frigidaria*, the cold water rooms. Then, on either side of those, are the *apodyteria*, the dressing rooms. And so we have this marvelous mirror image set of two suites of baths. We believe the men's are on the left and the women's are on the right. The men's are larger, better decorated, and there is evidence that that decoration reflects male elite culture. But in either case, that's what we're looking at here at the Stabian baths. As I say, it's our best evidence here for local bathing culture. And as I pointed out, it shows us the limitations of the extent of Roman culture because this sort of division is something we find nowhere in the city of Rome itself. It is, in fact, unique to the small local baths where they're going to have these separate suites for men and women. And so I think this is important to keep in mind.

It also brings up a number of interesting questions, and that is, the role of the decoration. Can we see gender decoration? I think we can. It also brings up another point, and that is the culture of the baths. Roman poets, who write about the baths in the city of Rome, emphasize the role of the baths as a place to pick up girls. The question becomes here, how is that going to happen if you have separate entrances and separate suites? It would have to occur out in the common areas, in the *palestra*, in the *natatio*, or the latrine. I can't think of anywhere else in the common areas. Otherwise, it's not occurring here. And so there's a potential here that the cultural expectations for the baths are actually slightly different.

Nonetheless, we do have evidence for what's going on in these rooms in terms of the bathing. We have a very clear male suite here with the male bathing going on, again at a smaller level than we have in Rome. The scale is much smaller, but still, people are coming in here and spending hours a day in all those regular activities of exercise, and bathing, and haircuts, and doctors' visits and things like that.

The other thing that the baths represent is an outlet for local beneficence. At Rome, the baths are pretty much exclusively an imperial proposition. Only the emperor has the funds to build one of those lavish buildings. But here on the local level you can add to them. We have a marvelous example here from the forum baths at Pompeii. This is not the Stabian baths, but another neighborhood complex. Here at the end of the *caldarium* in a little niche, a little semi-circular niche, we have one of those standing marble basins. In the center of that marble basin is a lead water pipe, and so it constantly fed cold water out into that marble basin. At the opposite end of the room we've got the hot plunge and here in this *schola*, this little semi-circular niche, we have the cold water basin, and all the way around the edge of that basin we have a dedicatory inscription. It must have been very expensive to bring this basin, which is about five feet in diameter. It's a piece of solid marble on a tall base about four and a half feet tall. Taking all this into Pompeii must have cost a lot. The marble itself is imported from North Africa, and then they would inset into the rim—it's largely gone now—a bronze inscription naming the man responsible. And so his name would be permanently associated with this improvement in the baths.

We can see it here in its context in the forum baths at Pompeii. It's much simpler than the Stabian baths. The decoration is much simpler, and you can see that basin down there. There's a skylight above it that had panes of glass in it so that you could see it there very clearly. This gives a great sort of centrality to his dedication. So these benefactions are a major component of the baths in the local communities.

We should also talk briefly a bit more about the decoration because there is an interesting question about the decoration of these local baths. I mentioned before how I think the decoration reflects the activities that are taking place, effectively self-referential. But there's another component of the decoration as well, and it's not just that the decoration reflects the actual activities that are taking place here, but there are forms of the decoration in terms of the iconography, as well as the subjects, which suggest that it's not a portrayal of the actual activities, but an idealization of the activities, and that what the

Romans are projecting here is not seeing yourself in the wall painting or the mosaic floor, but the ideal. It's what you want to believe is taking place.

Certainly there's nudity in the decorations, but there's also quite a bit of frank sexuality. There's not just nudity, but erotic imagery. This erotic imagery that we have shows individuals in the baths, but they're not actually bathing together. They're on beds. The decoration reflects very much the forms of Greek Hellenistic artistic conventions. The women have pale white skin, the men have that dark red skin. They're on Greek-style beds. In the background in these we see garlands hanging. They're very lavish sort of dinner scenes that these people have, again, with an erotic context, but they're not appropriate to the baths. They're not shown in bathing atmosphere. In this case the decoration isn't just, as I say, projecting the activities. These project a fantasy about what's going on.

In terms of the Greek identity, we also see a tremendous amount of Dionysiac imagery. We do know, for example, that there's a tremendous amount of drinking going on in the baths, wine drinking. Epitaphs talk about this. People who bemoan being dead on their tombstones say, "What I miss most are baths and wine, and baths and wine together." And so in the decorations in some of these, for example, in this illustration we have Dionysiac figures paired with images of warfare, that is, shields and weapons together to give us this sense of elite male cultural identity. It's both Roman and Greek together.

And so I think this is a nice place to sum up what we see in the local bathing culture. What we see here altogether in these smalls towns across the Roman Empire is a bathing culture that projects Roman cultural identity, but most importantly, brings with it Roman culture inclusiveness, a tremendous amount of Greek identity here in the mosaics, in the stucco decoration in the decoration of the baths, and we also see in the organization of space in these local bathing structures the limits of Roman identity as these local communities adapt them to their own needs and cultural expectations.

# Roman Harbors—Liminal Monuments
## Lecture 33

**Long-distance travel in the Roman world, especially transport of vital food and building materials, was largely by water and generally across the Mediterranean Sea, referred to by Romans as Mare Nostrum ("our sea").**

Roman harbor complexes, the largest building projects in the Roman Empire, were built to reorient travelers to Roman rule. The lighthouse at Alexandria became the model for many Roman imitations. The lighthouse was a multiple-story tower creating a raised fire platform. The lighthouse lay on the right to those entering the harbor, setting the standard pattern for all subsequent lighthouses.

The culminating structure at the harbor was a large podium temple to Poseidon designed to be viewed from a distance by those entering the harbor. The temple to Poseidon was built on a terrace overlooking and facing the harbor. The goal was to provide those arriving and departing with evidence of the religious authority responsible for their safety and to provide a tangible object for their arrival and departure sacrifices. It was augmented by a temple to Caesar that effectively redirected worship from Poseidon to Caesar, establishing the pattern followed in later Roman harbor foundations.

The Augustan-period harbor at Caesarea provides the best-studied and best-documented example of a developed Roman harbor, with emphasis on the harbor entrance and harborside for monumental display. The entrance to the harbor was designed with a lighthouse as well as other monuments establishing Roman authority over the harbor. Two sets of three columns surmounted by statues were placed on either side of the harbor entrance. The statues were probably an imperial portrait gallery with images of Augustus and his family.

A large podium temple adjacent to the harborside dominated the monuments of the complex. The temple was dedicated to Augustus and a companion deity who was jointly the personification of the local community and the goddess Roma. This temple was large, grand, and built of white marble so that it acted like the lighthouse to aid navigation into the harbor. Travelers made arrival sacrifices in the temple, thus showing gratitude to the emperors and acknowledging their power in promoting trade and safety at sea.

The Roman harbor of Portus, the facility for the city of Ostia at the mouth of the Tiber, was planned by Julius Caesar and constructed by Claudius. The Claudian construction at Portus created a harbor complex that for the first time gave the city of Rome its own formal opening onto the sea and projected its monument sets onto the coast. This harbor is not well understood because excavations have been difficult. The major monuments at the harbor mouth included the lighthouse, based directly on Alexandria's, with a statue of Claudius as the new Zeus, savior of sailors.

The Trajanic expansion of the harbor shows a shift in the imagery of rule as Trajan's monuments take on triumphal and military themes. The inner basin of the harbor was overlooked by a colossal statue of Trajan himself dressed as a triumphant general. Behind this statue on the edge of the harbor was a temple to Dionysus, a god Trajan used in his own identity as the new Dionysus to justify his campaigns against the Parthians.

The Severan harbor at Leptis Magna shows the extension of Trajan's triumphal imagery and further conflates imperial identity with Roman deities. The monuments at the mouth of the harbor were derived from and expanded previous themes of safety and imperial responsibility for security. Again we see the lighthouse on the right-hand side. The entrance was flanked by two small temples decorated with triumphal wreaths and dedicated to Dionysus and Hercules, the deities with whom the sons of the emperor identified.

The culminating monument was a large podium temple built directly opposite the harbor mouth as seen at Caesarea and Portus. The podium temple was dedicated to Jupiter, whose identity Septimius Severus adopted. Because Jupiter is the father of both Dionysus and Hercules, Jupiter's temple becomes a dynastic monument celebrating the Severan dynasty. ■

## Suggested Reading

Hohlfelder, *The Maritime World of Ancient Rome.*

Keay, *Portus: An Archaeological Survey.*

## Questions to Consider

1. How do Roman harbors operate to create an ideological display requiring that those navigating their spaces acknowledge and celebrate Roman power and imperial rule?

2. What developments do we see in the decoration and monumentalization of harbors? What forms of decoration are consistent throughout the empire?

# Roman Harbors—Liminal Monuments

## Lecture 33—Transcript

Welcome to this lecture on Roman imperial harbors. What we're going to be looking at in this lecture is not just the harbor itself, or a harbor as a piece of Roman infrastructure, but the sets of monuments that we find within Roman imperial harbors. I should warn you at the outset that this is actually the topic of my doctoral dissertation, and so I can, literally talk about this forever. But I'll try and restrain myself to a short period of time here in some actual, focused, salient examples.

I think Roman imperial harbors, and the monument sets that we find within them, are incredibly important to understand the visual Roman world. The reason for that is that most long distance travel, particularly of bulk commodities like grain, marble, and things like this, go through harbors. The road systems that the Romans built are just fantastic, but they were still very slow. The quickest form of travel, long distance travel in particular, is by sea. Roman imperial harbors ring the Mediterranean, what the Romans themselves refer to as the "Mare Nostrum," or "Our Sea." They serve a very important symbolic function, that is, when somebody sailed into a Roman imperial harbor, the set of monuments that you found there—and it was very often a consistent set of a very limited number of monument types—helped to reintegrate you into the Roman world. Through engagement with that monument set, what we see is individuals re-establishing their connection to the Roman world.

One of the best examples we have of this is from Suetonius's "Life of Augustus." We have a marvelous example from his life, as well as from the harbor where this event occurred, and that is the harbor at Puteoli, the second city of Italy and the largest harbor down on the Bay of Naples. We have a painting that shows a reconstruction of Puteoli.

In Suetonius's *Life of Augustus*, in an episode near the end of Augustus's life, a group of merchants have sailed their ship into the harbor dominated by a temple to Augustus himself. But instead of sacrificing toward that Temple of Augustus as they normally would, they saw Augustus himself sailing out of the harbor. So they turned their attention to him and made their sacrifices and prayers to the emperor himself rather to his temple. They say very clearly in Suetonius, it is to the emperor that they owe their prosperity and their very lives. This is the formula that we see as people sail into Roman imperial harbors. They are thankful, first, for having made it on a sea voyage in the ancient world, and they're thankful not just for their lives, but for their prosperity as well, and the emperor is responsible for that. So the religious component of this space added to the fact that people are actively engaging with it. The expectation is that you will turn and make a sacrifice as you enter or leave a Roman imperial harbor. This serves to reintegrate you into the Roman world. After you've left this transitional space of the open sea, you've come back, and you're literally rejoining Roman territory. That is the purpose of the Roman imperial harbor monument set. It's to allow you, or to force you, to reintegrate yourself and to take your place again in the Roman world.

The Romans themselves didn't come up with this monument set on their own. They actually adapted the monument set we see from the greatest harbor in the ancient world, and that's at Alexandria. Alexandria, on the coast of Egypt, was Alexander the Great's foundation. It was largely constructed under his successors, the Ptolomies, and what we see at Alexandria is a very standard monument set that we see replicated throughout Roman harbors. As you sailed into the harbor at Alexandria, and we have a wonderful reconstruction painting for you here, on the right hand side, and it's always on the right, is a great lighthouse. The lighthouse at Alexandria, the Pharos, is the typical monument. This is the type of monument for a lighthouse in the ancient world. It's the first and best example that we have of one of these multi-stage, multi-story towers with a lighting platform at the top, and that's all it is really. It's a large platform to host an open flame at the very top. It's always on the right as you sail in. When you enter the harbor, and we've got a great example here at Alexandria, across from the lighthouse, and across from the harbor mouth, there is a large temple, generally harborside, often a tall podium temple, set up so that it's prominent. This temple—in the case of Alexandria it's to Poseidon—is to allow you to sacrifice to the god who has made your safety possible. At Alexandria, we have a complex sort of division of authority. The lighthouse has a large statue on top of it to Zeus Soter, Zeus the Savior. And then we have Poseidon, the god of the sea, with his enormous temple on the harborside, so you have your choice between the savior god, Zeus, or Poseidon as you sail in or out of the harbor.

Once the Romans take over Egypt and Alexandria, they build a second temple just next to and slightly behind the temple of Poseidon, and this is a temple to the emperors, in particular, to Augustus. It's the so-called "Caesarion," the temple to Caesar Augustus. And so what we see here at Alexandria, although it's not part of the initial foundation, is the redirection of worship toward the emperors. This becomes the standard pattern throughout the Roman imperial harbors, that the main deity is the emperor. Because it is the emperor, who is responsible for the infrastructure, and who is responsible for, as Suetonius's merchants say to Augustus himself, for their prosperity and for their very lives. And so Alexandria provides us with a wonderful model, first constructed under the Greeks and then adapted by the Romans.

We see very rapidly after the Romans take over Egypt and Alexandria the construction of what we might call the first of the Roman imperial harbors. This is actually at Caesarea in the kingdom of Herod, king of Judea. So it's built under Herod, but there's very good evidence in the excavators of Caesarea Maritima on the coast of modern day Israel—I've written about this—that Marcus Agrippa, Augustus's right hand man, came out here and actually seems to have consulted on the construction of the harbor. Much of the harbor is actually constructed with Roman materials: Roman concrete, and in particular, materials from down on the Bay of Naples where we know Agrippa built a number of naval facilities for Augustus.

So Agrippa comes out here. Whether Agrippa is responsible or is just in a consulting capacity we don't know, but what we do know is that Herod decides to build this enormous city dedicated to and named for Augustus. We call it "Caesarea." Herod referred to it as "Sebastos," which is the Greek version of Augustus.

What we see in this Augustan period harbor at Caesarea is really the first of these types of Roman imperial harbors. This is—I have to give credit to the excavators here at Caesarea—it is the best studied and best documented of any of the large-scale harbors that we have around the Mediterranean. They've been excavating in Caesarea now for decades and have published everything in a remarkable series of publications. The vast majority is in English, so it's accessible to an English-speaking audience. It's a wonderful achievement and something you should take the opportunity to seek out if you're at all interested.

We have a great reconstruction painting here of Caesarea, and it shows us the monument set as it's described in ancient literary sources and through the work of the excavators here at Caesarea.

As you sail into the harbor we have one set of monuments out at the mouth of the harbor. There's a lighthouse on the right hand side, again, modeling itself after Alexandria, and that is actually joined here by subsidiary monuments. On either side of the mouth of the harbor are three large columns. Topping each of these columns is a statue. So we have a large statue group out here.

We have a nice description of this from the author, Josephus. Josephus talks about what it was like to sail in here and tells us about the parts. He tells us in particular that there was a large tower out here at the mouth of the harbor named "the Drusion." At the time this was constructed, about 15 B.C., Drusus was Augustus's prospective heir. Augustus, of course, lived a long time and ruled from 31 B.C. to A.D. 14, and he ran through a lot of prospective heirs. Drusus was only one of them. I get the feeling sometimes that somebody might have gotten a letter, a papyrus scroll saying Augustus has named you as his heir, and they might just burst into tears because everybody Augustus names as his heir for about the first 40 years of his rule dies almost immediately afterwards. It's a disturbing pattern, and getting that letter must tell you to update your will immediately.

At this point, about 15 B.C., Drusus is Augustus's heir, but he's not the only one and he's not the first. So what we have on those columns is a set of statues. These are believed to be an imperial dynastic family grouping. We have Augustus and his wife, Livia. Who the others are we're not sure about. Drusus is taken care of here, but what we probably have here are Tiberius and Marcus Agrippa, and perhaps his two sons, Gaius and Lucius. We're not sure what the grouping is. But these sort of dynastic family groups are actually found all over the Roman world in a number of different contexts: free-standing sculpture groups, reliefs, carved gems, all sorts of things, and so it's fairly standard here. The point here is that what we're establishing here at the mouth of the harbor is that this is where the dynastic group is. One would sail in and see the family of the emperor. When you pass through the mouth of the harbor, directly across from the harbor mouth over on the shore was a harborside temple. This was dedicated to Augustus and the goddess, Roma, combined in one worship. It was actually a form of Roma, whose identity is syncretized to the local community. The images we have from the ancient world looks like the personification of Roma, but she's also named Sebastos, and so they've created a very complex form of identity.

If we look at another very nice reconstruction painting again, we can see just how prominent that temple was. Here, in this reconstruction, they're just completing the breakwaters that surround the harbor, but the temple is already completed on the far shore. It's white, it's up on a raised podium, and it's gleaming, just as Josephus describes it. The temple itself acted as a lighthouse as the secondary navigation point. So after you pass the lighthouse and get into the harbor, you point your ship toward that Temple of Augustus and Roma, and you're literally navigating by members of the imperial family. That is your goal, to get to that temple.

We also have from Caesarea a really remarkable find. It's a little cup made of bronze inset with a very richly decorated scene, and it was found at Caesarea. It's now at the Louvre, so if you get a chance to see it, it's there on display. What it shows us is the arrival sacrifice taking place in the actual harbor at Caesarea. The cup itself was a votive. It was a dedication. Sea travel in the ancient world is incredibly risky. If you've read the Acts of the Apostles you know that the Apostle Paul sails from Caesarea to Rome, and along the way he is shipwrecked, and this a common occurrence. So as people set out on voyages they would make a prayer as they're leaving one harbor. Please, whatever deity it is, in our case probably a member of the imperial family, please, Augustus, if I survive I'll make a dedication to you, a votive. That's what we have here in the Caesarea cup. It's a marvelous votive. What it shows us is the temple here at Caesarea. If you look at this image of the cup, and they are difficult to photograph because the cup is round, but on the right hand side of your image there is the temple itself with the columns strung with garlands. In front of it we have an image of that wonderful syncretized feminine figure dressed as Roma, but named as Sebastos, the local community. So it's a personification that joins Rome and the local community together. She's on this side. Augustus is on the other.

In front of her is a procession. Coming from the harbor at the left we have a large group of people coming forward and making a sacrifice in front of that statue before the temple. The first person in front has their toga pulled over their head, as is appropriate while making a religious sacrifice, and this is the actual sacrifice taking place. And so the votive cup, which exists because of the vow, also shows the arrival sacrifice. This was, of course, a very powerful moment because you're not just thankful for being on dry land, which you would be after the threat of a shipwreck, but in fact, it shows this reflection, this establishment, this acceptance of Roman religious and political authority. This is all here in a city that's not actually in Roman territory at the time. It's in Judea. So I think it's a really remarkable example.

If we leave Caesarea, and it always breaks my heart to do so, we can see the repetition of this series of monuments throughout other harbors across the Roman world, but with distinctive differences. As different emperors create their own harbor complexes, they project their own identities on them. These harbor complexes are the largest building forms, the largest construction projects in the entire Roman world. A forum, such as the Forum of Trajan, is the largest construction project in the city of Rome, but it's dwarfed by the size of one of these harbors, and the technical complexity of building here on this liminal area between sea and land.

We have a marvelous painting here showing us a sort of a bird's eye view of the harbor at Portus. Portus, which just means "harbor" in Latin, is the actual harbor for the city of Rome. It's constructed just off the mouth of the Tiber River down by the city of Ostia. This is actually a double basin harbor because it was constructed by two emperors at two different times. The outer basin that you see here in the reconstruction was actually planned by Julius Caesar and constructed by the Emperor Claudius in the A.D. 40s. It consisted of the same sorts of monuments that we saw at Caesarea and Alexandria, although I have to tell you Portus is less well understood because much of the harbor actually is under the airport for the city of Rome. Leonardo da Vinci airport is built on it. The harbor silted up and they just laid out the runways and everything right there on the coast. It's a marvelous idea that in the ancient world you sailed into the harbor and now you fly in, same space. Nonetheless, it makes excavation kind of tricky. I've been out there trying to explore the harbor remains before and have been stopped by the police. They actually sent a helicopter after me one time. It was very exciting, but we'll tell that story some other time.

In any case, what we have here on the right as you sail in is the lighthouse. You come into the harbor itself, and there was an opportunity here to worship at a temple dedicated to the emperor himself, dedicated to Claudius. What they've done in this reconstruction is taken the large-scale statue off of the lighthouse and set it down kind of evocatively into the center of the harbor where it wasn't actually. It was placed up on the lighthouse, whereas Alexandria had that statue of Zeus Soter on the lighthouse, here what we're convinced there was, was a statue of Claudius himself. So it's effectively Claudius Soter, Claudius Your Savior, as you're sailing in. So the Claudian harbor, although it's, as I say, not as well understood and not as well excavated, we know it has the basic monuments of a temple, as well as the lighthouse.

The inner basin that we see here in this reconstruction is this large artificial basin that was excavated out by Trajan. Trajan decided to expand the harbor inward to create this wonderful double-basin hexagonal harbor. By the way, if you ever fly into or out of Rome always look out the window as you're leaving the airport or landing and you can very often get an excellent view of Trajan's harbor basin. It's still there.

Trajan's basin has a different ideological program because Trajan is projecting a different identity. His political and military needs were different than those of Claudius. So what we see in Trajan's harbor is all Trajan, all the time. There was a bust of Trajan at the mouth of the inner harbor; no lighthouse, of course, because that's out in the Claudian harbor. There's a colossal statue of Trajan as a conquering general with a *cuirass* and all, which really dominated the inner basin. And then behind that was a temple. Interestingly—I think it's interesting—that temple that really dominated the harborside in the inner basin was not dedicated directly to a member of the imperial family, not to Trajan himself, or to a previous emperor. This is unique among the harborside temples in the Roman world.

What Trajan did was he had a temple constructed here to Dionysus. This is kind of an interesting idea because it's a portion of his propaganda program. Trajan's construction here of the harbor at Portus is tied in with his great Parthian War, his great campaign to go out and attack and absorb the Parthian empire into the Roman Empire, which he largely achieved. He attacked and sacked the Parthian empire and added much of what is today modern Syria, Iraq, Saudi Arabia, much of the Middle East, into the Roman world. He justified this by conflating his identity with that of Dionysus. He is, in his coins and in his statuary, the Neos Dionysus, the New Dionysus.

In Greek mythology, Dionysus had an eastern triumph where he brought his culture all the way out to India, going east through what we would call Middle Eastern lands. Trajan is adapting this idea himself, so Trajan is the Neos Dionysus. So he has this colossal statue of himself as a conquering general built, and then behind it the Temple of Dionysus, and that axial arrangement links the two together. So we have a really complex identity here.

We have some ancient images of the harbor that give us a sense, and I wanted to show you these because they are some of our best sources of what's going on besides the literary accounts and the excavations. There's a coin that I wanted to show you which shows the grain fleet inside the Claudian harbor. This is the outer basin of the Claudian harbor before Trajan's harbor is constructed. What we see here are ships that are recognizably members of the grain fleet. At this time, Rome is bringing almost all of its grain. The staple of the Roman food supply is coming into Ostia, being imported from North Africa and from Egypt, so Ostia, or Portus here in particular, is a critical part of supplying the city of Rome with food. And so Nero has struck a coin here showing the grain fleet in the harbor, secure and safe.

Surrounding that harbor basin are the breakwaters that define the harbor. On the upper left side what we see is a temple. This is not the temple that would have been at the harborside across from the mouth. This is actually a temple that was on the end of the breakwater as you approached opposite the lighthouse. So the lighthouse is on the right as we see up here, and this little temple is on the left, and if you have extremely good eyes or a better television than I have at home, you can see somebody standing out in front of that temple sacrificing. If you have really good eyes, you can see the same thing in the sterns of two of these ships, men standing up with one hand out like this, making the sacrifice. They're all reflecting that arrival sacrifice, making a sacrifice to the emperor.

We see the same thing in another relief, this one also from Ostia, illustrating Portus. This is a marvelous relief because what it shows us is a conflation of all of the major monuments from the two harbor basins together. It shows a ship sailing into the harbor. On the sail of the ship we have images of the she-wolf with Romulus and Remus. In the prow of the ship there's the master and other members of the crew sacrificing over an open flame altar as they arrive. Just behind the ship with the open flame up in the sky is the lighthouse, and then off to the side, off to the right, we have the flank, the profile of a triumphal arch, probably built by Trajan here. And it's Trajan up there, we think, in a chariot, being pulled by four elephants. And then beyond that is the figure of Dionysus, the terminal figure as you sail into the harbor. On the far right hand corner above, there's the god Dionysus. And so it lays out really the entire monument set. I forgot to mention, on the next to last stage of the lighthouse just below the flame, there's that statue of Claudius right up there as well, taking the place of Zeus.

So the harbor at Portus has this marvelous dual identity, Claudian as well as Trajanic. With the Trajanic elements, what we see is the extension of military imagery. In particular, Roman military triumphal imagery, Trajan as this triumphal general outside the city of Rome, and this linkage between military campaigns and the monument sets of a harbor. We can see that sort of extended as well, this extension of Trajan's triumphal imagery, at Leptis Magna. Leptis Magna is a great city on the coast of North Africa. It's the birthplace of the Emperor Septimius Severus, who rules from A.D. 193 to 211. What we see in the imagery of the monument set at Leptis Magna in the great harbor, all built under Septimius Severus to honor his birthplace, is a conflation of the imperial identities of Septimius Severus and his sons, Caracalla and Geta, with standard pagan Roman deities. Septimius Severus regularly conflated his identity with that of Jupiter. Jupiter's most important, and I think most well understood sons, that is, the ones who are worshiped most in the Roman world, are Hercules and Dionysus, and so Septimius Severus's sons adopt, or syncretize, their identities with those of Hercules and Dionysus. So Caracalla and Geta become the new Hercules and Dionysus and their father, the god, is Septimius Severus as the new Jupiter. This is different than what we saw under Trajan. Where Trajan exists as the new Dionysus, son of Jupiter, Jupiter is effectively his "vice-regent on earth," as it's been termed by one scholar.

What we see at Leptis Magna is a full range of this set of monuments, as you sail into the harbor today, and I hope sometime to get this opportunity myself. Leptis Magna, by the way, is in the modern country of Libya, and I've never been able to go there. I looked into it one time and the State Department told me that I faced a ten year prison sentence if I went, so I didn't go. I know, it's shocking. But what we see as we sail in is the remains of a lighthouse on the right hand side as you come in, on that standard formation.

We also have here our best extant evidence, besides the coin of Portus, of small temples out on either end of the breakwater at the mouth of the harbor. In this case, we have small distyle temples, that is, small temples, just a small single *cella*, with two columns in front supporting a front porch with a projecting pediment. Here's one on the eastern side of the eastern breakwater, and you get a sense of, if you let your eye slide past, the warehouses along the breakwater. Out at the end there are the remains of the temple.

We have a mosaic here from just outside Leptis Magna, which is from a villa, but I think what it's showing us here is actually the harbor itself. On either end of the two breakwaters projecting out into the sea, and there's a ship sailing in, what we have are two pediments and distyle fronts. Those are the two entrance temples. And then if you follow that around all the way in the back, there projecting up taller than anything around it, is the harborside temple. This temple is poorly preserved, but we have the dedicatory inscription for it. We know it was dedicated to Jupiter as this identity conflated with Septimius Severus.

I have another image here to show you: the lighthouse at the mouth of the harbor as well. So we have the remains of that actually pretty well preserved, and the blocks around it. What we see at Leptis Magna is the harbor entrance flanked by two small temples, one to Hercules and one to Dionysus. Not just Hercules and Dionysus, though, but Caracalla and Geta, the sons of Septimius Severus. So, as we saw 200 years earlier at Caesarea, the emperor's family. The dynastic monuments are out here at the mouth of the harbor. This is where you come in and it's to reacquaint you with the dynasty. And then as you enter the harbor mouth, you point your ship toward docking and you guide yourself based on that large harborside temple. At Caesarea it's to Augustus. Here, it's to Jupiter as Septimius Severus. And so the entire complex works together to reinforce this notion of imperial dynasty.

It does more than that, however, because it also serves to extend that triumphal imagery that Trajan used in his harbor basin at Portus. We see the lighthouse at Leptis Magna being used on a great triumphal relief from the city of Leptis Magna, a great relief from the attic of a triumphal arch built, again, under Septimius Severus, being used as the monument that orients you and serves to give you the architectural context for where you are. It effectively acts as a triumphal monument the way triumphal arches in Rome are shown on the reliefs that decorate them. Here, the lighthouse is being used in the same way.

So what we're seeing here is a marvelous attempt to transition travelers into this space, which serves two key functions. First, to celebrate the Severan dynasty through these deities of Hercules and Dionysus, and then, finally, Jupiter Septimius Severus. Second, to reflect on the extension of this triumphal imagery away from Rome here into North Africa for the first timeAll of this is being accomplished in a very symbolic ideological way using the same set of monuments with different themes, which we see going all the way back to the harbor at Caesarea constructed under Augustus. This sort of consistency, I think, is deliberate. The Romans are using these monuments to create a sense of reintegration into the Roman world. As you sail into and actually literally re-enter Roman territory, you're reoriented through the lighthouse, the harbors, and the references to the imperial family. You're reoriented into Roman culture, and in particular, into Roman religious and political authority.

# Putting It All Together I—A Day in Pompeii

## Lecture 34

**In this lecture we follow a day in the life of a fictional traveler who has landed at the Bay of Naples and is now coming through Pompeii on his way to Rome.**

A traveler making his way to Pompeii starts by sailing into Puteoli, the major harbor on the Bay of Naples, and traveling by road until he reaches Pompeii itself. As he enters Puteoli, the second city of Roman Italy, he engages a series of monuments and buildings that reorient him to Roman rule en route to Pompeii. A triumphal-style arch sits along the dock, overlooked by the imperial amphitheater and grand public buildings. The road to Pompeii is flanked by an aqueduct, and milestones along the way celebrate the construction of this infrastructure.

As he approaches Pompeii, he sees local markers that establish the key identities of the city and its inhabitants. The roads immediately outside the walls of Pompeii are lined with the tombs of wealthy members of the community, announcing the important families in town and their role in defining the community. The inscriptions on them announce that the most prestigious locations were given by the local city council. These tombs are covered with painted announcements of upcoming gladiatorial games, testifying to a strong political system, beneficence, and public spectacle entertainment in a community with its own gladiatorial school. If he approaches from the east, he sees the amphitheater rise up on the edge of the city to define its role as a Roman colony with Roman cultural values. Approach from the west presents the traveler with the high terrace supporting the Temple of Venus, patron deity of Pompeii and of the Sullan family that founded the colony, projecting the religious identity of the community.

The first stop in the city might be the home of a patron or business associate. The route to and exterior of the house is devoid of the directional signals found in a modern city. Street corners do not have signs, only plaques to protect the crossroads from evil; directions are given by public buildings or prominent landmarks. The outside of the house has no name, address, or numbers; the only identifying marks are symbols of the crowns and recognitions won by its inhabitants. For elite houses, long benches along the outside walls by the sidewalk are available for those waiting admission and audience with the patron who lives within.

**Street corners do not have signs, only plaques to protect the crossroads from evil.**

Once in the house, the visitor is led through the atrium into the *tablinum*, decorated with images of the family's past accomplishments and contributions to Rome. The entryway and atrium are decorated with the images of famous family members, often busts or funerary masks. The wall paintings and sculpture reflect the family's cultural values. The *tablinum* presents the patron slightly raised above the floor of the atrium and in a position of power and superiority to the visitor.

Our traveler's business would almost certainly take him next to Pompeii's forum, where he would accompany his patron and see a variety of activities taking place in a mixture of public and private actions. The open space of the forum is dominated by the *capitolium*, as well as shrines that define the values of the community. The other buildings around the forum support a variety of activities taking place simultaneously on this average day. The markets that flanked the *capitolium* are in daily use; there are large numbers of women in particular in the forum at the north end. The public buildings such as the basilica and local council chamber are located on the south end of the forum, effectively creating a public, but male, space for local elite males to interact.

Time in the afternoon could be given over to hours spent in a local bathing complex, in the theater, or at the amphitheater if public games were being presented—all opportunities to benefit from the generosity of local benefactors. The baths represent the most common daily activity among men and women, with constant references to Roman social status, cultural values and visual clues to insider or outsider status. If a set of games were being held, the traveler would accompany his local host, effectively making up part of his retinue and extending the reach of the games into the population of other communities.

The evening would often be spent at the home of a member of the local political elite whose position obliges him to regularly host dinners for peers, clients, and guests. Dinner is served to a group of nine people reclining on couches in one of the dining rooms of the host's home. They are served by standing slaves. The dining room is decorated with Greek art and forms, including mosaic floors, painted walls, and Greekstyle furnishings. Entertainment might include performances such as poems, plays, readings, or even private gladiatorial shows. ■

## Suggested Reading


Aldrete, *Daily Life in the Roman City.*

Cantarella and Jacobelli, *A Day in Pompeii.*

Zanker, *Pompeii: Public and Private Life.*


## Questions to Consider

1. In how many different venues in Pompeii would a visitor encounter the names or images of local political leaders and their families? How does this compare to images or names of the imperial family?

2. How do the visual markers of the city operate in allowing a visitor to negotiate the city and understand its political, cultural, and religious identity?

# Putting It All Together I—A Day in Pompeii

## Lecture 34—Transcript

Welcome to this lecture on the city of Pompeii. In this lecture, we're going to do something completely different than any of the other thematic lectures that we've had in this course. What I'm going to try and do here is put all of our themes together into one lecture. So it's going to be very exciting and rather synoptic of the material we've had so far.

What I want to do today is try to follow a day in the life of a typical traveler, a young man we've named Lucius Cassius, a visitor to Pompeii. What we're going to do is follow his journey from, let's say, the Eastern Mediterranean up through Pompeii and his visit to the house of his patron in Pompeii. Through his eyes we will see the city of Pompeii in all of its components, from the outside all the way to its center at the forum, and into the very recesses of the private home. This, I think, will be an excellent way of giving us a good sense of all of those elements of what the city of Pompeii was like. So I really think about this as putting it all together, or sort of daily life in Pompeii.

If you've read the Acts of the Apostles and the account of Paul traveling from the Eastern Mediterranean up into Italy, then you know that you don't sail into Italy directly anywhere except to Puteoli. Puteoli is the main harbor on the Bay of Naples, and it is the major place where ships from the Eastern Mediterranean come in. So we've got a young man, Lucius Cassius, who's, let's say, in the perfume trade. There are connections we know between Pompeii and the perfume trade in the Eastern Mediterranean. He would sail in on a ship, and we have a marvelous painting from the ancient world that shows us what the harbor of Puteoli looked like as you sailed in. The harbor was dominated by a temple to Augustus, and as he entered the harbor on the ship, the captain and crew, and perhaps some of the passengers—although not Paul, of course—would make a sacrifice to the emperor in Thanksgiving of their successful arrival. He would sail past a number of monuments on the harborside, which would reorient him into the Roman world. There's a triumphal-style arch, which we see here in our painting, a number of standing columns with statues on them.

Up above the harbor in the background was the great imperial amphitheater of Puteoli, which is still there. You can see all that today as well.

They would dock and disembark at Puteoli, and from there walk up to Pompeii, just take the road up to Pompeii. As they walked along the road they would pass a number of monuments, milestones along the road, which would tell you who was responsible for the construction of the road and what mile you were at. And the aqueduct which fed the amphitheater, and the other major public buildings at Puteoli, these also served as great markers, telling you that you're back in Roman territory, that the infrastructure is here, and all aspects of government are working here.

As he approaches the city of Pompeii itself our Lucius Cassius would walk up one of the roads outside the city walls, and as he did so and approached the city he would pass a number of tombs. We've got a nice image for you to look at here of a number of tombs outside one of the city gates. We can see the rich variety of these as you approach. If you have good eyes, you can see the little white inscriptions on each of the tombs, little white marble plaques that name the families. Each one of these is a family tomb and it has the name of the family right on the outside.

So as you walk up, what you get is a rich visual display of all of the important individuals in terms of family names. There is the Cornelii, and the Lucretii, and so on, all the way up to the gates. And then outside the gates you'd have some of the most important officials. Notably here in this image we've got a long, low tomb outside the very gates of Pompeii, which has two marble plaques on it, and this is a tomb to a public priestess, Eumachia, given by the local city council. And so this tells you who is important, what the authority is, and who holds the public offices. These tombs actually serve as billboards. Many of these outside this gate are painted in large red advertisements for gladiatorial games, and those are announcements of upcoming games so you can see when there might be games in the amphitheater: gladiatorial contests, animal hunts, prisoner executions, maybe Greek athletes, things like that, and those will all be announced outside. So that sort of local beneficence is projected outside the walls of the local city as well.

Lucius Cassius may not enter Pompeii from this gate. If we look at a plan of the city we can see that whatever direction he comes in, it's very clear that he is going to face an ideologically charged monument, something that's really going to announce the greatness of the city of Pompeii to him. If he comes up from the southeast, he has the amphitheater out there which really tells him about the fact that this is a Roman colony and really establishes Roman cultural values. If he comes up from the seaside, the so-called Maritime Gate, there's an enormously high platform, a large terrace that projects out with the Temple of Venus on it. Venus is the patron deity of the Roman colony of Pompeii, as well as the personal deity of the Sullan family, and Sulla, the dictator, was the man who established the colony here at Pompeii. And so we have religious authority on one side and then we have this wonderful entertainment building on the other, so however you come in you're going to be reoriented to what's important to the Pompeians.

As Lucius approaches the city he will, of course, come through a gate in the walls. Let's say he's here in A.D. 77. We don't want him to be trapped in the eruption of Vesuvius in A.D. 79. By 77 the city walls are vestigial. They just mark the boundaries of the old city. They don't really serve a defensive purpose, but the gates are still here. As he comes in there will be this formal moment where he crosses into the actual city itself.

As he goes through the streets of Pompeii, he might have a problem knowing where he's going because his first stop will probably be the home of his patron. If he's here on business because of, as I say, the perfume business, he would be visiting his patron or business associate. In an ancient Roman city there are no street signs. Streets might have names, but they're not marked anywhere. Street corners also are not going to have signs telling you that you're at a particular intersection. The only thing that's going to mark the corners of streets at Pompeii are little plaques set into the walls, high up, sometimes 10, 12, 15 feet above the pedestrian level.

We have an example of one of these marvelous street corner plaques here and they're really interesting designs because they are geometric patterns They don't give a lot of information about where you are or the name of the street. These are apotropaic plaques designed to keep away evil because intersections, crossroads, are places that are religiously charged in the

Roman world. So you need to have these plaques to keep down the evil of these intersecting spaces because Roman gods are gods of space and place. So these are very important in the city. You have the apotropaic markers, and they're not going to do much for guiding our visitor.

Instead, he might have directions based on public buildings or landmarks, and we know about a few of these, you know, orient yourself by the major public buildings. Go past the Temple of Venus and things like that.

How would he know when he got to the right house? The outsides of houses don't have numbers. There are no street numbers. There are no little plaques saying, "Welcome to the Johnsons," or, "Welcome to the Cornelii," or anything like that. The only thing that's on the outside of these houses that denotes the occupants doesn't tell you their name. It tells you their status, and that is the collection of images of public awards that members of the entire extended family could have won, and so he might be told to come to the house with the civic crown over the door. We've got a good example of one of those still extant from Pompeii in stucco with the civic crown over the door. If somebody had had a military triumphal procession, it might say go to the house with the oak wreaths or the laurel branches on either side of the doorposts. This is really your only hope to guide you to the appropriate house.

Outside those elite houses, as we see here in this house, we have long benches for people to sit and wait for the patron or the occupant of the house if they're here to see the paterfamilias. Lucius, showing up by sea, is not going to have a firm appointment. Who knows when or if a ship is ever going to come in, and he would probably have to sit out here for quite some time. The patron might be busy or he might be out of the house, so he would just sit out here on one of these benches and just while away his time waiting for his appointment.

Once inside the house, Lucius would see an interior which, in itself, like the outside of the city, is designed to reorient him to the values and identity of the occupants. As the tombs and plaques outside the city walls tell you about who is living in the town, the decoration inside tells you about the values of the occupants or inhabitants of the house. Once he's inside he passes through a little foyer into the atrium. We've got a marvelous cutaway of a Pompeian house here. It shows us the rich decoration of the large double-storied atrium. Lucius might come into this atrium and see that the decoration on the walls reflects that of a Macedonian palace. We see that sort of faux massive masonry as is typical of Macedonian palace architecture.

He would also pass, and we have an excellent example here in the reconstruction, a little shrine as he went into the atrium. This is the shrine up on the wall. It looks like the front of a temple facade with a pediment and four columns. This is the shrine for the *imagines*, the images of the ancestors. These might be busts or they might be wax masks, death masks, of prominent members of the family, and those would be on display. So he could come in and he could see these people have decoration based on a Macedonian palace, and there are the images of the ancestors.

He might wait for a while in the atrium. There's a lot of activity going on around him, slaves coming and going, other people coming in to have meetings or to get audiences. The women of the household, who would be doing the domestic duties, mainly having to do with spinning and weaving fabric, would also be out here in the atrium, themselves extending the identity of the family through their work.

If it's a smaller house and a smaller atrium, it might also have a different form of projected identity. Instead of the pretentiousness, perhaps, of a Macedonian palace, it might actually emulate the decoration of an elite villa. Here's another example of a potential house. Here's the atrium and just behind those sliding doors in the back is the *tablinum*, where the master of the house meets with guests. Just to the left of the *tablinum* as we're facing it is another little shrine, again for the *imagines*. The wall paintings here have little insets in the center of them. They're little mythological figural paintings and these, again, show the cultural values of the family because these are scenes of Greek mythology.

There is a number of forms of these houses, and we can see a rich variety of them. If Lucius is coming to see a patron, he's certainly going to have an atrium with a *tablinum* behind for a formal reception, but if he's coming to visit a rich business associate, the man might not be a patron. He might, in fact, not have a house with a *tablinum* or reception rooms at all. He might have one of these houses that's an urban villa where, in fact, the whole center of the house is the garden area. We've got a nice reconstruction here with a sort of vestigial *tablinum* and as you pass through you can see a richly decorated garden behind the house. You might actually come to a house and pass back through there. If somebody wasn't wealthy enough to have their own villa, they would have one of these urban villas, and this is a sign, again, of middle-class status in Pompeii.

So there are a lot of possibilities as he approaches and comes into one of these houses, and Lucius would be able to read through the decoration, through the organization of space, and through the suites of rooms what was here and what wasn't, the status of his business associate, and his expected behavior. If there was an atrium with a formal *tablinum* as we see, for example, at the House of the Faun, his expectation is to await his patron in the atrium. The patron would stand there at the *tablinum*, which is generally raised about four to six inches above the atrium so that the patron is above him as he approaches him. The patron would greet him there from his raised position, and then invite him to step into the *tablinum*, his little office area, for a meeting.

In any case, the decorative scheme, the organization, and so on, establish who he is, what his relationship to the house is, and his expected behavior throughout here. He would certainly visit this house first, come and see his patron here, and then they might conduct business here together. The patron is expected to be at his house every morning, particularly on those days when the local city council meets, and so if Lucius came to Pompeii on a day when the city council was meeting, the patron would be up by dawn for the *salutatio*, greeting all of his clients and business associates, conducting personal business here in the *tablinum*, until they would leave the house. Let's assume that Lucius is here for one of these events and didn't have to spend hours kicking around outside waiting on the bench.

As the patron left the house to go into the forum, Lucius and the other clients would go with him. So they effectively created a visual display of the political and economic power of that patron. As they moved from the house into that formal space, the public space of the forum, they make this display, and you can get sort of a snapshot of everybody's individual importance in Pompeii as they follow the patrons throughout the streets, finally ending in the forum itself.

At the forum we see a rich variety of public buildings and a lot of complex activities taking place in this space. If we look at the north end of the forum, we can see the primary religious structure of the colony, and that is the *capitolium*. As Lucius is here in A.D. 77, as I mentioned, he might see the *capitolium* not a whole lot better than we see it right now because there was an earthquake here in 62, which destroyed much of the *capitolium*, and it hadn't yet been rebuilt by 79, before the great volcanic eruption that eventually buried Pompeii. What had been rebuilt were the shrines to the emperors showing a marvelous redirection of worship, and so as Lucius stands here he might see the ruins of the *capitolium* just below Vesuvius as we see it today, but on the right hand side he would see a series of small shrines to the emperors: to Augustus and to the deified Flavian emperors, Vespasian and Titus. These are very important because what they do is they add to the visual and religious complexity of the forum area.

We have that religious component of the forum, both the traditional as well as the new, but we also have other identities and other activities, and Lucius would see these, too.

At Pompeii we see the *capitolium*, and on either side of it, flanking it actually, in the surrounding buildings of the forum we have two markets, or "*macella*." There is a dry goods markets on the left as you're facing the *capitolium*, and what seems to be a market on the right for fresh vegetables, fish, and meat. Both of these will be very active. The decoration of these spaces is in poor condition, but it's been studied, and it looks as though the decoration here is gendered. It looks like it's actually intended for a female audience. And so as Lucius would look at the *capitolium*, here, sadly, in ruins, he would see a lot more women on the north end of the forum. We have a nice image of the front of that *macellum*. This is the fruit and vegetable market with room inside for fresh fish and meat. We know that from the excavations of the drain system underneath here in remains.

Lucius might walk by this or certainly see it. There are a lot of women coming and going. But then he would see on the outside of this a whole line of statue bases. Each one of these statue bases originally held a bronze statue to a local political official, somebody who was voted space here in the forum by the *decuriones*, the members of the local city council. These are all lined up here in front of the market and it's a curious display as Lucius would see it because these are all lined up in what seems to be an un-prominent space, that is, in front of what might be gendered female space. The reason for that is that they were actually moved out of the center of the forum to make room for a large number of imperial statues, that is, statues to the family of the emperors, and there are a lot of statue bases larger than these in the center of the forum, and we can recognize the remains of statues, too, for example, Caligula and Nero.

So what he can see here as he looks at the *macellum* is really a snapshot of both male identity through the images of these prominent individuals who were voted statues, and then female identity as women go about their domestic tasks of marketing. And then the interior of the market, as I said, is decorated with paintings that we believe are intended to project female identity and virtues to a largely female audience. So that gives the northern end of the forum a curious, sort of unsettled idea of what is male identity on the outside and a tremendous female presence throughout.

If we go down to the south end of the forum, and this is almost certainly where Lucius and his patron would end up, because down at the south end is where we see all the civic buildings, the curia, the local senate house or city council chambers. There is a whole range of buildings down there. The most prominent and important of these is the basilica. The basilica is down here at the south end of the forum. It's a large columned hall, which is a multiple-use space. It's for a lot of business activities, but most importantly, it is for law cases. The basilica provides large, open inside space for law cases to be heard so that inside here lawyers would be arguing cases to large juries. There would be a lot of public business taking place.

We have a nice shot here of the facade of the basilica. In front of the basilica is a white marble colonnade, which is actually the colonnade of the forum. You go in and you step up two steps into the basilica itself, and you see the remains of these brick columns which separated the central aisle from the side aisles. These in the ancient world were all heavily stuccoed so they looked like marble. We see behind the wall there is better preserved with all stucco decoration. As Lucius would see it, it would look like a Greek Macedonian hall. The stucco is carved to look like huge blocks of marble. All of this material looks all so enormous.

At the very end is a large tribunal, that is, a large platform where the judges would sit. The usefulness of this tribunal is somewhat mitigated by the fact that right in the center of it somebody put in an enormous statue. There's a great equestrian statue on a tremendously high base, which would have actually blocked the view of the jury, and would have made it very tricky to see and hear legal cases in here. But it emphasizes the importance of projecting that local identity. This is actually not an imperial statue, but a statue to a local benefactor of the community.

The morning would probably be spent here at the basilica. If Lucius is here with his patron, they might attend a legal case or listen to the lawyers. These are public spaces and that was a common thing for people to do, to go down to the forum and listen to the lawyers or attend a city council meeting or whatever your public duties were, and that would take place in the morning. Much of the morning would be given over to that sort of activity.

The afternoons would be somewhat different. Time in the afternoon could be given over to hours spent at the local bathing complexes. Here at Pompeii there are a number of these: the forum baths, the Stabian baths, the so-called "Central baths," and since only twothirds of the city has been excavated, who knows how many more there are. But if Lucius is going to the most prominent of these, he might actually go to the Stabian baths just down the main street from the forum, a large, lavishly redecorated bath complex after the earthquake of 62.

He would go in and go through the bathing, and as I mentioned in another lecture, the Stabian baths were very gender-divided. You would have suites of rooms for men, and another suite for women. Here is a reconstruction of what we think is the women's *caldarium*, with women seated in here in the hot plunge, or standing around that cold basin splashing water on their faces.

The baths, again, are a very common social activity, common meaning ordinary, but also common meaning shared. Everybody bathes together here at the baths. And so you would see everybody here has an opportunity to network and to conduct business. The baths also serve to reinforce the identities of the elite members of society because elite members like Lucius's business associate would show up with retinues, with their own clients or slaves in tow, and so you would know who the important individuals were.

He would also see names carved on some of the material here in the baths, like that basin that we see, or on chairs and benches and things like that, naming dedications. So you would see who the prominent people were in town.

He would go into the baths and enter the *apodyterium*, the changing room, take off his clothes, maybe do a little exercise out on the *palestra*, and then come into the *frigidarium*, the little cold plunge right off the *apodyterium*, and splash into the cold water for a while to cool down after exercising. Then he would make his way casually through the rooms of the bath. There is no set prescriptive pattern here. Instead, he could come and go as he pleased through the set of rooms.

He might spend, as I say, hours at the bath, but there might be other things in town to do in the afternoon. We have a nice schedule of the spectacles at Pompeii, and we know that they occurred all times of the year. There might be a set of games at the amphitheater. If he passed into the city through the gate and passed those tombs he might see painted on one of them an announcement of a set of games: May 23rd, 24th, and 25th, set of games at the amphitheater, ten pairs of gladiators a day, animal hunts, prisoners executions. The awnings will be used. That's a standard sort of format. So if his patron wanted to attend the games at the amphitheater, Lucius would as well.

Let's say he's a good middle-class businessman, not a member of the upper-level elite, but a wealthy up-and-comer. He would come into the amphitheater, not through the restrictive upper-class seating, but through the regular seating with everybody else, the exterior stairways leading up, and come down into the cavea and take a seat maybe halfway down with the regular common populous. He wouldn't sit by himself, of course. He would sit with his patron and his patron's entire retinue. This, again, extends the authority of his patron, but also extends the audience for these games. We know, for example, that people did travel long distances to come to these gladiatorial games. Even at Pompeii we know that they traveled sometimes hundreds of miles to attend a set of games. And so this reinforces the local political system because these are all, of course, being paid for by local political officials as part of their official duties or running for office.

Games, of course, can only be held in the daylight. There is no good artificial light in the Roman world, no reliable artificial light. You have little smoky oil lamps and candles, so theatrical performances, games, and visiting the baths are all daytime activities. All of these things would occur in the afternoon.

In the evening, it's time for dinner. If, in fact, Lucius has come a long way, his patron would be expected to have a lavish dinner for him, an almost formal banquet.

Banqueting in the Roman world is a regular activity, and it is an accepted thing that patrons have to do. You're expected to make regular invitations to your peers, as well as your social and political inferiors, your clients. You're supposed to invite them on a regular basis into your house to dine. It's one of the expectations of rank in the Roman world.

So the evening would be given over to entertainment at the home of his patron. They would pass back into the house, but they wouldn't linger in the atrium or the *tablinum* because those are areas for business or reception. Instead, they would pass through to the *triclinium*, the dining room. The name comes from the three dining couches that are laid out as large dining couches, three people on each couch. And so you would have a standard dinner party of nine individuals. These could go on for hours, and we have lots of evidence of that from the ancient world.

There's a marvelous wall painting here from a house at Pompeii that shows one of these dinner parties. What we have here are five individuals; six really, but one of them isn't a guest, actually. There are two pairs of couples, and then on the far left is a woman who is ready for a dinner party. She's got a garland on her head and she's ready for a party, and she has a slave holding her up. She's got a loose grip on her wine cup and she looks like she's just about to fall over. A slave is holding her up. This gives us a sense of what's going on at this dinner party; lots of drinking.

The dinner itself would be multiple-course food, a rich variety of things: stuffed lettuce, stuffed dormice, all parts of animals that we generally don't eat, or at least I don't. I'm not big on brains and dormice, but they're a regular part of Roman fare. I have had oxtail soup, which was actually pretty good. But the Romans have a rich variety of foods that are designed to show the sophistication of the host. Those would all take place in these dining rooms that are lavishly decorated with scenes from Greek mythology, mosaic floors, painted walls, which again, all project the cultural identity of the patron. It's an inclusive cultural identity.

There would be entertainment here as well, plays, poems, readings of literature might be performed, or even private gladiatorial shows here, maybe in the dining room and maybe in the gardens behind the house. The patron is obliged to entertain his guests at a level, no matter what their social status, which reflects upon his tastes, and the tastes of all of elite Romans.

When the evening was over, Lucius would spend the night here at his patron's house. Inns were for lower-class individuals and people who just had no friends in the area. So he would be expected to be put up by his patron. At the end of the day, when the night was over and the next day, he might leave Pompeii and make his way up to Rome. But that, I think, is a topic for our next lecture.

# Putting It All Together II—A Day in Rome

## Lecture 35

**This lecture takes a fictional Roman, Marcus Cassius, through the capital city in the year A.D. 115. We follow his visit from his arrival at Portus to his exploration of the city.**

A visitor to Rome might approach the city as did the majority of people, through the harbor at Portus, sailing up the Tiber and then entering the city on the north side. Sailing into Portus, Cassius passes a series of monuments with layers of meaning, from the exterior monuments in the Claudian harbor to the Trajanic one in the inner basin. The lighthouse, with its colossal statue of Claudius, would mark the end of the dangerous sea voyage. The temple and altar at the end of the quay provide an opportunity to give thanks to the emperor for safe arrival. The Trajanic monuments of the inner harbor, a colossal statue and triumphal arch, change the theme to one of Trajan's recent wars.

After a short boat ride up the Tiber, Cassius would enter Rome from the docks along the north edge of the city, where the area outside the city walls was transformed into a monumental landscape of imperial commemoration. The area adjacent to the docks was developed by Augustus into a park containing his mausoleum, a large inscription recording his lifetime achievements, the Ara Pacis (his altar of peace), and a tremendous sundial. As Cassius walks down the Via Flaminia into Rome, he passes other imperial tombs and monuments in the Campus Martius.

On entering the city itself, the visitor is faced with a range of public spaces and activities, although Cassius's attention would probably be drawn to the Capitoline Hill and the new addition to the imperial forums added by Trajan, both immediately ahead of him at the end of the Via Flaminia. On reaching the end of the Via Flaminia, he would climb the Capitoline Hill to the Temple of Jupiter Optimus Maximus. He could then walk through the small valley of the asylum of Romulus to the Temple of Juno Moneta. From the Capitoline Hill itself, one gains a panoramic view of the city that would display the changes that had occurred particularly under the emperors, with the largest and grandest buildings in Rome built in the past 100 years.

The Forum Romanum itself might look quaint compared to the new imperial forums adjacent to it. The largest of the imperial forums was that of Trajan, just at the base of the Capitoline Hill to the north. From the Forum of Trajan, one would naturally pass into the Forum of Augustus. From the Forum of Augustus, those of Caesar, Domitian, and Vespasian are accessible, and Cassius crosses the latter two as he makes his way to the entertainment district to the east. As Cassius crosses the Forum of Augustus, the statues of the *summi viri* and the rich variety of military trophies under the colonnades echo the military motif of Trajan's forum. In the Forum of Domitian, the imagery changes dramatically to that of domestic virtues, with the temple and reliefs of Minerva and female domestic virtue balancing the otherwise warlike public areas. Finally, the Flavian Forum of Peace returns the imagery to war with the spoils of the Jewish war on display. Cassius then leaves these formal integrated spaces for those around the Colosseum.

**On entering the city itself, the visitor is faced with a range of public spaces and activities.**

The Flavian construction projects continue beyond the Forum of Peace with the Colosseum, Baths of Titus, and various monuments that connect this area back to the triumphal route and the Forum Romanum. The Colosseum, with its four-story facade and immense bulk, dominates this building program along the east end of the forums. Just beyond the Colosseum are the Baths of Titus and the Baths of Trajan. From the Colosseum, Cassius might follow the other Flavian monuments to the Arch of Titus on a small hill along the Sacred Way overlooking the Forum Romanum at the base of the Palatine Hill.

The Palatine Hill might be considered a monumental synopsis of the history of Rome, so as Cassius climbs the hill along the path from the Arch of Titus, what he encounters will reveal a visual history of Rome. From the forum side of the hill, the palaces of the emperors dominate the view and the majority of the land on the Palatine. The palaces of Tiberius and Caligula as well as sections of the palace of Nero are visible. The buildings around the House of Augustus encapsulate the development of the hill and of Rome. Just down the slope from the House of Augustus and the House of Romulus is the Lupercal, the traditional location where the wolf rescued Romulus and Remus. Near the House of Romulus are the remaining republican monuments, the Temples of Victory and Magna Mater, dating back to the Second Punic War. The final temple in this corner is that of Apollo, built by Augustus. It is the first temple in Rome completed in marble; it links the imperial constructions with the republican victory temples here and just below the hill along the triumphal route. ■

## Suggested Reading

Aldrete, *Daily Life in the Roman City*.

Carcopino, *Daily Life in Ancient Rome*.

Stambaugh, *The Ancient Roman City*.

## Questions to Consider

1. During the course of Cassius's walk through Rome, how do monuments of imperial power create zones of thematic decoration and identity?

2. In what ways do the imperial monuments reference earlier works, and how do they compete or compare with them?

# Putting It All Together II—A Day in Rome

## Lecture 35—Transcript

Welcome to this lecture on a day in Rome. What I want to do here is take a look at Rome in a different way than we have previously. We've spent a lot of time in the city so far, looked at quite a few monuments, but we looked at them in one of two ways: either by subject, looking at temples, or palaces, or particular spaces like imperial forums, or by area, dissecting the Forum Romanum, for example. What I want to do here is very different. What I would like us to focus on throughout this lecture are the intersections and interconnections between those monuments that we've already introduced throughout the lectures. You can see how all the public areas of Rome, all of the monuments that we see, and the urban spaces that they are created in, work together to give a visual impact about the identity and values of the city of Rome.

Now we might do this as a daily life thing, somebody waking up in the morning, leaving their house, and walking down the street. But to be honest, most people's daily lives are kind of dull and the sorts of things that we would want to explore in a daily life, where you're going to market and things like that, we don't know about ancient Rome. We don't know where people went grocery shopping in ancient Rome.

We do know a lot about the public buildings and monuments, so what we're going to do is follow the route of a fictional traveler. We've given him the name Marcus Cassius. Marcus Cassius will enter the city of Rome as a tourist, and we know from the accounts of Pliny the Elder that people did this in the Roman world. People came to Rome as tourists and Pliny tells us where you should send somebody or take somebody when they come to Rome, what buildings they should see. And we are going to see those; don't worry. We'll follow what Marcus Cassius sees and try and see Rome synoptically, in the spaces, looking at the types of monuments and the types of urban environment that we've built up separately altogether here. We'd better get started, then, because that's quite a bit to accomplish.

Let's start with our visitor, Marcus Cassius. He's going to enter Rome the way the vast majority of people in the ancient world would, and that is by sea. Cassius would sail into the great Roman harbor at Portus. I say harbor. It's two harbors, constructed first under Claudius and then Trajan. We have a nice mosaic here from the area, which is actually in a museum in Rome now, and you can go and see it. We'll see Marcus Cassius's ship sailing past the lighthouse in the Claudian, or outer harbor of Portus. The lighthouse with its colossal statue of Claudius is there, welcoming him back into Roman territory and telling him once again, or reminding him, of Roman authority and Roman religion. He'd pass the lighthouse on one side of the harbor mouth, and on the other would be a temple and an altar so that as he's coming through, and this would certainly be the case for most ships, the captain and crew would make a sacrifice as they passed in thanksgiving for having made a successful sea voyage. That would all take place as they would not just view these monuments, but engage with them. They might sail into the inner harbor, where we see the great Trajanic monuments, a colossal statue of Trajan and a temple of Dionysus with Trajan's identity as the new Dionysus. All of this would flow by as he sails into that great inner harbor basin of Trajan's.

From that point, he would probably transfer to a small boat and sail up the Tiber because the large seagoing vessels can't make it up the Tiber. So a very short boat ride would take Marcus Cassius from Portus and up the Tiber River to the city of Rome itself.

When he got to Rome, he would encounter Rome from the south side up to the north side, where the ship would dock, so we'll take him along that route. As he's passing the city of Rome, we see most of it on the right as he's going up the river. What we see along the edge of the river, and you can still see this today if you go to Rome, is a variety of monuments from a rich number of periods, from the very earliest periods of ancient Rome to what is the period that he is in, the 2nd century.

As you are going up the river, you would first pass the early republican areas outside the walls of Rome, the old cattle market, the Forum Boarium. And then you'd pass—and Cassius would certainly recognize these—the small Hellenized temples of Portunus and Hercules built in the late republic when Rome had just started to adopt Greek-style architecture on a small scale. The temples would be there, and then he'd pass under a series of bridges, all constructed starting in the late republic, the first of these in 73 B.C., still there for Cassius and still there for us today. All of these would help define the city of Rome. As he passed the city of Rome, sailing up the Tiber, the area to the right of where he is, is called the Campus Martius, the great flood plain of the Tiber. Because it's a flood plain, it was developed late and because it was developed late, it was developed much more thematically in an organized way than the center of the city. Remember, Livy tells us that Rome looks like it was occupied rather than settled. The Campus Martius is an exception, and we see here a great example of thematic development.

Sailing up the Tiber, he would pass three major theaters: the theater of Marcellus first, the theater of Balbus second, and then finally, the greatest and earliest of all the Roman theaters in the city of Rome, the theater of Pompey, instantly recognizable and, in fact, dominating this area of the Campus Martius. The theater of Pompey, dedicated in 52 B.C., is there as a prominent marker out in the Campus Martius, but he would see it from the Tiber.

When he got up the Tiber, he would disembark at a little port, or a little harbor facility, on the banks of the Tiber just north of the center of the city. That area is right next to where the Emperor Augustus built his mausoleum and reconfigured the area around it into a park. So Cassius would step off his boat, step up the steps that lead up to the banks of the Tiber, and before him would be the mausoleum of Augustus. He'd see the park around that, Augustus announcing his rule and his dynasty, but also bringing the benefits of his rule to the Romans by creating this wonderful green space.

Cassius would [walk] past the mausoleum of Augustus, past Augustus's great *horologium*, his great sundial and enormous pavement laid out there in the Campus Martius with its obelisk, reminding the Romans of Augustus's capture of Egypt, and then past a smaller monument, the Ara Pacis, the Altar of Augustan Peace.

Just past that is the route leading into the city of Rome itself, and that's the Via Flaminia. It's still the route you take today from this area. If you came up the Tiber and walked across the northern Campus Martius, you'd go down the Via del Corso, which is the Via Flaminia. Cassius would walk down the Via Flaminia, and as he did he would pass, again, this time with the Campus

Martius on his right, a number of different thematic monuments. Along with the mausoleum of Augustus, we see in the northern Campus Martius a rich number of imperial funerary monuments and temples to emperors. Campus Martius redefines the exterior of the city of Rome based on its imperial rulers.

So we have the mausoleum of Augustus and the temple to the deified Hadrian. He would also pass some of the most powerful and notable, and certainly the largest, of all of the great monuments out here in the Campus Martius, and that is the set of imperial victory columns. The great column of Antoninus Pius is out here and the great column of Marcus Aurelius. He would walk within 60 feet of that going down the Via Flaminia and see that great column of Marcus Aurelius off to his right, again, 100 feet tall, all carved in relief decoration, richly painted, giving a vivid account of Marcus Aurelius's battles. And so again, by the 2nd century, the whole Campus Martius is developed as a means for the emperors to display their rule and their identities. And they are separate identities to those who are passing into the city.

As you pass down the Via Flaminia, you pass through the Campus Martius and enter into the old city of Rome as it was in the ancient world and, as I say, you can still do this today. In the 2nd century, as Cassius is coming down here, he would pass through one set of walls, and that is the old Serbian wall from the 4th century B.C., now seemingly very close to the old Roman city and seeming kind of quaint in how small it is.

The Via Flaminia terminates down at the base of the Capitoline Hill and that hill, with the great Temple of Jupiter Capitolinus, is the largest monument in Rome in that it is the highest area. It's the tallest peak with the tallest building on it. It would serve as a beacon, and you would make your way toward that. Cassius, as a tourist here, would certainly do that, making his way through the Campus Martius and the more recent buildings, but inexorably being drawn, as people are today, to the Capitoline Hill.

He would head down the Via Flaminia and come to the base of the Capitoline Hill with the great Temple of Jupiter above him, and he'd notice that the Capitoline Hill is, in fact, not just one large mound, but two small mounds, with a little valley in between. He would head up that switchback road leading up to the Capitoline Hill—you can still follow much of the same route today—and eventually make his way up to the little valley or saddle in between, and then gradually up to the highest of these peaks.

When he got there, what he would see up on the Capitoline Hill was the great Temple of Jupiter Optimus Maximus. Now the Temple of Jupiter is the earliest of the extant temples in Rome. It was built under the last of the Roman kings, Tarquin the Proud, and dedicated in 509 B.C., when the Roman Republic was founded. But by this time, in the 2nd century, the temple is not alone. It's not standing by itself. It is, in fact, only the first and earliest of a whole series of religious monuments that fill this end of the hill. You've got other temples to Jupiter Tonans, Jupiter the Thunderer, and Jupiter Feretrius, Jupiter the Stayer of Light, and then altars and dedications. A whole line of dedications of military diplomas are nailed up on the outside podium of Jupiter Capitolinus. Every time a member of the military served out his allotted period of enlistment, which could be 20 or 25 years, he would get a diploma stating that he had completed his service, and a copy of that is nailed up on the outside of the Temple of Jupiter as an example of Roman military service. So there's a rich variety of monuments here that are agglutinative; they add over time. So it becomes crowded, not just with monuments, but with meaning as well.

We might pass across that high rise of the Temple of Jupiter, across the little saddle in the center, which was never built over. The little saddle between the two slopes of the Capitoline is always kept open because that is actually one of the oldest monuments in Rome. It's the open area where Romulus had asylum, that is, he set up an altar there so that anybody who wanted to could come and could become a Roman citizen by touching that altar. We'll pretend my podium is the altar. This is a very powerful space for the Romans because it marks the origins of their notion of inclusive citizenship, something that is unique in the entire ancient world and it's always preserved here. They don't build over that. The area is still open today, but it's been reconfigured by Michelangelo. So you go up there in that wonderful piazza by Michelangelo on the Capitoline and you'll see the same spot where the asylum altar was.

From there you can cross up to the other part of the Capitoline Hill and the Temple of Juno Moneta. While Cassius is up there, he might see the flock of sacred geese that are up there continually, different geese, of course, over time. These geese have been here since the early republican period, and they are credited with saving the republic by honking in warning as invaders tried to take the Capitoline Hill at one point.

He might stand and turn while he's up here at the Capitoline Hill, and get spectacular panoramic views down below. This is an excellent place to turn your back to these Temples of Jupiter and Juno and the best place to do this is at the auguroculum. It's a great open square where you can stand today and look out over the forum down below you the way Roman augurs did. In the ancient world it was a spot for augurs to examine the skies and look for flights of birds and things, and try to divine the will of the gods.

Today, it's a great place to get a sense of the great sweep of Roman art and architecture and truly the history that it represents down in the forum below you because the Capitoline stands just above the Forum Romanum. So if you stand there at the auguroculum and look down on the forum, you can look over here on the left and just at the edge of the forum, almost below your feet, you can see the senate house, the curia, as it was rebuilt by Julius Caesar. In front of that the spot is marked where Romulus's apotheosis took place, the Lapis Niger, the black rock, the black pavement. Looking around, you can see a whole range of monuments added together that make up the Regal, republican, and imperial identities of the Forum Romanum. There are the Regal monument of Romulus, the republican monuments of the senate, and the great basilicas rebuilt by the emperors, but still on the same ground plan so you can see the monuments that tell us about civic government and law and how important those are.

And then, of course, there are the imperial monuments. The senate house to the left is rebuilt by Caesar. Just in front of that is the great Arch of Septimius Severus, his great triumphal arch, the last one in the forum, which dominates the western end.

Going past that you see the Basilica Aemilia, and then at the far end of the forum, immediately across from you, is the Temple of the Divine Julius

Caesar. Just beyond that you might be able to make out the Temple of the Divine Antoninus Pius. And if everything is just right, in the far distance you can see the Arch of Titus and the Colosseum just beyond the limits of the forum. Looking slightly to the right, past the Temple of the Divine Julius Caesar, you can see Caesar's Basilica. And so laid out down here at Cassius's feet, and at your feet if you go, is the whole history of the forum. In stone, or marble, or concrete, we see a history of Roman political achievement, all of their political forums reflected in the building types and styles that we have down below.

Also from the Capitoline, Cassius could turn his attention away from the forum, which might look a little crowded, and frankly, somewhat quaint at this point, and he might turn his attention instead, slightly to the left, where we see the great additions to the Forum Romanum, those five major additions, the so-called "imperial forums," started by Julius Caesar and then added to by Augustus, Vespasian, Domitian, and then finally, Trajan. And these are laid out, again, like a panorama. Starting from left to right you'd see the Forum of Trajan, then Augustus, Julius Caesar, the Forum Domitian or Forum Transitorium, and then the Forum of Peace, of Vespasian, all laid out.

This would be a wonderful temptation to descend at this point from the Capitoline Hill and go down and walk through each one of these because they are all interconnected. Although they are walled discrete spaces, they do join one another. Pliny the Elder tells us that these are some of the finest buildings and, in particular, he notes that you have to send people through the Forum of Augustus and the Forum of Peace when they come to town because those are two of the three buildings everybody has to see, along with the theater of Pompey, which I named earlier. So, I think we'd be remiss if we didn't send Cassius through them.

He would descend the Capitoline steps at this point and pass through each one of these imperial forums. The largest and first that he would find on the western side is the Forum of Trajan, with his great rich collection of buildings, libraries, a basilica, and markets on the hillside beyond. But what Cassius might be most aware of is the decorative program. The decorative program of Trajan's Forum is dominated by Trajan's Column, easily visible from the top of the Capitoline, but easy to inspect down below, walking around it in the forum, with those images of Trajan's Dacian campaign. They are vividly colored and accessible as he goes down. As he walked past that, through the basilica Opia into the main piazza of the forum, he would see the great Trajanic frieze, this almost 10-foot-tall relief that goes for, perhaps, as much as 600 feet around the outside of the forum. And this is augmented by statues of Dacian prisoners, as well as images of triumphant Trajan himself, giving a real imagery of warfare throughout the entire forum.

Crossing out of Trajan's Forum, you would come next to the Forum of Augustus, recognizable for its adjacency to the Forum of Trajan and the great semi-circular hemicycles. The Forum of Augustus is dominated by a temple of Mars, and also has this consistent imagery of warfare. By the $2^{nd}$ century, the statues that make up the pedestrian level decoration of the *summi viri*, the great generals of ancient Rome, are still there. But they would, in fact, have a screen in front of them and it's a screen of Roman military trophies because by the $2^{nd}$ century, triumphant generals, by this point, have been coming back to Rome for over 100 years and depositing under the colonnades around the forum, in front of the statues of the *summi viri*, captured military standards: arms, armor, weaponry, and things that are characteristic of their great military achievements. So the decorations of the Forums of Trajan and Augustus are reflecting one another. He would pass through those, see these real monuments and, effectively, museums to Roman military achievements throughout both of these forums.

He might go through the Forum of Caesar, but it's a little out of the way. It also, of course, has the same museum aspect, but he would certainly have to pass through the Forum Transitorium, the little passageway forum of Domitian. As he did so, he would recognize, I think instantly, that this is not like the other fora that we passed through. The Forum Transitorium, with it's great Temple of Minerva, is decorated with reliefs along the inside of domestic virtues, particularly female domestic virtue. It's a very strong contrast to the two previous spaces, really richly decorated with Roman male military imagery.

Passing through the Forum Transitorium, he would go next to the Forum of Peace constructed by Domitian's father, Vespasian, and here he returns to the imagery of warfare, notably, the imagery of warfare in the celebration of the great Jewish War, the great Jewish Revolt under Nero that Vespasian subdued along with his son. Titus subdued brutally, giving him the money for this forum, and the museum aspect of this forum is the material from that Jewish Revolt here under the colonnades surrounding the open area.

The other thing about this forum that I think would be instantly recognizable to anybody who knew this area of Rome, or perhaps had a tour guide, is that this forum is not like the others. It's square, not rectangular. It's at one end, and actually, it's part of a larger building complex not originally planned to be attached to the other imperial forums, but to be attached to the building further east. Because what we see, and what Cassius would walk through, is the Forum of Peace and see the great fountains and the plantings in it. We have a marvelous plan to show you of the Forum of Peace and you can see long lines of greenery. It's a real lush greenness to the Forum of Peace that we don't have in any of the other imperial forums.

Just beyond that is the tremendous bulk of the Colosseum, the Flavian Amphitheater, also built by Vespasian. So after he passes through the Forum of Peace and gets a sense of the wonder and the tranquility of this, he would, I think, get a strong change of Roman identity when he comes to the Colosseum and sees this four-story tall tremendous building, about 120 feet tall. It's the largest amphitheater in the Roman world and, I think Cassius would just be awed to see this. Any visitor would because it just looms above you and it looks monolithic. When it's clean it's all gleaming white. The upper stories are long arcades all the way around of 80 arches on each story. Each arch has a statue in it, and you might walk around the outside if there are no games taking place and just look at this imagery of Roman power, the dedicatorian inscriptions saying that this was dedicated by Vespasian with the proceeds from the Jewish War, that same theme that he had from the Forum of Peace. It's also part of a great complex, however, of entertainment. Right next to the Colosseum are the baths of Titus. Cassius would see the baths of Titus there, and then on a hill above them, looming over them and dominating the baths of Titus, are the great baths of Trajan. In Cassius's terms, newly constructed there to augment and extend the notion that this is an entertainment district. Once again, we get that idea that the Romans are building thematically.

The Colosseum doesn't stand by itself. It's next to the baths of Titus, and eventually the baths of Trajan. And then further to the east, just beyond that, Cassius might walk over and see the four great gladiatorial schools that were set up here and constructed under the Flavians as well as under Vespasian, Titus, and the youngest and last of the Flavian emperors, Domitian. You might see the great Ludus Magnus, the great gladiatorial school, and the other three gladiatorial schools laid out here immediately adjacent to the Colosseum, giving this entire area of Rome a sense of public entertainment, with the baths, the Colosseum, the gladiatorial schools and the Forum of Peace. There's a great sense here of public dedication in this entire area, all from Cassius's perspective, very recent, all gleaming white and very new.

From here, a visitor probably wouldn't go any further east. There's not a lot more to see here. He'd probably backtrack a little bit and make his way up the Sacra Via, the portion of the triumphal procession route, passing a couple of triumphal arches, certainly passing under the Arch of Titus. At this point, having seen the imperial fora and Forum Romanum, he would probably turn left and make his way up to the Palatine Hill.

Up on the Palatine, what we see and what Cassius would instantly recognize, is a synopsis of all of Roman history. We see that at a distance if we look panoramically through the Forum Romanum, but you can see it up close on the Palatine Hill. On the side facing the Forum Romanum where Cassius is going to enter up and walk up onto the Palatine, what we see imperial palaces begun by Tiberius and added to by Caligula, Nero, and then the Flavians, all adding so that finally the entire top of the Palatine Hill on the north and east side is a palace, giving us our word "palace" from the name of the hill.

He might pass through some of the public areas of the palace because they are open, but then make his way across to the opposite side, to the south side of the Palatine. From there, he'd get a spectacular panoramic view down into the Circus Maximus looking down off the edge of the Palatine Hill and, again, parts of the palace are public area, so as far as we can tell everybody could enter them at any time, keeping in mind Vitruvius's dictum that gardens and peristyles are public areas of a Roman house, and the house would be no exception. He might look down and see the Circus Maximus laid out below him and Domitian's skybox over to the left, and really get a sense of the grandeur on this area of the hill.

If he turned around at this point and looked, he's right there on the southwest edge of the Palatine Hill. And here on the southwest corner of the Palatine is where we see this synopsis take place. If he's fortunate, he can look to the southwest and see a series of very small, and at this point, seemingly kind of quaint and small monuments, but these are some of the most vitally symbolically charged monuments in all of Rome. Down on the very edge of the southwest corner of the hill is the old House of Romulus, still preserved with its foundations cut into the bedrock of the hill, and it burns down occasionally as the city of Rome burns, but it's always rebuilt on the same ground plan. There's the House of Romulus right there.

Next to the House of Romulus is a pair of republican temples, the great and important Temple of Victory, and next to it a slightly larger Temple of Magna Mater, the great mother goddess, brought by the Romans from Phrygia, central Asia Minor, into Italy to get rid of Hannibal in fulfillment of an oracle of the Sibyl.

Looking past these, you would see the first Temple of Apollo inside the walls of Rome built by Augustus and a component of Augustus's now very small seeming house, the house of Augustus, and the complex of the Temple of Apollo.

The one thing he wouldn't see here from the top of the hill is perhaps the oldest monument. Down below, under the house of Augustus and under the house of Romulus is the Lupercal, the little grotto or cave where the she-wolf suckled Romulus and Remus, and that's still preserved as well; articulated and architecturally enhanced by Augustus, but still there. And Cassius's final step, sort of going back in time, he might go down there and reflect upon the origins of Rome in this simple little cave down below on the slopes of the Palatine Hill.

As we've walked through the city of Rome with Marcus Cassius, I hope you get a sense of how every emperor, every period in ancient Rome, adds to the city of Rome. It's all a tremendously additive monument with tremendous intersections and a great sense of interconnections between the monuments throughout every stage and every part of this urban space of the city.

## Conclusions and the Images of Empire

### Lecture 36

**Rome has been widely acknowledged as one of the most successful political structures in world history. Its success depended in large part on the visual elements that projected, defined, and established Roman power across its empire.**

Rome's success in projecting its values and culture still resonates today, as can be seen in the adoption of Roman standards, particularly (but not exclusively) in Western culture. The emulation of Roman urban planning and symbolic entrances is found through the use of gates and entrances along boulevards and avenues across the Western world. Perhaps the best and arguably most famous example is the Brandenburg Gate in Berlin, which combines Roman urban planning with passage architecture as found throughout the Roman Empire. The Golden Gate of Constantinople, the new Rome founded by Constantine, inspired many other examples as far away as Kiev. A very American version is the Roosevelt Arch marking the north entrance to Yellowstone Park, with its inscription, "For the Benefit and Enjoyment of the People."

Triumphal arches were probably the most imitated Roman monumental form, because they were erected with triumphal or other themes across the world. The Arc de Triomphe in Paris, like the Brandenburg Gate in Berlin, is a major arterial monument, but it is more directly modeled on Roman triumphal arches in its size, proportions, and decoration. Further famous examples of triumphal arches are found in London and New York, but variations are found across Europe, Russia, and Asia. Pyongyang, North Korea, erected one of the largest and most recent of these in 1982. Perhaps the most distant of these arches thematically and geographically is the Independence Gate in Seoul, South Korea, which is modeled on the Roman triumphal arch but celebrates Korean independence from China.

The emulation of Roman visual vocabulary reaches its greatest extent in the United States, with its self-conscious modeling on Roman government as well as building forms and monuments. The federal buildings in Washington

DC are deliberately designed based on Roman models, and the themes of law, liberty, and republican government are found repeatedly. The U.S. Capitol, with its rotunda and classical facade, is based on Roman architectural forms. The design of the Supreme Court building is based on the Temple of Jupiter Capitolinus, with its tall podium and its pedimental entrance containing a sculptural group of Liberty, suggesting that the role of law is comparable to that of Jupiter in this republic.

The monumentalization of the National Mall owes its inspiration to the Forum Romanum, with its monuments to the great men of Rome and its celebration of key values of the republic. The Lincoln Memorial is effectively a Doric temple to Abraham Lincoln. The Washington Monument reflects the obelisks brought to Rome and erected by Augustus, the first Roman emperor, who was also named father of his country. The Jefferson Memorial references the Pantheon in Rome, the best-preserved Roman temple to survive and also the inspiration for Jefferson's rotunda at the University of Virginia. The World War II Memorial contains reliefs evocative of Roman arches. The standing and equestrian bronze statues that decorate Washington are the descendents of the Roman versions that decorated the forum and religious precincts.

**The Roosevelt Arch at the northern entrance to Yellowstone National Park. This feature is one of many emulations around the world of Roman symbolic entrances**

## Suggested Reading

Elsner, *Art and the Roman Viewer*.

Greenberg, *Architecture of Democracy*.

## Questions to Consider

1. The proliferation of arches clearly marks them as the most popular Roman monument form. What contributes to that success? Is it the versatility of the form or the universal appeal of victory monuments?

2. In what ways do the Roman buildings and monuments of Washington DC emulate the values as well as the forms of Roman public buildings?

# Conclusions and the Images of Empire

## Lecture 36—Transcript

Welcome to this lecture on the reception of the visual vocabulary of ancient Rome. Now, the Roman Empire is widely regarded as one of the most successful, long-lasting, and certainly broad-ranging governmental forms in world history. Its success, of course, depended largely upon the visual aspects of the Roman world. It's through the visual that we've talked about so often now that the Romans defined and projected their power, and really shaped their world and announced their identities. These visual forms still resonate today, and we see that through their adoption.

What we're going to look at here is the adoption of Roman building forms throughout history. Not just the forms of monuments, but really the organization of urban space and the themes that the Romans used in their buildings that continued in later cultures. I think these serve as an important touchstone for power and for values. When people adopt the forms, and by people I mean not just individuals but governments and nations, whether they are democracies or not, they are really engaging with the ideas behind these visual elements. There's a strong connection between the form of a Roman monument and an idea behind it. And so when somebody, or some government, accepts these monuments to adopt or adapt for their own purposes, they are really engaging with what the Romans did here. And so I think it's very important for us to see how these forms are received and emulated and to think about what that means in terms of how these are used.

Rome, therefore, becomes a lens through which later people see and judge their own cultures. We constantly, as Americans, often reflect on how much we are like Rome. Are we like the Roman Republic? Are we like the Roman Empire? And we as Americans should do that because we have been particularly aggressive about using Roman forms, Roman monuments, and Roman urban space in our own monuments and urban space. So we'll take a look at those as well as bit later.

One of the most powerful and wide-ranging forms that we see from ancient Rome is the form of the gateway. When talking about triumphal monuments in Rome, I have termed these gateways and arches as armatures of celebration

And we see these repeated throughout history, not just in the western world, but across the entire world. I think this is a remarkable idea, and I want to show you some examples and talk about what these might mean as we see these emulations.

One of the best examples of this sort of armature of celebration is the Brandenburg Gate in Berlin. You may be familiar with this, and we have a great image of it here. The Brandenburg Gate is almost like a triumphal arch. It has, in fact, the culminating group at the top. We have a *quadrigae* being driven by the personification of Victory herself. There's Victory, this woman with the wings, driving a triumphal chariot, a *quadrigae*. But down below, the actual gateway doesn't directly emulate a Roman triumphal arch. Instead, it emulates a gateway. One of these very important liminal monuments that we see and, for the Romans, boundaries are really symbolically and religiously charged spaces. So the Romans articulate their gateways and celebrate these as openings through these boundaries. We can see the Brandenburg Gate and this may be more familiar to you, not from our image perhaps, but from newsreel images. John F. Kennedy and Ronald Reagan have both spoken in front of the Gate here, and perhaps you have seen those images as well.

In addition to the Brandenburg Gate, there are a number of gates that are deliberately designed to emulate Rome. In Constantinople, or modern day Istanbul, we see the new Rome with this form of gateway, here adapted into a style of Islamic architecture, but instantly recognizable to us now through our knowledge of the visual vocabulary of Rome. We have a triple-passage archway with projecting bastions and crenellations on both sides, a marvelous conflation of both passageway architecture and Roman fortification architecture put together to symbolize a formalized entrance, as well as the boundary around it. This is a great one. There is another one here I wanted to show you as well that gives you a sense of this single-passage arch here with the lower wall on either side, not in this case really a usable wall, but more like a wall around a Roman colony, a symbolic, demarcation of the boundary of a colony.

This form is amazingly flexible, the gate or arch, and we find these across the world, sometimes used the way the Romans did, as markers of boundaries, other times in very different ways that show the flexibility of the form and how important it is that the idea behind this be articulated.

One of my favorites here is the Roosevelt Arch. The Roosevelt Arch is a very American version of a triumphal arch. It marks the northern entrance into Yellowstone Park, and we're looking at one side of it here. As you get close, you see that there's an inscription, as there would have been on a Roman triumphal arch. The inscription here on the Roosevelt Arch says, as you're facing Yellowstone, "For the Benefit and Enjoyment of the People." So what we as Americans have done is taken a notion of triumphal arch, placed it in the native landscape as opposed to in the center of an urban environment, and with that idea, transferred the Roman notion of triumph over nature, which we see so often in Roman architecture. And we've brought it here, but placed a very non-Roman inscription onto it, this idea that this is for the benefit and enjoyment of the people. Certainly, for the Romans, their armatures of celebration claimed to have benefited the people, but it was never articulated as clearly as it is here, and the role of the people in this arch is much stronger than we have seen in ancient Roman.

Some of the arches that we see throughout the world—and we won't look at all of them because there are literally thousands—are much more traditional. I like to always show the Arc de Triomphe in Paris because this is a traditional adaptation of a Roman single passage arch. It looks very much like the Arch of Titus, which we've seen repeatedly throughout the lectures. It's a single-passage archway with Victories in the spandrels of the arch, a very strongly articulated attic story above, and then relief decoration on the arch. And it reminds us, perhaps, of the Arch of Titus or the Arch of Septimius Severus with those strong relief panels. The only thing missing here is the culminating statue group at the top which, of course, we also don't have from the ancient arches.

Further examples of triumphal arches, or the arch form, are found all over the place. There's one in London at Hyde Park, there's one in New York, of course, but some of the most interesting examples are actually the furthest afield. If we go to Pyongyang, which we can't do, but if one were to go to Pyongyang, in North Korea, what you would see is a marvelous example of a tetrapylon arch. And this arch is of the type that we saw in Leptis Magna, the great celebratory arch of Septimius Severus. It's a four-way arch built on a crossroads, and it's designed to have these four facades so you can pass through it, and it gives you a much richer image, and it breaks up what I term the "armature of celebration" so that you can cross through it both directions.

The arch here at Pyongyang is important because it shows how this imagery is sustained. The Pyongyang arch dates to 1982, so it's a very recent one. And here we've got a marvelous image of the arch at night lighted up with that dramatic up-lighting, and then in front is a statue of a soccer player. Again, it shows you how flexible this form is. Here it's a celebration of Korean identity through the arch, but also with the athletic imagery, something that the Romans never combined. Somebody has taken this form and really adapted it to their local identity, and this is a really interesting notion.

If we stay here in Korea, we can go just south to South Korea. And down at Seoul, there is something known as the Independence Arch, or the Independence Gate in Seoul. The Independence Gate is a really interesting monument because it's designed like a Roman single-passage arch, and we can see all of the elements of the single passage with the projecting columns, the very strongly articulated arch with the projecting keystone above it, a semblance of an attic story above here done as a balustrade. But the meaning is much different here. The Independence Arch in Seoul celebrates Korean independence from China. And so, what they have done is taken this notion of victory and used it in a completely different way than the Romans would. For the Romans, victory arches would universally celebrate dominance. In this case, the Koreans have created a victory arch that celebrates freedom, or, as they term it, independence. And so this shows you how exciting these monuments are because they are very flexible, but everybody here uses them with the knowledge that they have this inherent idea behind them. There's a symbolic charge to all of these. Whether or not they accept or reject what the traditional idea is, nonetheless, they are engaging with that. The mark of great architecture is that everybody walks by it and engages with it.

This is just an incredible wealth of arches and gateways to give you a sense of the articulation of space and urban form in the way the Romans did and the creation of armatures of celebration. These are important, but they stand alone as individual monuments. Most of these are set in piazzas or at crossroads, much as the Romans had, but they're not part of any sort of interconnected or interrelated set of monuments. They are individualized.

To really appreciate the emulation of Roman visual vocabulary, its extent and the notion of the interconnections, we need to come to the United States, in particular, to Washington, DC. Here, in Washington, DC, is where we see the most self-conscious modeling on Roman government and on these forms of architecture and monumentalization because these forms come with the ideas of government embedded in them. We can make the case here that the forms matter and that the lessons that they transmit are valuable and continue to resonate. We can make that case because people continue to make this style of monuments today. Washington, DC, in particular, is a fantastic example because Roman visual vocabulary permeates the city, and we find monuments that celebrate or memorialize one great citizen or another, or collective groups. Subsets of the citizenry are also celebrated in particular spaces throughout the city. And these are done in ways that very much recall the patterns that we saw in ancient Rome. So we're going to spend quite a bit of time here in Washington, DC.

If we look at the federal buildings, we see that they are deliberately designed on Roman models, not just with an empty use of the forms, but to resonate with the Roman themes of law, liberty, and republican government, which were so powerful when DC was laid out. These are found not just in one instance, but repeatedly, so we see a standard sort of leitmotif running through the monuments and building sets.

One of the best examples is the U.S. Capitol, a tremendous building in terms of scale. It's very Roman in the idea that it's designed on a hill, and it dominates the area around it. I think that is a deliberate choice. We can think back to the Temple of Jupiter Capitolinus or the Temple of Jupiter at Terracina for a similar monument built up on a hill to dominate down below. Think about imperial Rome, the palaces of the emperors up on Palatine Hill looking out over the Forum Romanum. The Capitol does much the same thing with its great Roman-style rotunda and its classical facade. Its design is based very much on Roman architectural vocabulary.

When you go inside, you see that this notion continues throughout the building. It's not just a facade that's slapped onto a generic office building. One of the best examples of this is in the House of Representatives, the chamber in the south wing of the Capitol. If you look at the House of Representatives, and you get to go in and sit in the gallery above the representatives, look down at the speaker's platform. There is the U.S. flag behind, and on either side of the U.S. flag we see low reliefs, bronze reliefs, set into the wall. Each of those reliefs is a *fasces*. The *fasces* is the axe, surrounded by a bundle of rods carried by the lictors, the bodyguards of Roman magistrates, and these are the symbols of Roman authority. Each one of these Roman magistrates had the power of life and death over Roman citizens and non-citizens outside the city of Rome. And so, these *fasces*, this bundle of rods with an axe in the center of it, represent the supreme power in the state. Placing these on either side of the speaker's platform in the House of Representatives makes a very clear statement. First, the people who did this represented that these were Roman monuments. This predates fascism, where these were adopted by the fascists and then stripped off our coinage. We don't see them any more on our money. What they tell us is that the people are the ultimate power in the American republic; not the elected officials, but actually the people that they serve. This notion of taking the Roman visual and making this statement with it is intensely powerful.

If we stay in the Capitol, walk back out into the great rotunda, just below that great Roman-inspired dome, we can look up into the rotunda, and we've got a great image of what that looks like for you. Again, it's very Roman-inspired. I want to focus on the painting in the center of the rotunda. The subject of this painting in the center is actually the Apotheosis of George Washington. This notion of apotheosis, or a bodily ascent into heaven, is a standard Roman motif. We find it throughout Roman visual vocabulary. It's a standard iconography for apotheosis of Roman rulers. Starting with Romulus and continuing through, Roman emperors make their bodily ascent.

Here, it's been adapted. George Washington is surrounded by Roman-style deities here, but each one personifies one aspect of the Roman Republic. And so this is a statement not just in celebration of George Washington and his values, but of the statement of the values of the republic. So if you've got a good pair of binoculars, or if you buy the guide book like I did, you can see details of aspects of the republic of law, and so on, guiding Washington. This is, again, a very deliberate attempt to make the statement that although we're using these Roman forms, we're adapting them for our republican virtues and values. I think these are just great.

This is all in the House of Representative and the Capitol, one of the branches of government. But we see the same notions in other branches as well, most notably, the Supreme Court building. The design of the Supreme Court building is based deliberately on the Temple of Jupiter Capitolinus on the Capitoline Hill. The great Temple of Jupiter on its tall podium with the front pediment is a temple, and it's a Roman temple. We didn't look at the reliefs in the pediment of the Temple of Jupiter because they don't exist any more, but we did look at the relief, or at the center of the relief, of the Temple of Mars Ultor, with this figure of Mars in the center, flanked and supported by Venus and the divine Julius Caesar, telling us that Mars is the primary figure and that the Julian dynasty supports the god, Mars.

Here, in the pediment of the Supreme Court, we have the notion, but with different values. What we have in the center of the pediment here is Liberty and it's a personification of Liberty, again, a Roman idea of creating an abstract value and personifying it as an individual. And it's Liberty supported on one side by order and on the other by authority. Liberty is the supreme goal of all of the branches of government, and this is an extraordinary statement about a celebration of specific values, well-articulated, and using these forms which bring with them the power behind them of, in particular, Jupiter Capitolinus. Jupiter is no longer the supreme figure; it is the Court itself which takes the place of the supreme god. I love that. It's a powerful statement about government values. It's also, arguably, a very ideal monument.

We've looked at a number of buildings in Washington, DC, and spaces within those buildings, the dome of the Capitol, the House of Representatives, and the Supreme Court. Washington, DC, is more than just the buildings. What we see is in the urban space, the organizational space, and the monuments around them are really monuments to individuals.

What I want to turn our attention to here is the National Mall. The National Mall owes its inspiration directly to the Forum Romanum or perhaps, more specifically, to a Roman colonial forum. I've pointed it out, the Roman colonial forum, Paestum in Pompeii, where we have a large open rectangle five times as long as it is wide. It's always kept as open area. The buildings of the forum surround that, and then, within that structure and generally surrounding it, we find monuments to particularly important individuals, either locally important individuals or nationally important individuals, members of the local city council or local benefactors in the colonial forum, but also members of the imperial family, great military leaders, and so on. And this is what we find today on our National Mall. Instead of the great men of Rome, we have the great men and key values of our republic. And these monuments are, by and large, to men. So we're going to focus on that.

If we look at an image of the Mall today—I've got a great map for you—we've already looked at the Capitol and the Supreme Court building on the right-hand side of the Mall, but if you go left, run down the center of the Mall you'll see, again, reflecting Roman urban organization, a strong emphasis, at least in the early monuments, on axiality. We see the Supreme Court, the Capitol, and then we go down and we see the Washington Monument and then, anchoring the far side, the Lincoln Memorial. We have other monuments in between. The World War II Memorial is in between. Flanking it, and there is a symmetry involved as well just as we saw in Rome forums, we see the Korean and Vietnam Memorials and then, somewhat by itself off to one side is the Thomas Jefferson Memorial. Let's take a look at these as we go down.

One of the earlier of these, and as I say, it anchors one end of the Mall, is the Lincoln Memorial. The Lincoln Memorial is really interesting because it is, effectively, a temple. It's a temple to Abraham Lincoln. It's a great Doric-style temple done in a form that combines the Greek elements—the classicizing elements—with Roman design. You come up these high steps because it's got this great podium just as a Roman temple does, and you enter in and just across from you there is the cult statue, Abraham Lincoln himself, seated as though he is Jupiter. He is the new god. It's really a powerful monument. I always go up there and I get kind of misty when I see it. It's moving. It really tells us about who we are celebrating and for what. The notion here is taken directly from the Forum Romanum where we saw the Apotheosis of Romulus. The monument marking that spot is always preserved and then, later on, the spot marking the place where Martius Curtius gave his life for the Roman Republic. I always think of the Lincoln Memorial as the equivalent of the monument to Martius Curtius, the man who gave his life to the republic.

The parallel, I think, for the spot of the Apotheosis of Romulus is better given to the Washington Monument. It's in the center and it celebrates the founder of the country. But the form here is interesting. It doesn't really follow the form of early Roman monuments. Instead, it's a tremendous obelisk. That obelisk form is the standard one that we find in the city of Rome, but we don't find it until the time of Augustus. If we look at the obelisk of the Washington Monument, we can compare it to one of the six obelisks that Augustus brought to Rome.

The form of the Washington Monument reflects these obelisks very well, but even more so, George Washington's title, the one we give him informally, "father of his country" is a title he shared with Augustus. Augustus was known as the "*pater patriae*," the father of his country as well. And so the fact that the obelisk form associated with Augustus is brought to Washington DC and associated here with George Washington, I think is not a coincidence. There's this symbolic charge in this monument, and it carries that meaning and theme with it as we re-interpret it for our monument.

In terms of the monuments to man, I think the most symbolically charged and visually fascinating is the Jefferson Memorial. Here we have a president, a leader of the country, who was himself an architect who designed his own buildings. We have here a marvelous memorial to Jefferson with a great rotunda dome and a projected porch out to the side. The form of this is based directly on the Pantheon in Rome; not the Pantheon built by Marcus Agrippa, but the Pantheon of Hadrian, who himself was a ruler of Rome and was an architect who designed the Pantheon. And so there's a marvelous symbolic relationship here. It's directly self-referential. We have an architect ruler and his iconic building celebrating another architect ruler, in our case, a president and not an emperor.

I've got a great image here giving you that three-quarter view of the Jefferson Memorial with that front porch with the pediment projecting out, and the great rotunda dome behind, again, based exactly on the Pantheon in Rome. So we get a great sense here not just about the inspiration for Jefferson's Memorial, but for the inspiration for a lot of American government.

These are all monuments to individuals, and great individuals, but all leaders. But as a republic we don't just celebrate our leaders. We also celebrate the contributions of the citizens. This is a more recent phenomenon that we find in Washington, DC, but it's also one that we see parallels for in ancient Rome. I think one of the best examples is the War World II Memorial. In its design it's very nonRoman with the great pool and the fountains out in the center. But in its details, it's very Roman. The archways that we see, the tetrapylon arches, are based on Roman tetrapylon arches. We saw one of Septimius Severus. The standing pylons between them are decorated with symbols of eagles and wreaths, again, victory images that we see in Roman triumphal or celebratory monuments.

The remarkable thing that set the World War II Memorial aside from other memorials are the reliefs. We have a huge series of bronze reliefs that show images of regular individuals during the time of war. These are really extraordinary because they show the war from the battlefield all the way to the home front. This extension of victory imagery, away from just images of great leaders, great generals, or great political figures, reflects explicitly what we see in ancient Rome, starting with the Column of Trajan. The Column of Trajan showing the Dacian campaigns begins in Roman territory and then carries through with very circumstantial images of the war. And we have that here, circumstantial images that show the home front, people listening to the radio trying to hear news about what's happening in the war. Images of battle itself—here is a marvelous one which shows the Normandy invasion, and there in the front you see the traps trying to keep the landing craft off the beach, and behind the landing craft they're coming up, and the first wave of men have just made it to the beach, some alive, some not. Like the Column of Trajan, it brings home to us, not an image of celebration of war, but an image of the actual costs of war.

One of my favorite of these reliefs shows paratroopers in a plane preparing to jump, and over on the right we see this line of men preparing to jump out of this plane, I think, in the dark, just going out, preparing for a battle. On the left we see their commander directing them with his hand outstretched, pointing at them, telling them to go on, what they are doing is the right thing to do, and to carry on and he, of course, will follow them. He's going to jump out of the plane as well. The image here, as we see, with the composition and the iconography is directly from the great Column of Trajan. It's really a marvelous parallel.

We also have tremendous equestrian statues that show, again, direct parallels, equestrian statues of the emperor Domitian as well as our great commanders. Here's one of Phil Sheridan, a great Civil War general from New York.

Scholars still argue about how aware the founding fathers were about details of Roman government and culture. Did they really know about the republic, and how much did they know about how that should work? However much they were, they certainly were keenly aware of the visual forms of Roman culture. They readily adopted them and expressed a clear desire to extend the imagery of Rome and to develop deliberate, explicit associations with Roman republican government and our new American republic. This, of course, is just one example of this practice, showing the reception and extension of the visual vocabulary of ancient Rome, which has been continuing since the fall of ancient Rome and continues on today as we've seen even in the most recent World War II Memorial.

As we come to the end of this course, it seems time to reflect upon what concepts I'd like for you to take away from it, and since this is the last lecture, it's clearly now or never. Certainly I'd like you to take away the subject of Roman art and architecture, the power of these visual forms, and their importance in Roman culture. But the real subject here is not really the Roman world. What I'd like for you to take away most is an enhanced awareness of the meaning of the visual, not just in the Roman culture or other historical cultures but in our own contemporary world. And I would consider this course to have been a success if, as you're driving down the road, or attending a football game, or even going to the grocery store, you spend some time, perhaps, unconsciously, thinking about urban forms, and the organization of space, and the meaning of what you see around you in the world. I think that would be a sense of achievement from this course, and what I hope that you would take away from it.

Thank you.

# Timeline

**B.C.**

753 ............................ Rome founded by Romulus.

753–509 .................... Regal period (Rome ruled by kings).

509 ............................ Roman Republic founded; first games, the *ludi Romani*, held in Rome; Temple of Jupiter Capitolinus founded.

364 ............................ First theatrical performance in Rome.

338 ............................ Ostia, Rome's first colony, established.

273 ............................ Colonies at Paestum and Cosa founded.

264 ............................ First gladiatorial games held in Rome at the funeral of Junius Brutus Pera.

264–241 .................... First Punic War.

218–202 .................... Second Punic War.

212 ............................ Sack of Syracuse.

186 ............................ First games to include animal fights held; first appearance of Greek athletes at Roman sporting events.

146 ............................ Destruction of Carthage and Corinth.

80 .............................. Roman colony of Pompeii founded by Sulla.

73–71 ........................ Revolt of Spartacus.

62............................... Pons Fabricius built.

61............................... Pompey's Triple Triumph.

55............................... Pompey's Theater, the first permanent theater in Rome, built.

46............................... Forum of Caesar dedicated.

44............................... Assassination of Julius Caesar.

31............................... Naval Battle of Actium; Octavian (Augustus) defeats Mark Antony and Cleopatra.

31 B.C.–A.D. 476 .... Principate (rule of Rome by a princeps or "first citizen").

**Julio-Claudian Emperors**

31 B.C.–A.D. 14 ...... Reign of Augustus.

29............................... Augustus's Triple Triumph.

12............................... Theater of Marcellus dedicated.

2................................. Forum of Augustus dedicated.

**A.D.**

14–37........................ Reign of Tiberius.

20–26........................ Tiberius resides at Sperlonga.

37–41........................ Reign of Caligula.

41–54........................ Reign of Claudius.

43............................... Invasion of Britain.

54–68........................ Reign of Nero.

59............................... Amphitheater riot at Pompeii.

62............................... Earthquake along the Bay of Naples extensively damages Pompeii and neighboring communities.

after 62 ..................... Temple of Isis and House of Octavius Quartio rebuilt at Pompeii.

64............................... Great fire in Rome.

67............................... Nero in Greece.

**Flavian Emperors**

69–79........................ Reign of Vespasian.

71............................... Flavian Triumph for Jewish war.

75............................... Forum of Peace dedicated.

79............................... Mount Vesuvius erupts, destroying Pompeii, Herculaneum, and Oplontis.

79–81........................ Reign of Titus.

80............................... Inauguration of the Colosseum; fire and plague hit Rome.

81............................... Arch of Titus dedicated.

81–96........................ Reign of Domitian.

86............................... Stadium of Domitian built.

## Antonine Emperors

96–98........................ Reign of Nerva.

98–117...................... Reign of Trajan.

100............................ Colony founded at Timgad.

103............................ Trajan's new harbor, Portus, begun at Ostia.

113............................ Forum of Trajan inaugurated.

117–138.................... Reign of Hadrian.

120............................ Hadrian's Wall begun in Britain.

125............................ Pantheon built.

138–161.................... Reign of Antoninus Pius.

142............................ Antonine Wall begun in Scotland.

161–166.................... Parthian wars.

161–180.................... Reign of Marcus Aurelius.

165............................ Plague sweeps Rome.

180–193.................... Reign of Commodus.

192............................ Column of Marcus Aurelius completed; Commodus appears in the Colosseum as Hercules.

193............................ Civil war; Year of the Six Emperors.

## Severan Dynasty

193–211.................... Reign of Septimius Severus.

197............................. Invasion of the Parthian empire.

203............................. Severan family's triumphal entrance into Leptis Magna; Arch of Septimius Severus dedicated in Rome.

204............................. Celebration of the 950$^{th}$ anniversary of Rome.

211–217.................... Reign of Caracalla.

216............................. Baths of Caracalla inaugurated.

## The Tetrarchy

284–305.................... Diocletian and Maximian reign as joint rulers.

300............................. Villa of Piazza Armerina built.

306............................. Baths of Diocletian dedicated.

# Glossary

**amphitheater**: Oval or round building for *munera* (see below); the name means "double theater."

***apodyterium***: Changing room in a Roman bath.

**arena**: Performance floor of the amphitheater.

**atrium**: Main room in a Roman *domus* (see below) that was lavishly decorated and where the achievements of the family would be displayed for visitors to see.

**augurs**: Religious officials who foretold events by observing and interpreting signs and omens, especially the flights of birds.

**basilica**: Hall used for law courts, civil administration, and business, characterized by a central hall with flanking aisles and often a porch on one end and a raised tribunal on the other.

***caldarium***: Hot room in a Roman bath; generally a heated room with a plunge bath of heated water and a separate basin of cold water.

***capitolium***: Temple to Jupiter, Juno, and Minerva that dominated the forum of a Roman colony; generally sited in the center of the short end of a colonial forum.

***cardo maximus***: Major north-south street in a Roman colony that established the central line in the layout of the community.

**cavea**: Seating area of a theater or amphitheater, always divided into sections by rank.

**circus**: Performance space for chariot racing, including the building and track. The largest and grandest of these is the Circus Maximus in Rome.

***collocatio***: Viewing of the deceased, which, for elite Romans, occurred in the atrium of the *domus*.

**Colosseum, the**: Properly called the Flavian Amphitheater, an amphitheater built in Rome and dedicated in A.D. 80 by the Flavian emperor Titus.

**curia**: Roman senate house both in Rome and in her colonies.

***damnatio ad bestias***: Condemnation to the animals as a form of capital punishment in the Roman world, carried out in public, generally as part of spectacle entertainment.

***decimatio***: Component of Roman military discipline in which every 10th man of a rebellious unit was beaten to death in front of the unit.

***decumanus maximus***: Major east-west road in a Roman colony that was surveyed to intersect the *cardo* at the exact center of the community.

***domus***: Town house; more than a residence, it was the headquarters for an extended family.

**Domus Publica**: Public house of the kings on the edge of the Forum Romanum.

***edicta munera***: Painted announcements of upcoming spectacles preserved only at Pompeii, where they reveal the role of gladiatorial games in the local community, the place of politics, and Pompeii's own gladiatorial school.

***euripus***: Low, narrow barrier in a circus over 350 yards long and 10 yards wide that kept chariots from head-on collisions.

**Flavian Amphitheater**: Proper name for the Colosseum, built by the Flavian emperors and dedicated in A.D. 80.

**Forum Romanum**: Most important public space in Rome, which included buildings and spaces for legal, commercial, civil, and religious activities, most notably government functions.

***frigidarium***: Cold room in a Roman bath consisting of a round cold plunge bath.

***gladius***: Sword, from which gladiators got their name.

***hoplomachus***: Heavily armored category of gladiator; often pitted against a *thracian* in combat.

***imagines***: Images of distinguished Roman family members in the form of masks displayed in cabinets in the atrium of the *domus* and removed and worn for triumphs, funerals, and major family events.

**Jupiter Capitolinus**: Temple of Jupiter Optimus Maximus ("best and greatest") founded on the Capitoline Hill in 509 B.C. and replicated in Roman colonies across the empire.

***laconicum***: Hot, dry room of a Roman bath.

**Lacus Curtius**: Swampy spot in the Forum Romanum that marked the location where Marcus Curtius galloped into a void to save Rome.

***laudatio***: Eulogy for a deceased Roman that was given in the Forum Romanum by a son or other male family member.

**Leptis Magna**: North African birthplace of the emperor Septimius Severus, who lavishly rebuilt the city with a new harbor, forum, and monuments celebrating his rule and family.

***limes***: Border defense system established along the frontiers of the Roman Empire. Portions of it stretched across Britain, Germany, North Africa, and the Near East.

***ludi***: Name for the whole variety of theatrical exhibitions, games, and contests that were held at Rome on various occasions but chiefly at the festivals of the gods. Sometimes, however, *ludi* were also held in honor of a magistrate or of a deceased person.

**Lupercalia**: Very ancient festival associated with Romulus and Remus observed on February 15. Rituals were performed to avert evil spirits and purify the city as well as to ensure fertility in the coming year.

**Mare Nostrum**: Roman name for the Mediterranean, meaning "our sea."

***mens sana in corpore sano***: Roman ideal of a "sound mind in a sound body" that informed the structure of Roman baths.

**mime**: Despite the name, a spoken form of theater consisting of spoken, usually short, vignettes that were either serious or comic but often satiric in nature that rose in popularity throughout the Imperial Period and overtook pantomime (see below) after the 2nd century.

***munera***: Literally "gifts"; public spectacles featuring gladiatorial combat originally held at funerals but later expanded to broader presentation.

***natatio***: Outdoor swimming pool.

***naumachia***: Large artificial basin built to host aquatic spectacles, including naval battles, that could be viewed by a huge audience at Rome.

***nymphaeum***: Dining complex incorporating statues, paintings, and water features.

**pantomime**: Roman theatrical performance form similar in many ways to modern ballet that portrayed themes of love and adultery along with mythological scenes through dance and gesture. It originally consisted of a solo dancer accompanied by music and a chorus. The performance was without dialogue, but the story (either comic or tragic) was conveyed through music, dance, costume, movement, and attitude.

***paradeisos***: Enclosed or walled park generally used for hunting wild game such as lions. The concept came to Rome from the Greeks, who encountered them in their conquest of Persia.

**Piazza Armerina**: Villa in Sicily identified by its excavators as the home of the emperor Maximian (r. 286–A.D. 305).

***pomerium***: Sacred and legal boundary of the city of Rome established in a ceremony in which priests plowed a furrow indicating the boundary.

***pompa***: Roman ceremonial parade that was an important component of funerals, triumphs, election campaigns, and religious and secular spectacles.

**Regia**: Ceremonial home of the Roman kings in the Forum Romanum, taken over by priests after the founding of the republic and continually used for rituals and public displays.

***retiarius***: Popular imperial gladiator wearing almost no armor and armed with a net and trident as well as a short, bladed weapon. He usually faced the heavily armed and armored *secutor*.

***rostra***: Speakers' platform in the Forum Romanum named for the bronze rams taken from Punic warships and attached to the front.

***salutatio***: One of the most important political ceremonies, in which a Roman patron would receive his clients at dawn in the atrium, after which they would escort him to the forum.

***samnite***: Gladiatorial category of the republic, heavily armored and armed with a large shield and a short sword. Imperial categories of *murmillo* and *secutor* developed from the *samnite*.

***secutor***: Most heavily armed type of gladiator, who usually faced the *retiarius*.

**Sperlonga**: Location of the villa of the emperor Tiberius (r. A.D. 14–37), where the colossal statue groups were found in the grotto dining room.

**stadium**: Performance space for Greek games such as running, javelin throwing, boxing, etc.

***stichomythia***: Dialogue in a Greek or Roman play with short lines like a tennis match.

***sudatorium***: Sweating room of a Roman bath; essentially a steam room.

***tepidarium***: Warm water room in a Roman bath.

***thracian***: Gladiator who wore a crested bronze helmet, greaves, and a rectangular shield and fought with a curved sword.

**triumph**: Roman victory parade for a victorious general and army, viewed as the culmination of a military career.

***venationes***: Games with animals; generally professional animal hunts, although could refer to animal fights that were staged in the amphitheater.

**Vesuvius, Mount**: Volcano along the Bay of Naples that erupted in A.D. 79, wiping out the cities of Pompeii and Herculaneum and surrounding areas such as Oplontis.

***via***: Roman for "road." The most important and famous Roman roads are the Via Appia, which ran south out of Rome down the length of the peninsula, and the Via Flaminia, which was the most important route to the north.

***virtus***: Roman quality that defined manhood, meaning courage or martial prowess.

# Biographical Notes

**Aeneas**: Legendary founder of Rome, a Trojan refugee who left the burning city with his son, father, and followers to sail to Italy to establish Rome.

**Alexander the Great** (356–323 B.C.): King of Macedon from 336 to 323 B.C.; conquered the Persian empire. He served as a model for Roman rulers and elites who emulated his public image and associated themselves with him through actions and art.

**Augustus** (63 B.C.–A.D. 14): Known also as Octavian. Nephew and heir of Julius Caesar and the first Roman emperor, ruling from 31 B.C. to A.D. 14. Came to sole power after the defeat of Mark Antony and Cleopatra at the Battle of Actium in 31 B.C.

**Caesar, Gaius Julius** (c.100–44 B.C.): The last in a line of Romans who sought sole control of the Roman state, leading to the end of the republic. His adoption of Octavian led to the beginning of the principate. His building program in the Forum Romanum and construction of the Forum Iulium were models for the emperors who followed him.

**Caligula** (A.D. 12–41): Emperor from A.D. 37 to 41; the first princeps to appear in public as an entertainer.

**Cicero, Marcus Tullius** (106–43 B.C.): Roman author and politician whose letters make clear the role of government officials in procuring animals in the late republic.

**Commodus** (A.D. 161–193): Emperor from A.D. 180 to 193 whose disastrous rule led to a civil war. Appeared as a gladiator and animal hunter in the arena and emulated Hercules.

**Hannibal** (247–c. 181 B.C.): Carthaginian general of the Second Punic War whose battlefield tactics defeated the Romans in many large battles before his final defeat at the Battle of Zama in 202 B.C.

**Nero** (A.D. 37–68): Ruler from A.D. 54 to 68. Performed as a singer and charioteer in public. The great fire in Rome in the year 64 was during his rule and was blamed on him, which led to the first Christian persecution in his attempt to assign blame to others.

**Octavian**: see **Augustus**.

**Octavius Quartio**: Owner of a house at Pompeii that exemplified the urban villa form of the middle classes.

**Ovid** (43 B.C.–A.D. 17): Roman poet who lived and wrote under Augustus. His works include the most extensive Roman engagement with Greek mythology as well as love elegies and a handbook on love for Roman men.

**Perpetua** and **Felicitas** (d. c. A.D. 203): Two 3rd-century Christian martyrs. Perpetua was a 22-year-old married new mother. Felicitas was her servant. They were martyred in the amphitheater at Carthage. The record of their sufferings was left by Perpetua and completed by another member of the Christian community and become one of the most famous and important of the passion accounts.

**Pliny the Younger** (c. A.D. 61–c. 113): Roman governor under the emperor Trajan and author of many works. His letters illuminate his values and his administration of his Roman province.

**Quintus Aurelius Symmachus** (c. A.D. 345–402): Held the offices of urban prefect of Rome in 384 and 385 and of consul in 391. Began to collect animals in 398 for his son's praetorship in 400. His letters reveal the details of preparing for spectacle entertainments.

**Romulus**: Legendary king of Rome credited with founding the city and establishing Rome's traditions of military conquest, triumphal processions and inclusive citizenship.

**Septimius Severus** (A.D. 146–211): Founder of the Severan dynasty and victor of the civil war following the rule of Commodus, he emulated Trajan in launching a Parthian war, constructing a large building program, and extending triumphal imagery across the Roman Empire.

**Suetonius** (A.D. 69–c. 122): Roman administrator and friend of Pliny the Younger who wrote a series of biographies of the first 12 emperors (Caesar to Domitian).

**Tacitus** (A.D. 56–c. 120): Roman historian and author of two influential and insightful works on imperial Rome, the *Annals* and the *Histories*, which covered Roman history from the death of Augustus to that of Domitian.

**Tarquin the Proud** (d. 495 B.C.): Final king of Rome who reigned from 534 to 509 B.C.; overthrown when the republic was founded.

**Trajan** (A.D. 53–117): Princeps from A.D. 98 to 117, oversaw major wars in Dacian and Parthian territory and saw the Roman Empire to its greatest extent. He was also responsible for massive public building programs in Rome and across the empire, including military triumphal monuments in Rome and Dacia.

**Vespasian** (A.D. 9–79): Founder of the Flavian Dynasty, he ruled from A.D. 69 to 79 and commanded the forces that subdued a Jewish revolt and destroyed the Temple of Solomon in Jerusalem.

# Bibliography


Aldrete, G. S. *Daily Life in the Roman City: Rome, Pompeii, and Ostia.* Westport, CT: Greenwood Press, 2004. An excellent, accessible, and well-written account of daily life in three key cities.

Anderson, J. C. Jr. *The Historical Topography of the Imperial Fora.* Brussels: Latomus, 1984. A thorough description and analysis of the development of the imperial forums from their creation to later rebuilding.

———. *Roman Architecture and Society.* Baltimore: Johns Hopkins University Press, 1997. A survey of Roman buildings and their relationship to society, focusing on the city of Rome itself.

Auguet, R. "Chariot Races, Stables and Factions." In *Cruelty and Civilization: The Roman Games.* London: Allen and Unwin, 1972. This book explores the origin and social role of spectacle entertainments, with emphasis on the responses of the audience.

———. *Cruelty and Civilization: The Roman Games.* London: Allen and Unwin, 1972. In this work, Auguet briefly describes the origins and process of the Circus Maximus, the gladiatorial combats, the hunts, and the patrons and factions that fueled these extravagant spectacles.

Beard, M. *The Roman Triumph.* Cambridge: Belknap Press, 2007. A thorough and insightful reconsideration of triumphal processions. Beard bases her arguments on the primary sources and frequently disputes scholarly opinion.

Beard, M., J. North, and S. Price. *Religions of Rome.* 2 vols. Cambridge: Cambridge University Press, 1998. An excellent two-volume work creating a survey of Roman religion backed by a tremendous number of translated sources.

Bishop, M. C., and J. C. N. Coulston. *Roman Military Equipment: From the Punic Wars to the Fall of Rome.* Oxford: Oxbow Books, 2006. Based on the remains of arms and armor from across the empire, this book provides the definitive look at what soldiers wore and fought with throughout Roman history.

Bodel, J. "Death on Display: Looking at Roman Funerals." In *The Art of Ancient Spectacle*, edited by B. Bergmann and C. Kondoleon. New Haven, CT: Yale University Press, 1999. The best brief account of the spectacular aspects of Roman funerals, with an extensive bibliography and excellent illustrations.

Bomgardner, D. L. *The Story of the Roman Amphitheatre* (London: Routledge, 2002. This work traces the origins and development of the amphitheater and its central role in the social and political life of ancient Rome through examples across the Roman Empire.

Bradley, G. and J. P. Wilson, eds. *Greek and Roman Colonization: Origins, Ideologies and Interactions*. Oakville, CT: D. Brown Book Company, 2006. A collection of masterful essays on key aspects of colonization.

Breeze, D. *Roman Frontiers in Britain*. London: Duckworth, 2007. This accessible, well-illustrated account places the frontiers into their context both in Britain and in Europe, examining the development of frontier installations over four centuries.

Brilliant R. *The Arch of Septimus Severus in the Roman Forum* Philadelphia, PA: University of Pennsylvania Press, 1987. A detailed study of the best-preserved triumphal arch we have. Brilliant analyzes the construction, decoration, context, and history of the monument in turn. His thorough analysis of the rich sculptural decoration that covers the arch is the book's greatest contribution.

———. "'Let the Trumpets Roar!' The Roman Triumph." In *The Art of Ancient Spectacle*, edited by B. Bergmann and C. Kondoleon, eds. New Haven, CT: Yale University Press, 1999. A thoughtful, brief analysis of triumph and the visual sources for studying it.

Cameron, A. *Circus Factions: Blues and Greens at Rome and Byzantium*. Oxford: Clarendon Press, 1976. An authoritative work of impressive research based directly on the ancient sources, this book is the ultimate source on the subject.

Cantarella, E. and L. Jacobelli. *A Day in Pompeii: Daily Life, Culture and Society*. Naples, Italy: Electa Napoli, 2003. In a series of short thematic chapters, the authors introduce all of the aspects of Pompeii in which a resident of the ancient city might engage during a typical day.

Carcopino, J. *Daily Life in Ancient Rome: the People and the City at the Height of the Empire*. 2nd ed. New Haven, CT: Yale University Press, 2003. A chatty, discursive, creative, and well-written attempt to reconstruct life in the Roman capital largely from the perspective of the man in the street.

Carter, M. J. "Gladiatorial Combat: the Rules of Engagement." *Classical Journal* 102 (2007): 97–114. This article argues that gladiatorial combats may also have been governed by an unwritten "code of conduct" enforced by the gladiators themselves: to fight bravely in hope of victory but not to wound or kill needlessly.

Cary, M., and H. H. Scullard. *A History of Rome Down to the Reign of Constantine*. 3rd ed. New York: St. Martin's Press, 1975. A standard and comprehensive survey that avoids polemic or ideology in presenting the long sweep of Roman history.

Castelli, E. *Martyrdom and Memory: Early Christian Culture Making*. New York: Columbia University Press, 2007. Carefully argued work on the role of martyrdom in creating early Christian culture, especially as a revolutionary culture that subverted Roman ideology.

Claridge, A. *Rome: an Oxford Archaeological Guide*. Oxford: Oxford University Press, 1998. An extremely clear, well-supported, and illustrated survey of the vast archaeological remains in Rome.

Clarke, J. R. *The Houses of Roman Italy, 100 B.C.–A.D. 250: Ritual, Space, and Decoration.* Berkeley, CA: University of California Press, 1991. In case studies of 17 excavated houses, Clarke demonstrates how patterns of Roman decoration signal the cultural, religious, and social imprints of the people who lived with them.

Coleman, K. M., "Fatal Charades: Roman Executions Stated as Mythological Enactments." *Journal of Roman Studies* 80 (1990): 44–73. A seminal article that connects prisoner executions with Roman penal theory and practices, as well as with Greek myths, in spectacle.

———. "Launching into History: Aquatic Displays in the Early Empire." *Journal of Roman Studies* 83 (1993): 48–74. The first and best analysis of the form and meaning of these, the largest spectacle entertainments in Rome.

de Grummond, N. T., and B. S. Ridgway, eds. *From Pergamon to Sperlonga: Sculpture and Context.* Berkeley, CA: University of California Press, 2000. A significant collection of essays that explore important sculptural groups and the meanings of their display in the Roman world.

Dillon, S., and K. E. Welch, eds. *Representations of War in Ancient Rome.* Cambridge: Cambridge University Press, 2006. This book examines how, in both visual imagery and in literary accounts, Romans represented war, which dominated Roman life to a degree unparalleled in other ancient societies.

Elsner, J. *Art and the Roman Viewer: the Transformation of Art from the Pagan World to Christianity.* Cambridge: Cambridge University Press, 1995. Based on ancient art images and texts, Elsner presents a fresh analysis of why the arts of late antiquity moved away from classical naturalism toward spiritual abstraction. This shows how an understanding of Roman viewing practices greatly deepens our insight into this fundamental transformation.

Fagan, G. G. *Bathing in Public in the Roman World.* Ann Arbor, MI: University of Michigan Press, 1999. This book approaches the baths as historical, cultural, and social phenomena, illuminating their contribution to Roman society.

Favro, D. "Rome: The Street Triumphant: The Urban Impact of Roman Triumphal Parades." In *Streets: Critical Perspectives on Public Space*, edited by Z. Celik, D. Favro, and R. Ingersoll. Berkeley, CA: University of California Press, 1994. Favro's work argues that triumphal processions moved through a set of monuments built by previous triumphal generals, creating a spectacle that engaged the history of triumphal parades in a reenactment of their events, reinforcing the key values of the ritual for viewers and participants alike.

Fredrick, D. *The Roman Gaze: Vision, Power and the Body*. Baltimore: Johns Hopkins University Press, 2002. This work contains sophisticated and theoretically informed discussions of a broad range of literature, art, and social components of the Roman world.

Futrell, A. *The Roman Games: a Sourcebook*. Malden, MA: Blackwell, 2006. The most comprehensive collection of translated and annotated ancient sources on Roman spectacle entertainment in English.

Greenberg, A. *Architecture of Democracy*. New York: Rizzoli, 2006. A recent work that links the forms of American government buildings with their classical, especially Roman, meanings.

Hallett, C. H. *The Roman Nude: Heroic Portrait Statuary 200 B.C.–A.D. 300*. Oxford: Oxford University Press, 2005. A comprehensive re-interpretation of the meaning and form of nude sculpture attempting to analyze it from a Roman perspective.

Hohlfelder, R. L., ed. *The Maritime World of Ancient Rome (Supplements to the Memoirs of the American Academy in Rome)*. Ann Arbor, MI: University of Michigan Press, 2008. This volume of papers contains the results of research on major components of Rome's maritime world, including ships and shipping, maritime life and commerce, and harbor construction and monumentalization.

Humphrey, J. H. *Roman Circuses: Arenas for Chariot Racing.* Berkeley, CA: University of California Press, 1986. A huge and meticulously written analysis of all of the evidence for this building type that is found across the Roman Empire.

Jacobelli, L. *Gladiators at Pompeii.* Los Angeles: J. Paul Getty Museum Press, 2003. A specialized look at gladiators and their role in one community where we have the best evidence for their arms, housing, careers, fan base, and role in political spectacle.

Jennison, G. *Animals for Show and Pleasure in Ancient Rome.* Philadelphia, PA: University of Pennsylvania Press, 2005. A work based on a massive number of ancient literary sources that illuminates every aspect of animals in Roman spectacle, including collection, transport, display, and show.

Johnson, A. *Roman Forts of the 1st and 2nd Centuries A.D. in Britain and the German Provinces.* London: A. & C. Black, 1983. A massive and detailed survey of the best-preserved Roman fortifications along the frontiers.

Keay, S. J., ed. *Portus: An Archaeological Survey of the Port of Imperial Rome.* London: British School at Rome Press, 2005. This meticulous work concludes that the harbor at Ostia was designed to make an ideological statement about the supremacy of Rome in the world and was, therefore, of key importance to understanding Rome and her relationship to the empire.

Keppie, L. J. F. *The Making of the Roman Army: From Republic to Empire.* Norman, OK: University of Oklahoma Press, 1998. Supported by a large bibliography and many illustrations and diagrams, this work is a solid introduction to the army and its development into the empire.

Kleiner, F. S. *The Arch of Nero in Rome: A Study of the Roman Honorary Arch Before and Under Nero.* Rome: G. Bretschneider, 1985. The putative subject of this book is an opportunity to survey and analyze this key monument form in Rome from its origins into the 1st century.

Köhne, E., and C. Ewigleben, eds., *Gladiators and Caesars: The Power of Spectacle in Ancient Rome*. Berkeley, CA: University of California Press, 2000. Published to accompany an exhibition at the British Museum, this volume contains an excellent survey of essays on all the major spectacle entertainments and entertainers.

Lander, J. *Roman Stone Fortifications: Variation and Change from the First Century A.D. to the Fourth*. Oxford: B.A.R., 1984. An extensive survey of the design and form of Roman fortifications.

La Regina, A. *Archaeological Guide to Rome: The Roman Forum, the Palatine, the Capitol and the Capitoline Museums, the Imperial Forums, the Coliseum, the Domus Aurea*. Milan: Electa, 2004. A comprehensive and useful guide to the ancient remains in the city of Rome.

La Rocca, E. *The Imperial Fora*. Rome: Latomus, 1995. A thoughtful analysis of the design and use of the imperial forums by the former director of the sites.

Lepper, F., C. Cichorius, and S. Frere. *Trajan's Column: A New Edition of the Cichorius Plates*. Gloucester, UK: Sutton, 1988. The most complete illustrations published of the reliefs that cover the exterior of Trajan's Column.

Lomas, K. *Roman Italy, 338 B.C.–A.D. 200: A Sourcebook*. New York: St. Martin's Press, 1996. This work consists of a superb and wide-ranging collection of translations of ancient sources, arranged topically with commentary and introductions.

Mazzoleni, D. *Domus: Wall Painting in the Roman House*. Los Angeles J. Paul Getty Museum Press, 2004. Gorgeous, lavishly illustrated work with essays on many of the best-preserved Roman houses from Pompeii Herculaneum, and Rome itself.

McKay, A. G. *Houses, Villas, and Palaces in the Roman World*. Ithaca NY: Cornell University Press, 1975. A thorough survey of Roman domesti architecture from apartments and small houses to the palaces of Rome's emperors, with dozens of plans and illustrations.

O'Connor, C. *Roman Bridges*. Cambridge: Cambridge University Press, 1993. In this book a civil engineer presents a thorough listing and description of all known bridges, with chapters that place the bridges in their geographical and historical contexts. Offers detailed maps of the empire-wide system of Roman roads and discussion of how these came to be constructed.

Orlin, E. M. *Temples, Religion, and Politics in the Roman Republic*. New York: E. J. Brill, 1997. A study of the construction of new temples in the Roman Republic, a process that illuminates key features of both their political and religious systems as well as the relationship between the individual and the community.

Plass, P. *The Game of Death in Ancient Rome: Arena Sport and Political Suicide*. Madison, WI: University of Wisconsin Press, 1995. An analysis of the Roman arena as a space in which forces harmful to society, such as criminals and wild animals, are neutralized under the power of government.

Potter, D. S. "Martyrdom as Spectacle." In *Theater and Society in the Classical World*, edited by R. Scodel. Ann Arbor, MI: University of Michigan Press, 1993. An insightful study of martyrdom in the context of Roman spectacle and its theatrical elements.

Salmon, E. T. *Roman Colonization under the Republic*. Ithaca, NY: Cornell University Press, 1970. A historical survey of the process, mechanisms, and results of colonization.

Scarre, C. *The Penguin Historical Atlas of Ancient Rome*. New York: Penguin, 1995. A brief survey of Roman history accompanying many maps illustrating key events and areas of Roman history.

Scodel, R. *Theater and Society in the Classical World*. Ann Arbor, MI: University of Michigan Press, 1993. A collection of thorough essays on the intersections between theater and the Greek and Roman social world.

Sitwell, N. H. H. *Roman Roads of Europe*. New York: St. Martin's Press, 1981. As the title proclaims, a survey of the Roman road system that crossed the continent and linked the provinces, including maps and technical information on creating roads.

Slater, W. J., ed. *Roman Theater and Society: E. Togo Salmon Papers I.* Ann Arbor, MI: University of Michigan Press, 1996. The authors of these papers discuss theater in Rome, incorporating not only stage performances but also dinnertime entertainment, sporting events, and political events and focusing on the social and political roles of Roman theatrical spectacle.

Stambaugh, J. E. *The Ancient Roman City.* Baltimore: Greenwood Press, 1988. A handbook on the organization of space in the city, from urban planning to the various forms of public space. Illustrated with case studies from Rome and selected colonies.

Stamper, J. W. *The Architecture of Roman Temples: The Republic to the Middle Empire*. Cambridge: Cambridge University Press, 2005. This book examines the development of Roman temple architecture, including the temples' formal qualities, the public spaces in which they were located, and how they accommodated changing political and religious contexts.

Toynbee, J. M. C. *Death and Burial in the Roman World.* Baltimore: Johns Hopkins University Press, 1996. A classic work on a critical topic that defines Roman culture and its evolution through Roman history.

Turcan, R. *The Gods of Ancient Rome: Religion in Everyday Life from Archaic to Imperial Times*. New York: Routledge, 2001. This book examines what their gods meant to the Romans and the rites and rituals connected to them, with key sections on religions of the family and land; religions of the city; and religions of the empire.

Versnel, H. S. *Triumphus: An Inquiry into the Origin, Development and Meaning of the Roman Triumph*. Leiden, The Netherlands: Brill, 1970. A massive work that tackles every aspect of triumph, based on the ancient literary sources.

Wallace-Hadrill, A. *Houses and Society in Pompeii and Herculaneum.* Princeton: Princeton University Press, 1994. A social history based on the archaeological remains of houses from the ashes of Vesuvius.

Warrior, V. M. *Roman Religion: A Sourcebook.* Newburyport, MA: Focus Publishing, 2002. As the title says, a sourcebook of ancient authors on religion, as well as descriptions of rituals and texts of prayers and dedications, all translated into English.

Welch, K. E. *The Roman Amphitheatre: From its Origins to the Colosseum.* Cambridge: Cambridge University Press, 2007. The title says it all.

Whittaker, C. R. *Frontiers of the Roman Empire: A Social and Economic Study.* Baltimore: Johns Hopkins University Press, 1997. A detailed study of the frontier zones as more than military boundaries but as areas where imperial policy intersected with economy and local societies.

Wiedemann, T. *Emperors and Gladiators.* London: Routledge, 1992. A short but thorough account of Roman gladiatorial spectacle interpreted as metaphors of rebirth.

Wilson, R. J. A. *Piazza Armerina.* Austin: University of Texas Press, 1983. An interesting but lightly illustrated guide to this villa, including descriptions of the mosaics, the highlight of the building.

Wistrand, M. *Entertainment and Violence in Ancient Rome: The Attitudes of Roman Writers of the First Century A.D.* Göteburg, Sweden: Acta Universitatis Gothoburgensis, 1992. Offers firsthand accounts from Roman authors revealing their true feelings on gladiatorial combat in particular.

Yegül, F. *Baths and Bathing in Classical Antiquity.* New York: Architectural History Foundation Press, 1992. A comprehensive work focusing on the architecture and technology of Roman baths and their development in Roman history.

Zanker, P. *Pompeii: Public and Private Life*. Cambridge, MA: Harvard University Press, 1999. A serious but readable analysis of aspects of life in Pompeii by a senior scholar who often advances innovative interpretations.

# Notes

# Notes